D0908635

'Til Politics Do Us Part

'Til Politics Do Us Part

A Political Wife's Declaration of Independence

By Paula Blanchard

A&M

Altwerger & Mandel Publishing Company, Franklin, Michigan

ISBN 1-878005-01-4

First Edition 1990

Designed by Mary Primeau

To
Genevieve Lynette Beardslee Parker
and
William Oliver Parker,
my mother and father

Preface

Today is June 10, 1990, nearly six weeks before this book hits the stands, and already it's the subject of speculation and controversy. I can count on less than two hands the number of people who have read the manuscript, but this week *Time* magazine declared that my book will have a substantial impact on my ex-husband's re-election campaign as governor of Michigan. As far as I know, no one at *Time* has seen a word of the book, so they're just guessing.

Because this book is being published three months before the election, people at *Time* and others rumor it is vindictive and will have a damaging effect on Jim Blanchard's second re-election attempt. It's just this kind of gossip which goes to the heart of why I wrote this book.

Because many of my married years were lived in the public eye as the wife of a member of the U.S. Congress and as First Lady of Michigan, my life has been ripe for rumors and conjecture. Speculation about our divorce—which Jamie and I agreed was best for both of us—has been particularly rampant because we played out the drama of the last days of our political partnership behind a drawn curtain.

Our divorce was not a tragedy and Jamie and I were not victims. It was something we chose and something we desired. I have no regrets that I was Jamie's wife and no regrets that I left. I hope to end speculation surrounding our marriage and divorce by revealing in my own words what my life was like and why I made the choices I made. I would have brought the book out earlier if I could have finished it sooner. I began writing the book on July 13, 1989, and completed the first draft on April 1, 1990, after working on it nearly every Saturday and Sunday during that time. It was not possible to work on it during the week because I live independently and support myself with a full-time professional position. I could have held the book until after the election but chose not to do so in the belief that the book will not damage Jamie's prospects and that it is time to tell the story which celebrates its third anniversary this month.

I've had an exciting life which my instincts tell me readers will find interesting. I have wonderful memories of Michigan's people, products, places and pride from my travels around this great state. I have a sense of satisfaction that I enjoyed, in many ways, an extraordinary marriage.

One of my greatest sources of pride is that I helped Jamie achieve the position of governor. I encouraged him to seek the office. I encouraged him to run in 1982 and again in 1986 and campaigned for him during both elections. I believe he has been an excellent and effective governor—one of Michigan's best— and deserves to be re-elected. I am supporting him in this election as I have in all the others. When people read this book, they will realize I would not do anything intentionally to diminish or damage the reputation of the man of whom I remain so proud.

In addition to writing the book to set the record straight, I also wrote the book for myself. I made a dramatic change in my life three years ago, a change which required enormous adjustment. Writing helps me articulate thoughts and feelings about which I could ruminate endlessly. Writing the book has been an exercise in introspection, an examination of my past that I hope will enlighten my future. The book is the period on my past, my Jane Hancock on my declaration of independence.

I have tried to bring fairness and a balanced perspective to this account of marriage and divorce. I have attempted to tell a truthful story as I remember it. In the end, however, it is my side of the story and my view of our life together. My hope is that readers gain some understanding of the exorbitant price politics demands from its worshippers—an escalating price I became unwilling to pay.

Paula Blanchard

Acknowledgments

Writing this book has been a solitary endeavor. My only companion was my computer as I spent nearly every weekend for the past year putting my story into words. Those words have come directly from my heart as I sought to bring the account of my twenty-one-year marriage to the page.

As I wrote each word, many people guided, encouraged, assisted and supported me. It is no mere cliche or exaggeration to say that without these wonderful people this book would not have been written or published.

Bill Haney's support was the turning point. Serendipity has played a frequent role in my life, as it seems to do in the lives of lucky people. Meeting Bill at an Adcraft meeting was enormously fortunate. He has a remarkable talent for many things, including writing and publishing. He was my mentor and guide from the beginning when I said to him at that meeting: "Bill,

I'm thinking about writing a book. . . ." Simply put, without Bill, there would be no book.

Eleanor and Kurt Luedtke were instrumental in the formative stage as I grappled with the decision of whether to write the book myself or work with a writer. They encouraged me to try my own hand first with the counsel that the story would have more authenticity and strength if told in my own words. The three of us had dinner on July 13, 1989 and by midnight that same evening, I had written the beginning and the end of the book. The following day, Eleanor, Kurt and Bill Haney read what I had written and sped me on my way with some very heartwarming words of encouragement.

Robert Mandel, my publisher, has nurtured this book lovingly and carefully. We built a remarkable level of trust and I appreciated very much his patient, calm, informed and supportive counsel which sustained me in times of doubt. His firm command as he led the book through the publishing process and we made each decision together was especially reassuring.

Dena Mandel's belief in my ability to tell my story and her support of my efforts to finish it when the last difficult chapters remained to be written were invaluable. She brought empathy, understanding, skill and devotion to the task of editor.

John Klemme's expert light hand in editing invariably improved the expression of my thoughts without changing the essence. His confidence in the value of the project gave me strength when I needed it.

As always, I turned to my parents for help. They believed in the worth of the book and pored through albums, boxes and drawers in search of photographs. They also assisted me in recollecting my early years and contributed some family history I hadn't known before.

I'm grateful to:

—Steve Thomas, Kelly Rossman and Carlene Carey for their assistance, one more time. The three of us worked together during my years as First Lady and they have never failed me when I needed them. They read the manuscript and helped to get facts, events and recollections right.

—Camille and Maryalice Abood, Jack Casey and Mary Lou Butcher, the readers, whose judgment and advice I have valued in my career and whose counsel I called upon in reading the manuscript.

—Debra Burke, Nora Paulson and my other colleagues at Casey Communications Management, Inc. As Manager of Computer Services at Casey Communications, Deb's assistance was invaluable in getting the manuscript into and out of the computer. Nora, Executive Secretary, helped me keep the manuscript organized as I made revisions. My co-workers have expressed enthusiasm and support for the book by giving up their time after work to assist me.

I'll be eternally grateful to Jamie who helped me fufill many girlhood dreams. I'm now fulfilling my dreams on my own, but I couldn't do it without the benefit of what Jamie taught me or the personal growth and confidence I acquired as First Lady.

I'm also grateful to him and our son Jay, for letting me share our private lives with you, the reader. Neither wanted me to write this book, but neither stood in my way or made it difficult.

Finally, I am grateful to the people of Michigan. It was your support during my years as First Lady, and your concern and interest since, that propelled me to write this book.

To all of you, thank you.

Paula Blanchard

Chapter One

In spite of the fact our marriage ended in divorce after twenty-one years, I'd marry Jamie all over again because I truly believe our marriage was meant to be—for both of us.

Our wedding preparations, ceremony and honeymoon were packed into a very tight timetable—a sign of things to come.

We were married on June 18, 1966, one week after my college graduation, one week after Jamie's return from his first year of law school at the University of Minnesota, and less than a week after my parents finished their end-of-school-year classes and paperwork.

During our wedding ceremony, I was very nervous and shy. My hands perspired, so luckily fashion dictated gloves. My flowers shook in my hands. My father walked too fast for the music, thank God, because we got down the aisle faster. Guests were standing, and all eyes were turned to me. I tried bravely to return their gaze with a smile, but failed. I bowed my head and hoped they thought I was a demure and modest bride.

1

Our wedding followed the prescribed pattern of the 1960s. It was a traditional wedding given for a daughter by her parents. The 250 assembled guests saw ushers in summer formal attire, bridesmaids in yellow summer dresses with daisy baskets, a flower girl and ring bearer. They saw a nervous bride in a wedding dress made by her mother and a confident groom in a rented tuxedo. They witnessed the wedding of Paula Lynne Parker and James (Jamie) Johnston Blanchard at the Clarkston Methodist Church. I wanted a romantic wedding with candlelight so we were married at 7:30 in the evening. I forgot, of course, that it didn't grow dark until much later in June, so the candles burned brightly, but to no effect. I dimly remember noticing that as I made my way down the aisle.

I went through the motions of the twenty-minute Methodist ceremony trying to relax and enjoy it, but it took all my willpower not to faint in a heap. Being in front of groups made me self-conscious, and even the joy of my wedding day couldn't overcome my unease. I felt immense relief when Jamie and I ended our walk down the aisle together as man and wife. At that moment, I turned to Jamie to share this intimate moment with a kiss. Jamie was scanning the audience and didn't return my embrace. Of course, I couldn't know it at the time, but that was my first glimpse of what it was going to be like to be a politician's wife.

We had three days for a honeymoon before we had to depart for Minnesota and a summer job Jamie had lined up for us near the university. We left our wedding reception about 11:00 P.M. after being gently reminded by my dad that he and Mother needed time to clean up the house from the reception and get organized for him to leave by car for North Carolina in the early dawn. I found out later that he never went to bed that night, but helped Mother and set off about 5:00 A.M. I never understood until years later how the joy of our wedding celebration must have been diminished for my parents by the prospect of his departure early the next morning.

To my surprise and disappointment, Jamie had waited until he arrived home for the wedding to make honeymoon arrangements. We were counting on going to Michigan's most magical place—Mackinac Island—on the Straits of Mackinac, but Jamie

2

placed one call and discovered the island was booked for the Lilac Festival. We decided instead on the Colonial Inn in Harbor Springs, a resort town in northern Michigan near Lake Michigan.

We spent our first married night in Flint, Michigan, in a Holiday Inn across from an automobile assembly plant—not romantic, but handy. It was about forty-five minutes from my home and on our way north. I have three memories of that one-night stay. The first is our joint discovery that we were starving. I had eaten nothing all day but wedding cake. We sat on the bed and went through the phone book to find a pizzeria to deliver a pizza to our room. The second memory is our love-making which was tentative and tender. The third was my discovery the next night that I had left my peignoir somewhere in the bedsheets in the Holiday Inn.

We arrived late the next morning, Sunday, at the Colonial Inn for a memorable three days. It is a grand place with an elegant tradition, but on June 19 it wasn't quite ready for the summer season. I'm not sure what Jamie had told them when he booked our room, but the porter ushered us into a dark and musty room without a bed. After I exclaimed my surprise, he showed us how the two day couches swung together to make a double bed. There they remained for the duration of our short stay.

We wanted to make the most of our short idyll so we planned to dress for dinner that night and take in one of the area's fine restaurants. We put on our "going-away" suits, I pinned on my wedding corsage, and we set off for the dining room at the Inn about 8:00 P.M. Too late! The dining room closed at 7:30 P.M. Sunday evenings. "No problem," we said, "there are other places around."

Harbor Springs neighbors Petoskey where I had worked the previous summer. Jamie and I were dating very seriously and he had visited me there every weekend. We knew all the places to go and for the next two hours we made the rounds of all of them. Only the Big Boy was open. Crestfallen, in tears, with corsage wilting, we ordered two hamburgers.

The weather favored us the next morning with a beautiful summer day. We set off for the hotel swimming pool after

3

breakfast. Too early! The pool hadn't opened for the season and was a slimy mess with last year's leaves floating on last year's water. Undeterred, we ordered a box lunch from the hotel kitchen and set off for a day on the beach on Lake Michigan. That day was glorious, as was the one that followed on Mackinac Island. We romped, biked, played, teased and loved. We even managed a champagne dinner at a favorite restaurant, Chimney Corners.

The honeymoon ended all too soon. Yet the prospect of leaving for Minnesota and our first home together was exciting, too. Without regret, we left the Inn to return to my parents' home to pack up our things and be on our way.

Our destination was Chaska, Minnesota, on the outskirts of Minneapolis, and the site of a new town development, Jonathan. Jamie had monitored the placement board at the university for summer jobs for us and had landed something that seemed ideal. We were hired as resident managers of Carver's Green, the residential section of the new town. My responsibility was to manage the guest house, and Jamie's was to tend the lawns, gardens and grounds. A darling one-bedroom furnished apartment had been added to the back of the guest house and would be our new home.

We lived and worked at Carver's Green that summer and got to know each other. It turned out that we were two people in love who were essentially strangers. We shouldn't have been surprised. For the ten months before our marriage, we had been together a total of about one month.

We had started dating in April 1965. Two months later I left Michigan State University for a summer waitressing job in Petoskey, Michigan, while Jamie stayed in East Lansing to do an internship in the Secretary of State's office. We saw each other only on weekends when Jamie made the four hour drive after work on Friday to the Bay View Country Club in Petoskey. I worked on Saturdays so we had only late Friday night, late Saturday night and Sundays to spend together before he left about 9:00 P.M. to drive back to East Lansing.

I returned to Michigan State in September for my senior year, and Jamie left for his first year of law school at the University of Minnesota. The little time we spent together over the

4

next ten months was full of activity and distractions: school preparations, the Christmas holidays and our engagement over New Year's. Our time at Easter was consumed with June wedding preparations.

Our regular communication over those ten months consisted of costly long-distance twenty dollar phone calls and daily letters back and forth full of love, longing and loneliness. Very romantic on paper, but risky.

At Carver's Green, we found ourselves married to someone we really hadn't spent much time with and knew very little about. In retrospect, it's a miracle we stayed married as long as we did. The daily responsibility and routine of living together and making a marriage work was a far-cry from our long distance courtship.

We weren't married very long before we discovered our compatibilities and incompatibilities. Some troubling things surfaced. I discovered Jamie had little sense of the clock—he didn't even wear a watch and was usually late. This was frustrating to me because I had been taught that being on time was a virtue and being late was rude. Politics had a very tight grip on him, and I was disappointed to discover he had little real interest in anything else. And unlike my father, he had little interest in helping at home. He discovered I had a quick temper and a moody disposition. That was hard on him, a person who rarely becomes angry and is even-tempered. I also had little patience, whereas Jamie is a person with a great deal.

These differences troubled our marriage for twenty-one years. These were the seeds of our divorce, planted before we were married and sprouting as weeds in the garden of our life together. Periodically, we'd pull some of them out and flowers would blossom. In later years, however, we became tired, negligent and resentful of the weeds' tenacity. Eventually we gave up and let the weeds grow wild, and they triumphed and took over. In the end, there were too many to tackle, so we left the weed-filled garden to plant flowers elsewhere.

Chapter Two

I married Jamie Blanchard because I loved him, and he loved me. He fell in love with a small town girl from Clarkston, Michigan, where my family's roots and traditional values strongly influenced me, as they did my parents before me.

Both my parents were born in Clarkston. My father, William Oliver Parker, the last of seven children, was born on Holcomb Street, and my mother, Genevieve Lynette Beardslee, the oldest of three, came into the world on the family farm just outside town. They grew up in Clarkston and knew each other from the time they were children. They were high school sweethearts. Each left Clarkston for college but came back to be married in the First Methodist Church, the predecessor to the one where Jamie and I were eventually married. They decided to marry on Pearl Harbor Day, December 7, 1941, and the ceremony was three weeks later.

My parents were teachers and taught for many years. When they were married, my mother was teaching in Bayport, Michigan, near Bay City, and my father was finishing college at Eastern Michigan University in Ypsilanti. On weekends, my father would hitchhike to Bayport to see my mother because he didn't have a car. After his graduation from Eastern, he enlisted in the Coast Guard during World War II and served for three years in Erie, Pennsylvania and New York City. After his tour of duty, my parents were reunited and moved to Montrose, and after a year, to Romeo, Michigan, where my father taught industrial arts and coached several sports. He left teaching for many years and went into sales. When I was in high school, he returned to teaching and taught junior high school science in Birmingham, Michigan, for about twenty years. In her nearly thirty years of teaching, more than twenty of which were in Clarkston, my mother taught home economics, science and geography at the junior high school level. She loves to travel so geography was her favorite subject.

I come from a long line of teachers. My maternal great-great-grandfather, Major John J. Knox, was the first of many in my family. He taught grades one through eight in a one-room schoolhouse prior to the Civil War. His granddaughter, my grandmother, Emily Knox Beardslee, taught elementary school for over thirty years after she was widowed in her twenties with three small children. She never remarried and taught until she retired in her sixties. Her sister was also an elementary school teacher for many years in Hamtramck, Michigan, to which she commuted daily from the family farm in Clarkston, a round trip of over 60 miles in the days when there were no freeways. There were teachers on my father's side, too, one being my Aunt Charlotte Parker Wixom who taught in a one-room schoolhouse near Clarkston.

Education was greatly valued in our house and my parents were proud of their profession. Their expectations of my brother and me were high, especially regarding our performance in school, and we couldn't blame our teachers if our grades weren't up to par.

I was born in Pontiac, Michigan, on November 13, 1944, during my father's tour of duty in Erie, Pennsylvania. My brother, Larry, was born in Pontiac on October 3, 1949, almost five years later. I have a clear recollection of the day my new

7

brother was brought home from the hospital. My Grandmother Parker was staying with us and was babysitting when my dad went to pick up Mother and Larry to bring them home. I knew they were coming and was too excited to stay inside and wait. So I went across the street to a friend's house and insisted on playing outside in the front yard so I could watch for our car, a 1949 Studebaker. I jumped up and down when I saw it coming down the street and caught a glimpse of Mother holding my baby brother in her arms. I didn't see much of him because he was all wrapped in blankets. Dad was driving slowly, and I ran after the car as it pulled into our driveway. All I wanted to do was hold Larry. When we got inside, Mother sat me down and let me hold him in my lap. I was satisfied and ran back outdoors to play.

Life didn't change much after Larry joined our family. I was happy and secure. My parents let me keep my bedroom all to myself, putting Larry's crib in their room. I had started school that September at Webster Elementary, just a few blocks from our apartment, and that had as big an impact on me as my new brother. I have some vivid memories of the two years I went to school there.

I remember being in a play in kindergarten, in which I was dressed as a clown. I hid behind a fellow student while we did our act on stage because I felt shy. My mother was seated proudly in the audience and smiling her encouragement, but I did the entire routine peeking out from behind another clown because I had stage fright at five.

I must have lost my stage fright somewhere in the next year or two, because my second grade teacher told my parents I clearly had acting ability. She was a creative teacher and was always staging plays and little performances. She gave me the lead in the Christmas play, the part of Mary. I forgot my lines and adlibbed the entire part. At one point, or so my mother tells me, I piped up and said, "OK, Joseph." I also recall singing "Rudolph the Red-Nosed Reindeer" when we made records for our parents for Christmas. The same teacher who liked my acting wisely made no recommendations about my singing! I also liked boys in the second grade and had a boyfriend named Victor Schramm. He told me his father had the Schwinn bicycle store near school. I don't remember what Victor looked like, but I do remember his fabulous name. What a tongue-twister: "Schwinn Store—Schramm speaking." I found out later his father was really a pharmacist at a local drugstore.

In the middle of the second grade, our family moved back to Clarkston. We had outgrown our small apartment in Pontiac, and my parents' hearts were still in Clarkston. My Grandmother Parker lived there, as did most of my parents' friends. We rented half of a two-family house on Washington Street, about a block from town, and lived there until I was in the sixth grade when we moved into a new home which my parents bought on East-lawn Avenue. It was from there that I left for college in 1962.

Clarkston, in retrospect, was a wonderful town in which to have grown up. It was a warm, safe, nurturing environment where everybody knew everybody and kept track of each other and each other's kids. From my point of view, however, it was dull, with a capital D, and boring with a capital B. Being the daughter of two teachers, one of whom taught in the Clarkston schools, made it confining with a capital C. I whiled away my entire senior year waiting to leave and go to college.

Clarkston, then as now, was a small town. Its main street is still two blocks long and one block wide. There were no movie theaters and no restaurants. There are still no movie theaters, and one restaurant, The Clarkston Cafe—so chic today—was a smoky poolroom and cafe known as "The Greasy Spoon." It was a quiet, conservative, Republican town.

My family was Republican and proud of it. They were clearly disturbed when Jamie and I announced our intention to marry, because a Democrat with political aspirations would be up to no good. The only thing that saved him with my Grandmother Beardslee was his other ambition to practice law. Her grandfather, John J. Knox, the teacher and Civil War major, was an attorney when he was invited to the White House by President Grant, a Republican of course. She always proclaimed loudly whenever politics came up that she had always voted Republican and always would. Her son, my Uncle Alvin, was a truck driver, a UAW member and the only Democrat in the family. He loved to rile everyone at family gatherings by starting heated political discussions and was delighted to have a Democratic

9

ally when Jamie joined the family. He had doubled his Democratic ranks and felt strength in numbers. Jamie joined those discussions, but with too many facts and too much reason for Uncle Alvin, a man who preferred political passion to political reality. To her credit, my grandmother stayed true to her word: she didn't live in Jamie's congressional district when he ran for Congress, and she was in a nursing home and unable to vote when he ran for governor.

My mother and dad were Republicans, too, but more open-minded than my grandmother. They were conscientious and caring parents who took their parenting responsibilities seriously. They set high standards for themselves in everything they did, and expected my brother and me to do the same. They were honest, straightforward, determined, diligent, organized and hardworking and expected Larry and me to exhibit the same qualities. They loved us and took great pride in our accomplishments. They trusted me completely, and gave me freedom and independence. They valued me and made me feel very special. They taught me and convinced me I could do anything I set my mind to if I had enough education and determination.

From the time we moved to Clarkston until she retired in 1980, Mother worked in the Clarkston school system, first as a secretary in the school office, and later as a junior high school teacher. She preferred teaching to staying at home. She is a wonderful homemaker and cook but didn't find complete fulfillment in being at home all the time. She had a reputation as a strict teacher which I could understand. She didn't put up with any foolishness at home, either. She tried, without success, to get me interested in cooking. Jamie had to teach me how to fry an egg after we were married. To this day, I cook only when I have to, or when I entertain, which I actually enjoy. She did succeed in sparking my interest in sewing, needlework and home decorating, things in which she excels.

Those were interests I cultivated as an adult. When I was young, I preferred to follow my dad around, assisting him where I could as he built furniture, wallpapered and painted rooms in our house, and took on and completed one home-improvement project after another. I learned a great deal about all those things from spending hours and hours at his side. He also is an

10

athlete and an avid spectator of sporting events. He and I spent many afternoons together watching sports on television while he taught me the rules and strategies of baseball, football, basketball and golf. I was a cheerleader who actually understood the games we cheered. On the day of my wedding, we whiled away the afternoon together watching the Detroit Tigers play baseball on television.

Their lives reflected the values of small town, mid-America: home and family, achievement, self-reliance, independence, hard work, loyalty, belief in education and in the principles of thrift and moderation. Their lives also reflected years of living through the Great Depression, and they set great store in predictability, certainty, control, routine and financial security. In their strong belief and unfailing practice of these values, they instilled them in me, principles which have served me well at various times in my life, particularly in the past three years as I struck out on my own.

During my marriage, however, some of these ideals were a continual source of anxiety and conflict. When I attempted to reject them, I found myself at odds with myself and my parents. My conformity to others put me at odds with my husband.

I didn't want routine—I wanted adventure. I didn't want security—I wanted to take risks. I didn't want thrift and moderation—I wanted to see the world. I didn't want to live in a small town with another school teacher (I was preordained to become one)—I wanted to live a fast-paced life in a city with a husband who would cut a wide swath. What I wasn't prepared for was the high cost of it all—the trade-offs and sacrifices I would have to make to have adventure and the thrill of such a fast-paced life.

I never succeeded in completely shedding those values so dear to my parents and passed on so effectively to me. I wanted a successful husband who would slay those dragons, try those cases, and win those votes—all between eight and six, and be home for dinner, promptly, every night.

I wanted adventure, but on a regular, predictable basis.

I wanted risks, as long as they came with a guarantee.

I wanted to see the world and have money in the bank for a rainy day.

It took me twenty years of marriage to admit to myself that

in spite of the fact that my parents taught me I could do any-thing I set my mind to, and I had proven that adage to myself time and again, I couldn't manage to have it all, have it both ways, have my cake and eat it, too. It took me over twenty years to face the choices, the painful choices, which I had to make.

Chapter Three

I first saw Jamie on a campaign billboard—how appropriate! He was campaigning for class president at Michigan State University, and I walked by the Union Building on my way to class one day and saw his picture and campaign slogan on a board near the sidewalk. I remember thinking how sharp and handsome he looked and yet how pleasant and friendly. I had heard his name around campus all year because he was a leader, a doer, a mover, a shaker, a BMOC. I had never met him though, because I was a freshman at M.S.U. and we weren't moving in the same circles. It would be another year before I would meet Jamie, but I never forgot the kind face in that picture.

I probably would never have met him without the persistence of a dear and loyal friend and sorority sister, Linda Chapman (now Dr. Linda Stone). Linda was from Clarkston, too, and went to Michigan State. We had known each other only slightly at Clarkston High, but she was instrumental in my pledging Delta

Gamma sorority at M.S.U. where we became close friends. Linda was active in student government with Jamie and was convinced that the two of us would hit it off. She really liked and admired him and was determined to match us up. I held her off for over a year because I was skeptical about BMOC's who seemed arrogant, self-absorbed, first-class bores. She kept insisting he was different, but I was dubious.

Our first meeting did not bode well for the future. Linda and I both worked in the student loan office in the Student Services Building on campus. I worked two hours a day during the week for spending money and Linda ran the office. One of my duties was to do mimeographing for student organizations which had their offices in the same building. This was before the days of photocopying machines, and mimeographing was a messy business. It involved typing a master which was placed on a drum full of blue ink. Cranking a handle on the drum distributed blue ink over the master, printing the copies. I never learned the trick of doing all this cleverly and neatly, and I invariably ended my work day with blue ink on my hands, face and the white lab coat I wore over my clothes.

Linda knew an opportunity for me to meet Jamie was inevitable because he was active in many student organizations and was around the Student Services Building daily. She knew sooner or later he would deliver something to be mimeographed. She was right. What she didn't know was that he would pick a day when I looked like a garage mechanic.

On the day of THE meeting, I had been hard at work at the mimeo machine for two hours. The results of my efforts were there for everyone to see—on my face, my hands, my arms and my coat. I also remember feeling frazzled. Linda had been singing Jamie's praises and making it plain she wanted to introduce us so, my radar system went into alert when I saw him round the corner with mimeo master in hand.

The mimeo machine was housed in a small closet across the hall from the loan office with only enough room for gallons of ink, stacks of paper, the machine and me. When I wasn't cranking, I stood around in the hall outside the loan office. When he rounded the corner, there was no escape. It was either into the closet with the machine or into the loan office with Linda where he'd have to fill out the required paperwork. He approached me with the master and asked me very politely if I could do it for him yet that day. I mumbled that I could. I was praying Linda wouldn't see us talking in the hall from her desk in the loan office but no such luck. She did introduce us, but I got out of that conversation as quickly as I could. Linda has incredible determination and persistence, evidenced by her successful battle against age discrimination when she decided to become a physician at age thirty. She had that same determination at age twenty, and she tried her best every so often to fix us up on a date.

Our next encounter made our future relationship even more unlikely. It was the fall of my junior year at M.S.U. By this time, Jamie had graduated the previous June and was studying for a master's degree in Business Administration at M.S.U. I'd been dating a fellow who was a Sigma Chi and one night he asked me to be his pinmate. I'd never been pinned before, and I was thrilled. Our sorority had a special candle ceremony—as all sororities do—to announce when a member becomes pinned or engaged. We had curfews then, and as soon as our housemother locked the sorority house doors for the night, the candle ceremony began. Part of the fun of the ceremony was keeping the pinning or engagement a secret from the sisters until the candle ceremony.

As my sisters ran down the stairs to form the candle circle, I was eagerly anticipating blowing out the candle when I was called to the phone. I took the call because I thought it was my pinmate. It wasn't—it was Jamie, of all people! I was intrigued so I didn't tell him immediately that I'd just been pinned. We had a short, casual and friendly chat before time ran out and I had to return downstairs. I remember ending the conversation with something like, "It was really nice of you to call, it's been great to talk, but I have to go now. I just got pinned tonight and my candle ceremony is about to begin!" He laughed and became the first to congratulate me!

That pinning was a short-lived three months, but it might as well have been six, because it took that long for word to get around that I was "unpinned." I decided to take a job in the Student Book Store between terms. The bookstores always hired extra help for the week before the term started because they were busy selling books and supplies to students preparing for the next term. A sorority sister tipped me off that it was a great place for meeting and greeting other students and getting your social life going.

Jamie did come into the Student Book Store, and one of the reasons I say our relationship was meant to be is that I saw him when he came in. The SBS is a mammoth place with rows and rows and stacks and stacks of books. He could very easily have come and gone without me catching a glimpse of him. But we saw each other and had a long and friendly chat.

A month passed before he called me. It was on the eve of Easter weekend, and he asked me to go out the night I was planning to go home for the holiday. I had arranged a ride to Clarkston—with Linda Chapman—but she was delighted when I told her the change in plans. I knew if I turned Jamie down for that date he'd never ask me again. He told me later my instincts were right!

We went on a "study date" to the M.S.U. library and spent the whole evening in the smoking lounge talking. Rather, he spent the whole evening talking, and I spent the whole evening listening. The subject was politics. I thought he was a fascinating person to be with. He was a great conversationalist—if you were a good listener—and I was. He was well-read, up-to-date on current affairs and full of enthusiasm and ancedotes about politics.

By this time in my college career I was liberated from my conservative Republican upbringing and had developed definite Democratic party leanings. Jamie had been brought up in a Democratic household and everything he said about current events, Democrats and Republicans, elections, and politics made sense. His every word was a pearl. He did all the talking and I did all the listening. He lived politics, breathed it, dreamed it, worked it, and loved it. I didn't realize the extent to which it would consume his life, our life and our marriage, but I know now that his first love was politics.

We had great chemistry and became serious almost immediately. Our courtship lasted a little over a year. We dated for the remainder of my junior year while he completed graduate

16

school and kept up a long-distance relationship between M.S.U. and the University of Minnesota Law School the following year. Observing us, most people would have thought we were a typical couple. We went to parties with friends, to the movies, out to eat, to fraternity gatherings, on more "study dates." He was everything Linda Chapman had said—intelligent, ambitious, up-to-date on everything, interested in other people and a lively companion with a great sense of humor.

But to me our relationship wasn't typical at all. He was unlike anyone I had ever dated. He was more focused, more directed, more mature, more driven than anyone I knew. He exuded confidence, charisma, and power. There was a tremendous vigor, energy and excitement about him, and he infused me with it and swept me along. I had to run to keep up when he walked. I was completely entranced and captivated. He seemed the perfect man to fulfill my hopes for a wonderful husband and an exciting life.

In retrospect, I was young, very much in love and naive, with little notion of the complexities and responsibilities of marriage.

Chapter Four

That September of 1966, after our newlywed summer at Carver's Green, I embarked on a four-year teaching career. I taught fourth grade for two years at Portland Elementary School in Richfield, Minnesota, a suburb of Minneapolis, while Jamie completed law school.

We could have continued living at Carver's Green, and we even tried it for a short while. Staying at Carver's Green tempted each of us, for different reasons. Jamie saw it as an opportunity to develop a close relationship with a well-to-do and well-connected state senator, Henry McKnight. Henry was the developer and financial backer of Jonathan and Carver's Green. It was he who had placed the ad, he who had inteviewed Jamie and he who had talked politics with Jamie and hired him for our summer job. The Senator had taken quite a liking to us and wanted us to stay. For me, it was an opportunity to save a nice little nest egg. We paid no rent at the Green—our apartment was part of our compensation.

It would have been possible to keep up with our maintenance duties there in the evenings and on weekends, but it would have required working essentially two jobs. It didn't take me much longer than about two weeks of teaching to discover how emotionally and physically demanding my job was, and that I didn't have it in me to juggle the demands of teaching, my new marriage and a second job.

Besides, it wasn't financially necessary. My salary of $5,200 was enough to provide us with a very comfortable standard of living. I wanted to use my time after work caring for my husband and my own home—not maintaining someone else's guest house. And I wanted our weekends for catching up and leisure time. Even at this early stage in our marriage, I was trying to strike a balance between work and play, private time and public time, and time alone and time together.

We left Carver's Green in September for a one bedroom-apartment around the corner from the school where I taught. We furnished it with some furniture from a second-hand store, our wedding gifts and some hand-me-downs. It wasn't the decorator's dream that our Carver's Green apartment had been, but I liked it better. Everything in it was ours. We settled into a comfortable routine.

I was always the first one up in the morning. I showered and dressed and went into the kitchen to make our breakfast and lunches. In those days, I fixed Jamie a breakfast of bacon, eggs, toast and coffee every morning. Sometimes the smell of morning coffee was enough to rouse him from bed, but it usually took a backrub, too. He was a night owl and mornings were torture for him. I, on the other hand, was a morning person and chirped about plans for the day. I had my breakfast, packed brown-bag lunches for both of us, took meat out of the freezer for dinner, kissed a sleepy-head good-bye and walked around the corner to thirty eager and energetic fourth-graders.

In the meantime, Jamie would wake up with breakfast, coffee, the morning paper and a long shower before driving to campus for classes. Several days each week he clerked afternoons for a prominent attorney he'd met through Senator McKnight. After school, I came home and took a nap. I needed it to recharge my emotional and physical batteries. I was also a little lonesome in

19

the apartment without Jamie there, so a little nap pepped me up and passed the time until it was time to fix dinner.

In the evenings, I graded papers, prepared lessons, read, did laundry and sewed many of my own clothes while Jamie studied every night. We saw little television because our apartment was small, and it was a distraction for him. We often watched the news during dinner and there were some television shows we used as rewards for our labors—"Batman", "Perry Mason" and "The Avengers" were some of our favorites.

We lived well on my teaching salary. Jamie's mother paid for his tuition and books while my salary covered our living expenses. We lived modestly, but like kings compared to many of our fellow students and wives—especially those with children. We allowed ourselves only two credit cards—a gas card and a Dayton charge card. We used that one only for occasional necessary purchases or gifts and always kept it paid in full.

In all our twenty-one years—even during his busiest years as governor—Jamie always paid our bills and controlled the money. Right after we were married, he asked me who should keep the checkbook. Although I had always balanced my college checkbook to the penny, I deferred to Jamie to manage our finances. It seemed to me at the time something a husband should do. There were two reasons for that, I suppose. I just assumed Jamie would have a "better head" for money than I, and my dad always managed the money when I was growing up.

We even had our weekend routine. Friday night was Shakey's Pizza night. We always treated ourselves to dinner there, usually just the two of us. Going out to dinner Friday night was something my mother had always insisted on when I was at home because she had put in a hard week in the classroom and needed a respite at the end of it. I finally understood that.

On Saturdays we went together to the grocery nearby—a discount Target store—to do our weekly shopping. For twenty dollars we bought food, including meat for six nights, paper goods, cleaning supplies, and cigarettes for a week.

We usually got started later on our Saturday errands than I liked because weekends were also for sleeping-in. On Sundays especially, we'd sleep in until early afternoon. That usually followed a very late Saturday night bridge game. Bridge was a

20

popular form of entertainment in law school—cheap, friendly and challenging. Our bridge games pitted men against women since Jamie and I never got along as partners in bridge. I played by conventional bridge rules while Jamie would make bold, unpredictable bids and moves. Several other couples experienced the same thing. The men, our husbands and future lawyers, also usually engaged in endless table talk and side conversation which drove most of the wives mad. One rubber of bridge could take us well into the wee-hours. The women usually won, not by any superior skill or genius, but by paying closer attention to the game.

While Saturdays were busy days together with shopping and apartment cleaning, Sundays were lonesome. We were far away from our families in Michigan, most of my women friends in Richfield had children to care for, and Jamie had a day of studying to do. He often went to the law library on campus for the afternoon and evening. I did a lot of reading, sewing and thinking.

I was troubled during those two years in Minnesota because Jamie and I weren't as emotionally close as I thought husband and wife should be. I was puzzled and disappointed by that, but I couldn't put my finger on why. I cast around for reasons and complained to Jamie.

I thought at the time it was because we didn't spend enough time together, that he wasn't as helpful around the house as I expected and that he was almost always late. When I complained to him about these things, he would listen patiently and explain why things were as they were and why they probably wouldn't change. He fully expected that I would accept him just as he was. He didn't believe he should have to adjust or accommodate himself to my needs. He was genuinely puzzled that I was unhappy and disturbed about what he considered petty matters. He talked circles around me and I listened dutifully. He used his skills as an attorney very effectively because I never won an argument with him. He could placate me for a while and over the years we compromised on some things. We never fully resolved many of our early differences.

Later, I realized I was bothered by this basic disharmony, but even more troubled by our lack of intimacy—a lack of sharing

21

of thoughts, feelings, hopes, and dreams. It wasn't that we lacked those, but that we weren't sharing them with each other. I also realize, looking back, that Jamie didn't have his heart in the law or the life we were leading together. His thoughts, feelings, hopes and dreams were in Michigan—in politics.

Chapter Five

We were tempted to stay in Minneapolis when the attorney Jamie clerked for offered him a position just before he graduated from law school. He could have joined the firm and embarked on a very promising career as an attorney. We actually considered the offer seriously because we liked Minneapolis. It is a beautiful city and Minnesota is a beautiful state—not unlike Michigan in its greenness, its sparking lakes and natural beauty. We'd made friends there and knew the future was promising.

We were also comfortable with Minnesota politics. Hubert Humphrey was vice-president, and the country had gained much from his years of political vision. Jamie and I both admired him greatly, but in our idealism he wasn't liberal enough. We supported another Minnesotan, Eugene McCarthy, and later Robert Kennedy, in the presidential primaries of 1968. In our minds, Humphrey was too close to President Johnson and the tragedy of the Vietman War to merit our support. Against

Nixon, however, he was our inevitable choice. His son, Skip, was Jamie's classmate and enjoyed his admiration. Essentially, we recognized that Minnesota politics were grounded in the liberal Democratic tradition, and we felt right at home.

But Jamie wasn't entirely preoccupied with political ideology and tradition. His concerns were practical, and he was assessing where he had the best political base and the best chance of being elected to office. In our two years in Minnesota, he had established a political foundation: the potential support of a state senator, a prominent attorney and law school colleagues. That didn't compare to the political base he'd built up during his years of high school and college politics in Michigan. It may have seemed implausible at the time, but only five years later that support would be an important part of the realization of a political dream.

I was also eager to return to Michigan to our families and friends—our roots; I felt very far afield in Minnesota. Another practical consideration entered our decision to return to Michigan—we agreed Minnesota was too cold and winters were too long. We retraced our steps back to Clarkston, Michigan, and my parents' home with another U-Haul trailer packed with wedding gifts in tow. Our plan was to live with them for the summer while Jamie studied for the bar exam and looked for a job. He spent three months in their basement buried in his books while I worked as a secretary for the Oakland Intermediate School District in a job my mother had lined up for me.

Things were a bit tense at 6683 Eastlawn that long hot summer. My parents wisely planned some summer study away that year, but those times when we were all at home together were almost more than that little house could bear. It was a warm, cozy, charming house when I was growing up there and fit two children and two adults nicely. It had a small living room, kitchen with a dining area, a family room which my father had added on, a basement which he finished, three small bedrooms and one bathroom. With four adults, it bulged at the seams and creaked under the activity. All of us operated on different schedules so there was always someone eating, sleeping, showering or studying. I was the lucky one because I was up early weekday mornings, out of the house and at work all day. Jamie and my parents negiotiated the cramped quarters and tried to accommodate each other. Luckily for Jamie, the basement was given over to him for study, and he spent his days down there in the cool quiet. For my parents, who liked predictability and control even more than I did, it was a measure of true parental patience and love.

All's well that end's well, they say, and it did. Jamie passed the bar and accepted a job in Lansing where we rented an apartment. We packed up our wedding gifts once more in one more U-Haul trailer, merrily waved good-bye to Clarkston, and moved to Lansing. We had an eventful three and one-half years in Lansing. These were years with a lot of change; years which set us on a course we would chart for many years to come. In retrospect, these were some of our best years.

The Lansing area was our home from August 1968 to March 1972. In August 1968, we unpacked the U-Haul trailer, Jamie started work and I settled us into our new apartment, which didn't take long because our only furniture consisted of a bed, a card table and chairs, and an old chair from my parents' basement. We had sold most of our furniture before we left Minnesota. We were there only a couple of days when our apartment was livable, so I started looking for a teaching job. I wasn't concerned when I didn't have a job when we left Clarkston. In those days, there were more jobs than there were teachers and I was confident of finding a position. I visited the administrative offices of three area school systems, filled out applications and was invited for an interview at all of them for a position for the upcoming school year. Within days of the interviews, I was offered a job at each. I accepted a second-grade teaching post at Cavanaugh Elementary School in Lansing, because it was the one which paid the best salary, was nearest our apartment and was a grade level I knew I would enjoy.

We had found an apartment in Lansing Towers, a new high-rise building on Ottawa Street across from the state capital. Jamie had landed a promising job as legal counsel to the State Elections Division, a division of the Secretary of State's Office. His office was in the state office complex behind the Capitol, and he could walk across the street to work. I drove our only car to school and we weren't dependent on each other for transportation. This arrangement worked well because we continued to operate on different schedules. Jamie was usually still in bed when I left for school at 8:00 A.M. even though as a state employee he was technically bound by a schedule of 8:00 A.M. to 5:00 P.M. But in all the years I knew him, Jamie was never bound by a day-in-day out routine. He usually got to work about 9:30 or 10:00 A.M. and worked into the evening until about 7:30 P.M. I, on the other hand, thrived on routine and was always at school by 8:20 and home about 4:30.

I loved my second graders and settled happily into teaching and homemaking. Jamie and I had more free time and financial means than during our first two years together. Since his studies were over, evenings and weekends could now be spent in leisure time activities. Our income also tripled with both of us working. We had time to spare and money to spend and we enjoyed life. Our Lansing Towers apartment was outrageously expensive, but we justified the expense by its convenient location. We shopped for furniture, draperies, stereo equipment and accessories. We spent evenings together in the basement of the building "antiquing" and refinishing furniture to round out our purchases. Our wardrobes to date had been minimal, and we accompanied each other on shopping trips as we began to fill our "professional closets."

Predictably, we traveled to Washington, D.C. for our first vacation and then to San Francisco to sightsee and visit friends. We saw every movie that came to town, attended Michigan State football games and gave parties. We still played bridge.

After several months with the elections division, Jamie admitted to himself and to me that he was restless and bored. It was a difficult admission. He felt guilty because he liked the people he worked with very much and admired his boss, Bernie Apol, a great deal. The work itself—interpreting and applying election law was not challenging, however. More importantly, he was only moving around the edges of politics and was itching to become more involved.

Jamie's discontent was coupled with a bit of serendipity. Our next-door neighbor, Eugene Krasicky, was an assistant attorney general. In 1969, the attorney general was Frank J. Kelley. As I write these words in 1990, Frank J. Kelley is still attorney

26

general, or the Eternal General, as political punsters like to say. Frank had been A.G. for several years already and was a successful statewide elected official. Students of Michigan politics—and Jamie was an A+ student—talked about Frank's political prowess and acumen in reverential terms. Jamie began eyeing the A.G.'s office and its staff of young attorneys with growing interest. He became more and more intrigued with the possibility of joining the A.G.'s staff. He'd become casually acquainted with Gene Krasicky from seeing him in the hall, in the elevator, and around the building. Gene even asked Jamie once if he'd ever thought about practicing law with the A.G. which seemed the most logical career move for Jamie to make next.

Joining the A.G.'s staff became increasingly clear as the next step. I vividly remember a long, soul-searching discussion we had one evening, weighing the merits of staying with the elections division and the merits of joining the A.G. Jamie was torn between his loyalty to Bernie Apol and the appeal of working for Kelley who was on his way to becoming a political legend. Jamie asked me what I thought he should do. I thought he would become increasingly restless, unhappy and bored in his current position, that Bernie would understand, and that he should speak to Gene Krasicky, the sooner the better. He went the next night and their conversation is one for the history books. I wasn't privy to it, and I don't know what was said, but I do know the result. Jamie was hired by Frank Kelley, and our career in Michigan politics began.

It all began inauspiciously enough. Jamie was assigned to the Licensing and Regulation Division and he practiced administrative law regarding the licensing and regulation of dentists, nurses, cosmetologists and the like—anyone in Michigan who needed a license to practice their profession. I was outwardly supportive but hiding mixed inner feelings. Politics fascinated and intrigued me, and I was excited by the prospect of future involvement. I looked upon politics as a desirable and worthy calling. I admired politicians and I admired Jamie for wanting to be one. Jamie continued to be my teacher and my political mentor. Most of his words were still pearls. We were poised to begin the life he had dreamed about and I believed I wanted to share.

Even then I was jealous of the grip politics had on him and resented that he seemed to give more thought to politics than anything else. I didn't like the fact that he was preoccupied so much of the time, and that he wanted to talk politics to the exclusion of everything else. I had to compete with politics for his attention. I knew in my heart I was about to compete with it for his time. Most of all, I feared that I would also have to compete with politics for his heart and soul.

Meanwhile, I hid my inner doubts and continued to pursue my teaching career. Second grade is a perfect age to teach because the children are eager and fresh, and most of them love school and their teacher. Their first grade teacher has taught them the basics of the three R's, and the second grade teacher spends a year refining, enhancing and enlarging those skills. The second grade teacher has the opportunity to develop new and creative avenues of expression for the basic skills they've gained. I enjoyed those twenty-five second graders as grandparents enjoy grandchildren. I loved to see them arrive in the morning, I loved spending the day with them, and I loved seeing them return home at the end of the day!

I diligently taught my students their reading, writing and arithmetic but found real joy in giving them outlets and an appreciation for their natural creativity. I always believed it was totally unrealistic to expect seven-year olds to sit still at the same desk, in the same room, with the same people for six or seven hours a day, 195 days a year. They have too much energy, enthusiasm and curiosity. I attempted to relieve the tedium by changing the room and desk arrangement often and planning activities they would look forward to as they came to school each day. I tried to plan our days so that students would experience at least one thing every day which they enjoyed and were good at. After the pledge of allegiance and attendance, we started every morning with a chapter from a piece of good children's literature. I gathered them in the reading corner I always had in my room and we all sat on the floor together while I read the day's chapter. They shared their thoughts about it and I invited them to show the books they were reading and say a little something about them. I tried to instill in them my own joy of reading and an appreciation of literature. They had their chance to try their hand at writing, too, with many creative writing exercises we did as a group and individually. The enthusiasm and skill they brought to the reading of their own pieces and those of their classmates made Dick and Jane dry and dull.

I had an artist's corner in my room where a two-sided easel stood, ready with paper, brushes and paints. Each day four students took turns painting, two in the morning and two in the afternoon. They painted while regular classroom activities were conducted and we all enjoyed watching their paintings develop. When completed, each student hung his or her painting on the "Gallery" bulletin board reserved just for displaying the daily masterpieces. Every day four new paintings were displayed and the ones from the previous day were taken home by the proud artists.

We had music, too, when the music teacher came and conducted organized singing. Since I can't sing a note, the music I taught them came in the form of the classical music I played from the radio I brought into the classroom which provided background as they read or did assignments at their desks. It was relaxing for all of us.

We staged plays and performances, sometimes for an audience, but most often for our own enjoyment right in our own room. Some of the plays involved work over several weeks and others were completely spontaneous, brought on by an incident, event or something we'd read.

We ended every day back in the reading corner, sharing thoughts about our day and our plans for the next. I had fun teaching and I think my students had fun learning. Teaching was gratifying and gave me a feeling of worth. It satisfied my social conscience and my need to contribute in a positive, meaningful way to the lives of other people. The inherent value of my work and the belief I had in myself to bring my own value to it sustained me as I watched Jamie become more and more immersed in politics.

In 1969, Jamie and I returned to a new home at the end of our day. The novelty of spending $600 a month for an apartment wore off even before the end of our year's lease at Lansing Towers. The inconvenience of a high-rise was something we hadn't anticipated. Just transporting the week's groceries up from the underground garage was a logistical challenge, requiring numerous trips up and down the elevator carrying bags or negiotiating a stubborn and awkward flatbed cart. Shopping involved a complicated ordeal from the car, through several sets of doors, into and out of the elevator, unloading the cart from the hall into our apartment and back down again. We were also the only young couple, and we felt out of place and out of step with our neighbors.

Jamie's sister Suzanne and her husband Bob were living in a homey, large and comfortable apartment in Mason, the Ingham County seat about ten miles outside Lansing. We visited them frequently because they had two children and typical babysitter problems. A two-bedroom apartment became available there when our lease was up in Lansing, and we moved to Mason where we lived for the next two and one-half years.

With the money we saved in rent, we also could afford our first new car. Jamie made a scientific study of our big purchase. Consumer reports, blue books, comparison shopping, miles of surveying car lots, dealing, negotiating, and discussing resulted in the greatest car we ever owned—a 1969 Oldsmobile Delta 88. It was a red two-door sedan with a black vinyl roof and interior. And it was fast. It had a huge engine. In those days, the speed limit was 70 MPH and we could make the ninety-mile trip between Lansing and Detroit in one hour.

That trip began with regularity in 1970 which was an election year. A statewide election in Michigan can't be won without carrying Detroit and its suburbs—Wayne, Oakland and Macomb counties. Jamie had worked his way into Frank Kelley's inner circle of political advisors and was active in Frank's re-election campaign for Attorney General. He spent more and more time with Frank himself, accompanying him to events, even driving for him on occasion.

As was so often the case in his political career, an old friend had turned up for Jamie at the right time and in the right place. Larry Glazer was a boyhood chum who had gone to summer church camp with Jamie. When Jamie was governor, Larry went on to become his legal advisor and later was appointed a judge by Jamie. In 1970, Larry was on Frank Kelley's staff writing

30

speeches for him. Jamie hadn't seen Larry in years, but they ran into each other on the day Jamie was sworn into the Michigan Bar in 1969. Their paths crossed next when Jamie joined the A.G.'s office where they renewed their acquaintance, and Larry was instrumental in helping Jamie gain access to Frank and his top advisors.

Frank enjoyed dealing with young, bright attorneys, especially those who liked politics and had good political skills and instincts. Jamie qualified on all counts. Frank gave Jamie more and more political responsibilities on top of his legal work and Jamie responded enthusiastically. Much of our social life on weekends consisted of attending and "working" political events for Frank. Candidates frequently host receptions, called "hospitality suites," especially in conjunction with other larger events, like county, state and national conventions and fundraising dinners. Jamie and Larry staffed many of those receptions, accompanied by Larry's wife, Pat, and me. By and large these parties were fun because the people in politics are friendly, outgoing, and interesting individuals who are well-informed and not infrequently opinionated. They keep up with what's going on in the world and have opinions on all of it. Political cocktail parties—at least Democratic ones—are usually noisy, crowded places where major decisions are often made.

One of Jamie's tasks was to arrange these parties. That meant ordering the beverages and snacks, making sure nametags, signs, banners and literature were in the room, helping determine the guest list and getting invitations out. At party time, it meant greeting guests and helping Frank entertain them, getting them out of the room when the party was over and cleaning up. This was my training ground for what would come later. At these parties, I met hundreds of people active in Michigan politics—elected officials, candidates, party workers, precinct delegates, media, opinion leaders and other wives. Many of the people I met in 1970 would be helpful in 1974 when Jamie ran for U.S. Congress and again in 1982 when he ran for governor. Many would prove instrumental in his success.

I listened, observed and learned. I learned how to make conversation, mostly small talk, with anybody. I learned how to "work the room"—the art of entering a room and determining

31

at a moment's glance who you should be sure to talk to before you leave; the art of circulating throughout the room and through the crowd, shaking hands and talking, for at least a brief time, with everyone there; the art of reading a person's name tag before speaking to them so you can look them in the eye when you shake their hand; the art of meeting and greeting, gripping and grinning. I learned how to remember people's faces and many times their names. Remembering a person is the single most effective thing one can do to please someone. It became an easy and pleasant thing to do. The key is to give absolute concentration to the person you're conversing with, look at them in detail and repeat their name as many times during the conversation as possible. Jamie was the unchallenged master at it. He could remember everybody he met, what they talked about and where he met them. More often than not, he could also tell me where and when I'd met a person and what we'd discussed.

I learned that some of the most helpful things a politician's wife can do are to help entertain, "work a room," give people attention, fill up potato chip and pretzel bowls, keep a party going, and clean-up when it's over.

I received plenty of instruction and practice in all of this in 1970. There was pent-up demand in Jamie, and he couldn't get enough of politics just working for Frank that year. Besides, he was on Frank's staff as an attorney, being paid taxpayers' dollars to protect the public good, so there was a limit to the volume of political work he could do for Frank.

Where there's a will, there's a way, and Jamie found one. The hot race of 1970 was for governor and that one gripped Jamie's interest. The Democratic candidate was a state senator named Sander Levin, a fine legislator with a good record who was challenging the Republican incumbent, Bill Milliken, who had been governor for two years. Milliken had inherited the office from his predecessor, George Romney, who was appointed to the president's cabinet. Since he had been the incumbent for only two years, Milliken was beatable, and Levin had an excellent chance to win. Jamie wanted to help him win and he talked Frank into letting him work on Levin's campaign. Because of his other responsibilities, that meant Jamie did most of his work for Levin on his own time, during evenings and weekends.

As had been the case with Frank, Sandy soon recognized Jamie's natural political instincts, his gift for insightful analysis and good political strategy. Jamie repeatedly was given increased responsibilities and wound up being the field organizer for eighty of Michigan's eighty-three counties. Jamie was on the road constantly, traveling to and from many of those eighty counties many times. That new car of ours logged thousands of miles. I was still teaching so I could travel with him only on weekends. During the week I worried because he usually attended a meeting or an event in the evenings and due to the distances he had to travel, he often arrived home after midnight.

I remember feeling desperate one night when it was very late and he hadn't returned home yet. I couldn't sleep and I was beside myself with worry. Where on earth was he? What had happened? This was craziness, I thought, working all day at the A.G.'s office, then driving half-way across the state and back, working most of the night too. And Sandy wasn't even paying him. It made no sense to me.

By the time Jamie arrived home that night about 2:30 A.M. I was frantic. When he did walk in, my relief dissolved into anger. I raved about the worry he caused me, how unfair it was to leave me home alone every night, how I couldn't sleep until he got home, how I had to get up early to teach, how I couldn't understand all this.

He didn't listen to me. He never really did. He couldn't. He was doing what he loved. He resented it when I suggested, complained, reasoned and ranted that he was gone all the time, that he was consumed with this race, that he couldn't talk about anything else, that he didn't seem to care about anything else. It was that last part that haunted me—the caring. Jamie cared so deeply about politics that there was little caring left for anything else.

My fears about having to compete with politics for his time, his heart and his soul were coming true. And now there was going to be another person who would have to do the same— our son.

Chapter Six

J ames Johnston, Blanchard, Jr., "Jay," was named for his
father for two reasons: we couldn't find any other name we
liked better, and I knew Jamie would make that a name of
which our son would be proud.

Jay got his first taste of politics before he took his first bottle.
Jamie and I used to joke about the fact that our son attended
more cocktail parties, political events and parades before he was
born than most people do in their entire lifetime.

He was conceived right on schedule. When we were married,
we decided we would start our family after four years of marriage. That would give us two years during which Jamie could
finish law school and two years during which both of us could
work to acquire some possessions and save a little nest egg.

I had it all planned, and it was a pretty typical plan for the
1970s. Once we started our family, I intended to make my
husband, my children and my home my full-time career. I had
no intention of working outside our home. I had worked the

past four years to give us a head start on our future, and I had my teaching degree and my permanent teaching certificate for insurance should I need them in an emergency. It truly never entered my mind that I wouldn't be completely fulfilled by my responsibilities as a wife and mother.

In the fall of 1969, I started my fourth year of teaching. I had been on birth contol pills since our wedding, and I had read and heard about the difficulties some women had conceiving children after using oral contraceptives. Jamie and I talked it over and decided we were ready to start our family. In November of 1969 I stopped using any contraceptive, and in January I was pregnant.

We were stunned. We weren't really trying, thinking it would be a while before my body adjusted to being "pill-free." I went to Sparrow Hospital one morning before school for either the rabbit or the frog test and called that afternoon the minute school was over to get the results which were positive. I called Jamie at work and greeted him with the cliche, "Hello, Dad." He was as happy as I was, and we made plans to celebrate that evening at one of our favorite Lansing restaurants, Scofe's. We met there after work and were really quite shy and tongue-tied about the whole thing! I think we were both in a bit of a daze, and I vaguely remember we talked about the changes this would mean for me because I planned to quit teaching and stay at home with Jay. We knew it would change our financial situation and what the consequences would be.

I had a wonderful pregnancy. I anticipated our baby's birth joyfully. I never had a day of morning sickness and never felt healthier. I didn't gain too much weight and was in great spirits. I kept a daily diary about my pregnancy which I hoped to share with Jay when he grew up. I made most of my maternity clothes and couldn't wait to wear them. I bought a second-hand Jenny Lind baby crib and refinished it, and refreshened the bassinet in which all three of Jamie's nephews had slept and which Jamie's sister Suzanne had loaned to me. I painted other furniture in the red, white and blue color scheme I'd chosen for Jay's room, and I made colorful clown pictures from felt to hang on the wall. Everything was in readiness weeks beforehand.

My pregnancy passed happily, especially the summer months.

I was in good shape psychologically and physically, and I enjoyed statewide campaign travels by car with Jamie. The Levin campaign was nearing its peak and I enjoyed sharing the campaign with Jamie. I finally met many of the people I'd heard him talk about for months and saw the communities he'd worked so hard to organize. I was happy to be able to share the part of his life which seemed more important to him than anything else. I remember we spent our fourth anniversary, June 18, 1970, at a fundraiser for U.S. Senator Phil Hart. While we "worked the room," Jamie discussed the governor's race and I discussed the baby.

I was happy to share this time with Jamie, but I was secretly happier that the campaign would be over shortly. I was excited to begin a more normal life and have time to share our baby together.

Our baby was due in early October. On the evening of September 29, we were in Southfield, at the Raleigh House, attending a fundraiser for Frank Kelley. Frank joked about the fact that I looked just about ready to deliver, and he told us he was fully prepared to put me on top of the piano and deliver the baby then and there, if necessary. It may have been the power of suggestion, but as we were driving back to Mason I began having labor pains. Upon arriving home, we immediately called the doctor to report my labor pains, and he advised us to go to the hospital. We grabbed my bag which had been packed for months and set off eagerly. We had taken childbirth classes at the hospital together and felt confident we were in for an easy delivery because we were prepared and I was in such good health.

After arriving at Sparrow Hospital in Lansing, I was examined by a nurse who informed us I wouldn't deliver until morning. She sent Jamie home, and I was left alone at 2:00 A.M. in a dark labor room with a woman next door screaming with every labor pain. I became frightened and insisted the nurse call Jamie and ask him to come back to the hospital. She discouraged me, saying he was going to need all the sleep he could get, but she could tell I needed his moral support so she relented and called. She roused him from a deep sleep, but bless his heart, he said he'd be right there. He dressed and drove the twenty miles back to the hospital. He came in the labor room with a smile, kissed me, and climbed into the labor bed with me. There we slept through the night together, if a bit fitfully.

He stayed with me for the next forty hours, holding my hand, counting while I did deep breathing during labor pains, timing my contractions, rubbing my back, and giving me hope and encouragement. It was a long, difficult labor but he was with me every minute. Jay was born by cesarean section on October 1 at 6:16 P.M., after the doctor completed a Wednesday afternoon round of golf.

A C-section was considered major surgery in those days, requiring ten days of hospitalization. Jamie visited every day and brought me a dozen yellow roses and a gold baby-shoe charm, engraved with Jay's birthday, for my charm bracelet. I don't have that any longer—someone broke into our house in Virginia during our Congressional years and stole most of my jewelry, including that charm bracelet.

During those ten days, I sent the birth announcements which I had designed and made myself. Each announcement included a hand-written note about Jay and invited the recipient to come and visit us at home.

Jamie and I took Jay home to our apartment in Mason on a glorious, warm, sunny fall day. A neighbor took a picture of the three of us outside our apartment building to record this milestone in our lives. My parents came to stay with us for about a week which was a great help. I remember my mother was very concerned when they left; she wasn't certain I was ready to handle the baby on my own. I was eager to have Jay to myself but sorry to lose their company.

It was now just about a month before the November election and Jamie was completely tied up with the campaign. He was out every night or home from the office late. The pressure and the demands were mounting, and the campaign was running out of time. Levin had narrowed the gap but was still trailing the incumbent, and every moment and every vote was precious.

Intellectually I knew how important this election was to Jamie. If Levin could do as well as he was expected to do in Wayne, Oakland and Macomb counties, and do better than expected in the other counties—those that Jamie was organizing—that might provide the margin of victory. So much was

37

riding on the work Jamie was doing and had done for months outstate. I knew this was a great opportunity for him to prove himself, his strategic abilities and political skills. In my head, I knew this, but in my heart I wanted him home with me and Jay.

Sander Levin lost that election by less than one percentage point. It was heartbreakingly close. Even though Levin did better than expected in the counties Jamie organized, Jamie took the loss hard and was depressed for the next month. He worked through that depression with post-election post-mortems with other campaign workers after work. My hopes of getting him back as soon as the election was over were unrealistic, but by Christmas we were really into parenthood. We bought ourselves all of the baby paraphernalia with which parents load themselves down—playpens, wind-up swings, high chairs, and a movie camera. Our home movies from Christmas, 1970, show the family looking a little off-color as Jamie experimented with lighting.

As January, 1971, and a new decade began, Jamie was coming out of his post-election depression and I began to fight an eighteen-month battle with post-partum depression. The excitement of Jay's homecoming, the high drama of the election in November and the holiday festivities had been a swirl of activity. January, however, was a different story. With the onset of the long, cold winter and a small infant to care for, I was housebound and feeling like a prisoner in my own home. The reality of the responsibilities and demands of parenthood began to dawn on me. The caring and feeding and tending and worrying amounted to a twenty-four hour, seven-days-a-week duty. Every day was like every other. Weekends, those treasured days of the working world, lost their special meaning. They were days like all the others, completely bound-up with baby care.

I loved Jay dearly. He was a darling baby who came home from the hospital with a sweet and sunny disposition which he has to this day. He was an easy baby to love and care for, and he brought both of us immeasurable joy, but I didn't like staying home and taking care of him all the time. I couldn't really understand that ambivalence, and it made me feel enormously guilty. I was bitterly disappointed that I didn't find the role of full-time wife and mother as satisfying as I expected it to be. I felt tricked and trapped but hated myself for feeling that way. I was jealous and resentful that Jamie left the house every morning bound for work while I was bound to baby bottles. I was doubly resentful when he lingered at work and came home late. I turned this guilt, resentment and anger inward because I didn't like feeling the way I did. I didn't think I should have those feelings and didn't want to admit to them, so I buried them deep inside myself and pretended things were fine.

This denial of my true feelings, this ambivalence, this disappointment led to a deep, unrelenting and long-term depression with alarming symptoms which I fought for the next year and a half. The symptoms of depression are insidious and they crept up on me and grabbed hold before I knew what was wrong and what I was fighting.

I found it increasingly uncomfortable to be with people, to leave the house, to be in crowds, to go to the grocery store and to drive a car. Any activity out-of-the-house caused me extreme discomfort, anxiety and eventually severe anxiety attacks. When I had one, I became dizzy, I lost my equilibrium, my hands and arms became numb, I hyperventilated and felt I was about to faint. It was terrifying when it happened in a public place or while I was driving. I began to avoid going out or driving for fear I would faint in public or lose control of my car. It was exacerbated by my love and responsibility for Jay because my fear was compounded. I worried not only about what would happen to me, I worried far more about what would happen to Jay if I fainted in the grocery store or while I was driving. I found this extremely alarming and it caused me to be even more housebound than ever.

My life became a vicious circle. The more I stayed home, the more depressed I became, which caused my symptoms to become worse, which heightened my anxiety attacks, which increased my fear of going out, which caused me to stay home, which made me more depressed. Around and around and around. For a while, I struggled with this in solitary confinement. I was very ashamed that I couldn't get a grip on myself. I had read about post-partum depression and knew that's what I was fighting. I also knew that it usually went away of its own accord and I would lead a normal life again. Everyday I forced myself out of bed and prayed fiercely that this would be the day when I would begin to feel content and in control of myself, instead of a victim of this monster inside my head which caused me such torment.

In the spring of 1971, after about three months of this, I couldn't hide my problems any longer. It was a terrible strain to function normally when I felt like a complete misfit. Jamie hadn't said anything about my acting peculiar, but I suspect he just wrote it off to the emotional roller coaster many new mothers experience. I finally confided my inner terror to him and explained my feelings of impending doom which people with depression wear like a shroud. I described to him what happened to me when I had to leave the house, the anxiety it produced and the resulting symptoms. I was extremely alarmed and frightened, and I couldn't keep it to myself any longer.

Jamie's response was very calm, rational and understanding, and that was such a relief. I was afraid he would dismiss my problems or scoff at them or tell me I'd get over them if I just pulled myself together. I don't know what I would have done if he had said that because I'd been trying to pull myself together for months. He couldn't, however, offer any instant cure. I told him I wanted to talk to Bob Brook, Jamie's brother-in-law, who is a clinical psychologist. Jamie discouraged me because he thought Bob, as a family member, might be too close to be objective or helpful. He had another suggestion, however, and it's one I took him up on. He suggested that I talk to my internist about my problems.

I was so relieved when he suggested that because Dr. Paine was a special person in whom I could confide, and one with whom I felt a great deal of rapport. I went to him once a week for counseling for many months. Unfortunately, in 1971, depression was not understood to the extent it is today, and my sessions with Dr. Paine did not result in recovery. He was older, Catholic and conservative and believed that a woman's place is in the home. He did his best to convince me that I should be completely fulfilled by my role as wife and mother and when I truly believed that, my depression would lift. He shared with me the joys of his own family, the special role God gave only to women to bear children, and the readings of Anne Morrow

Lindbergh. He suggested that the best thing I could do for myself was to have another child as soon as possible in order to stimulate my motherly instincts. I was horrified. Dear Dr. Paine. The only thing he succeeded in, in spite of his good intentions, was to increase my guilt and depression.

I seriously considered going back to teaching as a means to achieve more self-fulfillment than full-time mothering provided. I couldn't bring myself to do it for a couple of reasons. I believed with all my heart that my place was home with Jay, at least until he started school. I believed Jay needed my love and my presence. I knew no one else would treasure him as I did and that any substitute for me was second-best. I couldn't bring myself to short-change him. We chose to bring him into the world, and he deserved our best.

My nature dictated, as well, that I accept the responsibilities of my actions. Once I make a decision and commit myself to a course of action, virtually nothing will deter me or alter my course. I had previously decided that I would stay home and be a full-time mother and I stuck with that decision.

The next year, 1971, was an eternity. Each day I had to fight dragons just to get through the day. The demons of depression transformed the easiest, simplest, most trivial things into impossible, gargantuan tasks. It took every ounce of my inner strength to give Jay the nurturing, loving care and attention he deserved and I wanted to give him. I made it my mission that no matter how lousy I felt, Jay received the best care and love I had to give. There wasn't much left over for Jamie, but he hung in there with me and did his best to understand.

He continued to bury himself in his work, usually arriving home about 7:30 at night. And we argued about that. In fact, we argued about it for twenty-one years. Dinner was an important time for me—in fact, it capped off all the day's events. In my youth, dinner had been a command performance at our house, and you just didn't miss it. It's ironic that it was so important to me because I really don't like to cook. It wasn't the meal that was important; it was the gathering, the coming together of the family, the togetherness and the sharing of the day's happenings. It always seemed to me that the best time for dinner was about 6:00 or 6:30 P.M. which would give us time to eat a

41

leisurely meal, sit around and chat afterwards, clean up and still have some of the evening left for relaxation.

I wanted Jamie to come home earlier. My days at home by myself with little Jay were long, and I yearned for Jamie's company and companionship. As my depression deepened and I became more and more withdrawn from other people, I needed his presence even more. At 7:30 when Jamie returned home, a leisurely dinner together was impossible because Jay would be tired and ready for bed. By the time dinner was finished, the dishes cleaned up and Jay put to bed, it was nearing 10:00 P.M. We were still on our different schedules; I was up early because Jay woke about 6:00 so I turned in about 11:00 P.M. That gave Jamie and me a very short evening together.

Each day doggedly followed the one before it. Jamie was still working for Frank Kelley, and had moved up to an assistant to the Deputy Attorney General, Leon Cohan. He continued to do double duty, practicing law in the Licensing and Regulation Division and functioning as one of Frank and Leon's lieutenants. Politically, 1971 was an important year because it set the stage for the Presidential election in 1972 and a Democratic challenge to a U.S. Senate seat in Michigan. Jamie was actively involved with both elections. He had remained close to Sandy Levin, and it was he who gave Jamie his next big opportunity.

After losing the governorship, Sandy became involved in Edmund Muskie's presidential campaign and was designated his campaign director in Michigan. Sandy had gained a great deal of respect for Jamie's political abilities during the 1970 gubernatorial campaign and asked Jamie to be his deputy in organizing Muskie's Michigan campaign. We faced another tough decision. Muskie's chances were slim, and Jamie knew that. He also knew that Frank Kelley would run for U.S. Senate against Robert Griffin. He knew he couldn't work on both campaigns and practice law, too.

Accepting the Muskie job required us to move from Mason to Detroit where the Muskie headquarters were located. I didn't welcome that prospect; I was still in the grips of depression and barely managing. Moving to Detroit would require a whole new series of adjustments which I wasn't sure I could handle. I

42

preferred to stay in the Lansing area which is what we could do only if Jamie continued to practice law with Frank Kelley and work on his Senate campaign. That was a set of circumstances which was predictable and familiar and there was comfort in that.

Jamie, however, was eager to move to the Detroit area, and he revealed that to me in the course of our discussions. In fact, he had been trying to figure out a way to do that ever since Sandy's loss, but he hadn't come up with anything sensible. He didn't want to join a private law practice, which he could have easily done, because law wasn't where his interests lay and the demands of private practice would have been too great to allow much time for political pursuits.

The opportunity to go to work on Muskie's campaign seemed to be the way out of Lansing Jamie had been looking for. I didn't have the strength to oppose the move and didn't have the heart to deny Jamie the chance to take another big step on the road to achieving his ambitions. We agreed to take Sandy up on his offer, risky though it was, and organized for the move to Detroit. I buried my fear of the unknown in the daily preparations for moving. The salary of the Muskie job wasn't great, but it was augmented by a rent-free apartment. Sandy knew several real estate owners in the Detroit area and one of them donated an apartment for us to live in as an in-kind donation to the Muskie campaign.

It was a dreadful place, and it became my prison. I saw it once before moving day, and I couldn't imagine living there. It was in Detroit in an old apartment complex near Livernois and Outer Drive on the third floor of a building with no elevator. The apartment itself was spacious, and we had two bedrooms. In its day it had been grand, but it was definitely at the seedy stage by March 1972, when we moved in. The public hallways were old, dim and dusty with threadbare, dirty carpeting. Our apartment was in somewhat better shape, but badly in need of new carpet and updating.

Our March moving day felt like the beginning of a death sentence to me. Our apartment in Mason had been light, airy and pleasant and was Jay's first home. I felt a real sentimental attachment to it and I hated to leave. I was fond of the town of

Mason, too. I had spent many hours walking with Jay in his stroller around the town square. Those walks were a real salvation and outlet after driving became so difficult. It was a safe, secure, familiar, comfortable environment.

I was unhappy leaving our home in Mason for an old run-down apartment in a big, unfamiliar city. I was beside myself with dread. Jay spent a few days with my parents while Jamie and I completed the move. We had two cars to drive to Detroit which meant I had to drive one. For someone who could barely drive around the block, the prospect of driving to Detroit, alone, and finding a new apartment building seemed as difficult as climbing Mt. Everest.

On moving day, the movers came, loaded up our furniture, and set off for our Detroit apartment. They were able to load up in the morning and wanted to unload that same afternoon. That meant that either Jamie or I had to go ahead of them and arrive at our Detroit apartment to let them in to begin unloading. The other one had to stay behind to clean the apartment and shampoo the carpet in order to get our security deposit back. It made more sense for me to go ahead of the movers, and I knew it. I also knew I'd have to make that drive sooner or later, and I wanted to get it over with. Filled with dread, and nostalgia to be leaving Jay's first home, I kissed Jamie a tearful good-bye in our empty Mason apartment as he began the shampooing operation. Feeling as if I'd never survive the trip to Detroit, I fearfully drove off.

I knew I'd have to fight terror, hot flashes, numbness, the sweats and feeling faint that entire trip, and I did. The trip from Lansing to Detroit is usually made on I-96 and for the first part of the trip that was my route. That didn't last long, however, because freeway driving is scariest when you're fighting an anxiety attack. The pressure to keep moving, to travel at fairly high speeds compounds the fear and the anxiety. You have the urge when you're frightened to slow down, but on a freeway you have to maintain a minimum speed. You feel trapped and even more frightened. I drove about half the trip on the freeway, hands frozen on the steering wheel, and eyes glued to the road, every inch of my body tense, my heart beating wildly and my breathing fast. I could only take about forty-five minutes of this before

44

I had to leave the freeway. I exited at Brighton and took the old Grand River Road into Detroit.

My anxiety lessened somewhat once I exited the freeway but as I neared Detroit I realized I had no idea how find our apartment on this route. I'd been there only once, and Jamie had driven the freeway the whole way. Again my anxiety flared because I had to arrive in advance of the movers who might not wait. I was hopelessly lost. At this point, I was panic-stricken and in tears. After several stops at gas stations to ask directions, I arrived at our apartment about an hour behind schedule, a complete wreck. The movers must have recognized that, thank God, because they were very sympathetic and didn't complain about waiting when I told them I'd been lost.

I did what I could to make the place comfortable and liveable, but it wasn't easy. We immediately went into another campaign mode with Jamie gone long hours, returning late, and completely preoccupied with Muskie's campaign. The loneliness was even worse now because we were in a strange environment and I didn't know anybody. I drove the car only to run absolutely essential errands because city driving nearly paralyzed me. I felt completely trapped. Going out of the house was more frightening than ever now because everything was strange, and I was virtually housebound in an apartment I hated. My depression worsened, dangerously.

Jamie was patient and understanding but he had his hands full with the campaign. He also didn't know what else to do but try to be sympathetic. He didn't complain, but I know he was wondering when I'd come out of the grip of this depression which had lasted for over a year at this point. Besides, I was managing, only barely, to keep things running at home and be a loving, caring wife and mother. Jay was loved and was thriving and that was the yardstick we were both using, in an unspoken agreement, to measure my ability to cope.

I was still trying to see Dr. Paine once a week in Lansing. He wasn't making me any better—that I knew—but I was afraid that things might grow worse if I stopped. He was a safety net for me, but it became harder and harder to see him because Jamie had to drive me there. On several occasions that spring, I cancelled appointments with Dr. Paine because Jamie couldn't get away from the campaign. Eventually, I stopped making appointments altogether.

I don't know if it was a self-fulfilling prophecy but things did get worse after I stopped seeing Dr. Paine. I lost my appetite, I couldn't sleep, I cried most of the day, and I finally lost my will to live.

Depression had me in its deathly grasp. Early one summer afternoon, I couldn't stand the anxiety, the fear, the impending doom any longer. I left the apartment while Jay was napping and as though in a trance I walked down three flights of stairs, out the door of the apartment building and straight into two lanes of heavy traffic. The screech of brakes and the honking of horns saved my life. I was jolted to my senses as traffic came to a halt inches from me. Screaming, I ran back into the apartment and called Jamie. I told him what had happened and that I had to go see Dr. Paine immediately. Something had to be done. I couldn't be trusted with my own safekeeping, let alone Jay's.

Jamie came home immediately, and we went to Dr. Paine's office in Lansing. Jamie and I must have talked about my near-accident and my problems on that hour-long trip, but the only thing I remember is Jay's chatter from the back seat. Dr. Paine saw me immediately so I think we must have called ahead.

After talking to me for some time, Dr. Paine decided I should be hospitalized. He spoke to both of us about it, and we nodded silently and dumbly because we didn't know what else to do. While he made the arrangements for my stay at the psychiatric unit at St. Lawrence Hospital in Lansing, Jamie and I went to a local park to talk and entertain Jay. I remember sitting with Jamie at a picnic table while Jay played on a jungle gym. I tried to explain to Jamie what was wrong, to describe how hard the simplest things were, to help him understand why I couldn't cope anymore.

I was admitted to the hospital that summer afternoon in 1972. Jamie and Jay were with me all the way. Up the elevator to the psychiatric floor, to my room, making arrangements for some clothes and toilet articles for me, and back to the elevator to say good-bye. I kissed them and waved goodbye to the two most precious people in the world as Jamie stepped into the

46

elevator with Jay in his arms. I was dumbstuck at where I was and grief-stricken because I didn't know if we would ever be a family again.

I returned to that same park about two years ago, to watch Jay play second base for the Okemos High School varsity baseball team in his senior year. I vividly remembered the scene there fifteen years earlier and thought about how much had changed in the intervening years.

Chapter Seven

It didn't take long to realize I didn't belong in the hospital. I was there a week and while I wasn't cured when I left, I regained my will and determination to recover.

During the week I was hospitalized, I saw a psychiatrist daily and attended daily group therapy sessions. Dr. Paine came to see me every day and Jamie visited me twice that week. None of the professional people in the hospital seemed very worried about me, and in the face of the serious mental illness suffered by others, my depression seemed to be a paltry problem. I knew it was real and I knew it had seriously debilitated me. I also knew I wasn't nearly as ill as those around me and that there were professionals who could help me get better. Most important, I saw how blessed I was and how much I had to live for.

I don't know if Dr. Paine put me in the hospital because he actually feared for my life or because he wanted to paint a clear picture for me of what my choice was. In any event, the stay clarified my choice—either find a way to overcome my depression or doom myself to a life of illness and hospitals. In this regard, my hospital stay had a dramatic effect on me. It gave me a week to talk and think about my depression. I confronted my problems head on, faced my depression openly, and learned to stop pretending that everything was normal. I listened to the options for treatment. I stopped feeling ashamed; I stopped feeling guilty. When I let those emotions go, I regained my strength and determination to cope.

I wanted to go home. I wanted my husband. I wanted my child. I wanted to rejoin my family and function as a family. One week after my admission to St. Lawrence Hospital, Jamie picked me up and we headed home. It was wonderful to be home, even to our dreadful apartment. For the first time it looked good.

Things did not improve magically or immediately. It took a long time and much determination on my part, and love and patience on Jamie's part. Jay being Jay helped immeasurably, too, because he was full of life, laughter, charm and delight.

In that summer of 1972, unforeseen factors serendipitously contributed to my recovery, too. Trivial as it may sound, the weather had a major role in my recovery. Summer arrived and Jay and I left the confines of the apartment for walks around the apartment complex. Just leaving the apartment, and going out into the fresh air and summer sunshine improved my health a great deal. I had made a friend, Sydney Pittman, who lived in our building and had a son six months older than Jay. She and I and our sons spent a lot of time outdoors together enjoying the weather and the companionship. The apartment complex had a swimming pool which our boys enjoyed. She and I and our sons are still friends to this day. The connection between the length of exposure to sunlight and depression hadn't been discovered in 1972. The sunny days of the summer of 1972 and the companionship of a good friend certainly helped alleviate mine.

Another factor involved some luck. I came out of the hospital determined to find a doctor who could treat depression effectively. One thing I discovered in the hospital is that depression is a disease that is treatable, and like most diseases, it requires therapy. It doesn't improve on its own. I also discovered there are doctors who understand depression and can treat it.

After I was released, Jamie drove me twice to Lansing to see privately one of the doctors who had counseled me in the hospital. He strongly suggested I find a doctor in the Detroit area and gave me two recommendations.

It was easier to pick up the phone now and call an unfamiliar doctor because I had talked openly about my depression in the hospital. While it wasn't as serious as many of the other problems I saw there, my depression was dealt with by the doctors and nurses as legitimate and shameless. The Lansing psychiatrist had given me two names to call and I picked one at random.

I sat on the kitchen floor to make the call because my legs felt a little rubbery. I instinctively knew how much was riding on this call. He answered his own phone and listened attentively as I briefly described my problem. He asked me how many times I'd told this story; it must have sounded rote. I told him that I'd been struggling with this for about eighteen months and had just recently been in the hospital for a week where I'd told it to many people. He said "I can help you." That simple sentence, and the conviction and sincerity with which he said it, brought a torrent of tears and sobs from me. I knew from that moment I would get better. He apologized that he couldn't talk any longer at that time because he was with a patient. He promised to call me back in thirty minutes and made me promise to wait by the telephone for his call. I did and he did. He returned my call almost to the minute and set an appointment for me to see him the next day. He again apologized that he couldn't see me immediately. At last, someone sensed and understood my despair, my urgency, my need. Someone existed who wanted to help me then and there.

That was the beginning of a six-month treatment program with Dr. Lawrence Cantow. He was a psychiatrist of uncommon good sense, practicality, sensitivity and skill. He immediately put me on anti-depressant medication and it took two attempts to find the medication which I could tolerate best. Initially, I had appointments with Dr. Cantow twice a week, but as I progressed I saw him once a week.

He believed in prescribing anti-depressants because they ease and eventually remove the anxiety symptoms which so paralyze

50

people with depression. Removing those symptoms made it easier for me to participate in my own counseling which is the secret to long-term treatment of depression. Dr. Cantow's prescription worked for me, and within a month I was beginning to feel like myself again. It was joyous to become reaquainted with my true self again, the individual I liked and the person who loved life.

Through all my trials and tribulations, Jamie had his problems to contend with. The Muskie campaign was rocky from the start and came to a tearful end when Ed Muskie emotionally defended his wife against vicious attacks from the media. In 1972, the country wasn't ready for a presidential candidate whom it decreed weak, sentimental and unfit because he wore his heart so touchingly on his sleeve. The campaign was disbanded and Jamie was left to look around for his next move.

He didn't have to look far. The attorney general has an office in Detroit and that became Jamie's next place of employment. It suited both Jamie and Frank because it kept us in Detroit where Jamie wanted to be for political reasons, and it enabled Frank to enlist Jamie to work on his campaign for the U.S. Senate. He was challenging the incumbent, Robert Griffin, in an election slated for November 1972.

I thought after the Muskie campaign collapsed we might return to Lansing, but Jamie was convinced we had made the right move in coming to the Detroit area and wanted to remain there. He had already begun to survey the local political landscape, especially the neighborhoods of south Oakland County where he'd grown up, and was beginning to plan the development of a political base of his own.

Our rent-free arrangement ended with the Muskie campaign and we had to make a decision about where to move. We had lived in seven different apartments in our six years of marriage, and since starting a family, we both felt it was time to settle down and buy our first home. Politically, it was a smart move, too. Jamie knew a family man who is a home owner in the community makes a much more appealing candidate than an apartment-dweller.

Looking for our first house was very exciting. We enlisted a family friend of Jamie's to be our real estate agent, so we had an ally we could trust completely. I hated our apartment so much that I was ready to buy five or six of the first houses we saw. They looked like palaces in comparison to our present apartment. Jamie, however, was more realistic and convinced me to hold out for the right house, in the right price range, with the right features, in the right political district. And we found it: One Woodside Park in Pleasant Ridge, eight blocks from where Jamie had grown up.

Purchasing our own home and leaving that dreadful apartment was another major factor in my recovery. We moved in on October 1, 1972, Jay's second birthday. From the first step through the front door on our first visit, it was a home we loved. We owned it for fourteen years and more than any other place we lived, it played a central part in the Blanchard family history. It was the only home we owned in Michigan, and I believe it is Jay's favorite of all the places we called home. It was the site of many family gatherings, many political pow-wows and parties and was the launching pad for Jamie's political career.

Chapter Eight

Moving into our first home gave me a new lease on life. This move contrasted sharply with the tension, depression and dread of our previous move. This time I couldn't move fast enough.

I clearly remember the day we moved. Again, I was the scouting party to the new abode while Jamie wrapped up things at the old place. This time I had no problem making the drive and I arrived at our new home before the movers. I had the empty house completely to myself, and I ran from room to room in complete delight, my head full of plans for redecorating, furniture placement, kitchen remodeling and the dog we could have in our fenced back yard. Our new home had a large picture window in the living room and I recall lying on the floor in the empty house, completely alone, with my hands behind my head, staring out contentedly at the bright blue, clear sky, basking in the happiness of that moment.

We settled right into the house and the neighborhood. We

couldn't have picked a better house, a better street or nicer neighbors. The house had a living room, dining room, kitchen, den, three bedrooms, two baths, full basement and a two-car garage. It fit our family of three perfectly and gave us growing room, too. It was in excellent condition and needed only redecorating. With the help of my dad who is an expert in a myriad of things around the house, we wallpapered and painted and added our own personal touches to make it home.

Woodside was home to many families with many children, and Jay was happy. Across the street was a large family with children just a little older than Jay, and he spent most of his waking hours there. He loved the action across the street. A family with five children had something going on all the time. Even at two years of age, Jay was an extrovert and spent every minute he could with the neighborhood kids. There were thirty-two houses on Woodside and about half of them had young children living in them. It was a perfect street for young families; I used to call it an Ozzie and Harriet neighborhood. We were heartily welcomed to Woodside by these families, and to this day I hear from some of them occasionally. They were loyal neighbors, friends and campaign supporters—even though many of them are Republicans!

For the first time since Jay's birth, I settled happily into the role of full-time wife, mother and homemaker. We moved in on October 1, and I spent the next three months busily making the house our home and preparing for the holidays. I had so much enthusiasm and energy that I handmade Christmas presents for everybody on our Christmas list of about twenty people.

I continued to see my psychiatrist once a week and take anti-depressant medication until the following spring. My outlook on life, my enthusiasm, my energy, and my patience all improved immeasurably. I was optimistic about the future again, my anxiety attacks ceased, Jay and I were out and about all the time and life was full and happy. I was able to cast off that shroud of impending doom which had so burdened me and my shoulders were back, my head was up and my eyes were bright. I was convinced a miracle had transformed my life, but in reality it was hard work. It took introspection, self-examination, and maturing for me to make the lasting changes which were necessary for a long-term recovery. Our weekly sessions provided me an outlet for expression and food for thought during the week.

During this time, I rediscovered my self-worth and my self-esteem. I also confronted my perfectionism and my unrealistic expectations. I learned how to keep things in perspective, to give other people the benefit of the doubt, and to allow myself the same benefit. I learned how to set and keep priorities in my life, how to keep in mind what is really important and how to act on it.

My Grandmother Beardslee always said things turn out for the best and I truly believe that. My experience with depression and my recovery from it are proof enough for me the adage is true. I wouldn't want to wish depression on anyone, but in my case, there was a silver lining. In the process of my recovery, I learned an enormous amount about myself and about other people. That knowledge has been invaluable during the many turns my life has taken.

Jamie, meanwhile, was as happy with the house as I but for somewhat different reasons. He felt as comfortable in it as I and liked the neighbors equally well. Its finest feature for him, however, was its location. It was strategically located in a newly defined congressional district.

Frank Kelley had lost his race for the U.S. Senate that November and remained Attorney General. That was propitious. If Frank had won a seat in the Senate, Jamie undoubtedly would have had an opportunity to go to Washington as one of his aides. As it was, Jamie continued to practice law for Frank in the AG's Detroit office and study the political landscape in southern Oakland County. Another propitious event occurred that November which set the stage for Jamie's entry into politics under his own banner.

As usually is the case following the ten-year census, the political map is re-drawn and new districts emerge. Such was the case in November 1972. Following the 1970 census, the Eighteenth Congressional District was created, covering most of southern Oakland County, including Ferndale and Pleasant Ridge, Jamie's political base. It was a new district, marginally Democratic, and everyone expected Dan Cooper, a Democratic state senator from the area who served in Lansing a number of years, to be elected to represent the voters of this congressional district in Washington, D.C. Dan was popular, but in November 1972, he lost in a surprising and unexpected defeat to Robert Huber, a conservative Republican from Troy. Dan was defeated on one issue—busing. Huber had incited fear in the hearts of the voters, had inflamed the issue and rode a bus of his own right to Washington, D.C.

While Democrats expressed disappointment and astonishment, Jamie saw another side to the results. He saw a chance to mount a challenge to Huber in two years for a seat in the U.S. Congress, and an earlier-than-expected opportunity to make a run for Washington, D.C. The possibility of the fulfillment of his life-time political dream stood before him.

In his previous studies of the political map, Jamie never expected that a seat in Congress might open up so early in the heart of his political home. He, like everyone else, expected the Democrat to take that seat and hold on to it for many years to come. Jamie fully expected that he would start his own political career in Lansing, in the state house or the state senate, serve there with distinction and position himself for opportunities down the road and up the ladder. Fate, however, set the stage for a big jump up several rungs.

For the next year, 1973, I hummed around the house, a very content "happy little homemaker." I got the house the way I wanted it, except for the kitchen which we were saving money to renovate, got to know my neighbors, watched Jay make friends with every kid on the street and learn to ride his tricycle, house-trained Abby, our new Labrador puppy, and joined the Pleasant Ridge Garden Club and the American Association of University Women. I was more contented with life at One Woodside than I had been in years.

Jamie, too, was happy. He turned our third bedroom into a small study, and it was in that room that he planned his first campaign. He spent hours during evenings and weekends in there. He had all the tools he needed: a phone, a calculator and the vote totals of Dan Cooper, Bob Huber, the State Board of Education, Sandy's 1970 campaign, and so on. He made room-sized maps of the Eighteenth Congressional District which he color-coded by using a variety of magic markers and a rainbow of push pins. He studied, analyzed, discussed and dissected those numbers and those maps until they were part of his every breath, his very being. He remarked once during his race for governor that he never went into an election better prepared than he was for that first race. He always remembered it fondly and proudly and recounted it hundreds of times to anyone who would listen.

He was in his element and I was in mine. He was happy, Jay was happy, and so was I, having recovered from the torment of the previous year. Jamie's excitement was infectious as he explained how good the projections looked, how vulnerable Huber was as a first-term, single-issue incumbent, and how taking the congressional seat was possible and feasible. For the first time in a long time, I felt the same excitement about politics that I felt when Jamie and I first met. He exuded enthusiasm, energy, will, conviction, and again he carried me along. I still had to compete with politics for his time, his attention, his heart and his soul, but I felt equipped to do so. I loved him and I was a loyal wife. I sincerely wanted to express that love by supporting him and helping him in his quest to fulfill his dream.

The resentment I felt when he gave so much of himself away on behalf of other candidates was very much diminished. The endless phone calls, the late night and weekend meetings and the preoccupation were still a source of irritation, but they bothered me less for several reasons. The effort was now expended on Jamie's own behalf—not another distracted, unappreciative candidate. Also, Jamie was in charge, for the first time, doing his own bidding and not someone else's, and he had more control over what was going on and that made it easier on me. Finally, because so much of the planning and work took place at our home, I could be an integral part of this campaign from the outset.

He did an enormous amount of research and planning during those months in 1973 and began putting a skeleton campaign committee together comprised of people he had known from high school, college and from previous political campaigns for Frank and Sandy. Two early key people were Susan Laird, a political organizer and strategist with whom Jamie had worked in Sandy's campaign, and Ron Thayer, a fundraiser and organizer whom Jamie met while working for Frank. Susan Laird eventually became Jamie's campaign manager and Ron Thayer remains a close political advisor and chief fundraiser.

Our home became campaign headquarters because the campaign was still in its infancy and no money had been raised to rent space elsewhere. Countless meetings were held in our living room and I participated in the majority of them. These living room meetings and that campaign group formed the nucleus of the Blanchard political machine, the most effective one Michigan may ever see. Some might say that Soapy Williams or Bill Milliken had a better one, but I predict that the Blanchard one will go down in history as the best. I was a founding member, because Jamie trusted my judgment about people and my political instincts. He often asked my opinion about whom to trust, about a person's strengths and weaknesses, and about the approach which would work best with a particular individual. He usually asked me to review his speeches and to listen to them as he practiced them aloud. He also thought I was a good bellweather and in touch with how an average voter would react to a campaign slogan, ad, billboard or other campaign strategy. He used me as a sounding board and trusted me to give an honest and forthright opinion. I never failed him in that and always gave him a sincere and frank appraisal, even it if was something he didn't want to hear.

I fulfilled that role for him throughout his career, to a great extent while he was in Congress and to a lesser extent while he was governor. He had many more advisors as governor, all of whom were anxious to tell him what he wanted to hear, and he solicited my advice less and less.

By fall of 1973, Jamie began to mount his effort in earnest. At this stage, our operations were top-secret and behind the scenes. An element of surprise was crucial. For his campaign to have the slightest chance of success, however, it required Jamie to obtain the support of a number of party and elected officials. That was no easy task. It is an understatement to say most people were skeptical. While Jamie had a great deal of political experience, it was not the kind which carried weight because he had never run for office and won, except in high school and college. Yet many seasoned politicans were impressed by

Jamie's research and analysis as well as the campaign framework and committee he had in place. His target for touching all the necessary political bases was December 31, 1973.

His strategy hinged on a sufficient number of political powerbrokers supporting him or at least remaining neutral in their support of someone else. Without an adequate number of opinion leaders, a successful campaign simply couldn't be waged. These meetings and conversations were crucial, and Jamie prepared thoroughly with his committee to anticipate questions and to practice persuasive replies. The success and effectiveness of these meetings exceeded Jamie's expectations; he met his target date and came away with the support he needed.

These strategic meetings were an essential campaign exercise. In presenting his case to the powerbrokers, Jamie needed to articulate his reasons for running, his campaign theme and key messages, and his strategy for implementing a winning campaign.

It became apparent that Jamie would have to a devote fulltime effort to the campaign in order to win. Frank had been generous about allowing Jamie flexibility in his schedule to accommodate the early stages of the campaign, but the campaign would have to go into full-swing in March. Jamie had been anticipating the problem and was drawing on all his resourcefulness to find a solution which would allow him to campaign full-time and still put a roof over our heads and food on the table.

I offered to go to work, but we decided that would be our last resort. We both believed strongly that the best thing for Jay was to be at home with his mother, even if he did spend most of his time with his cadre of friends, and we knew that I could be valuable in the campaign. Somebody had to be the anchor at home, especially since it was also campaign central, and it certainly was not going to be Jamie, so it had better be me.

Jamie managed a coup which solved the dilemma of managing these two full-time tasks. The Attorney General has the power to designate attorneys in private practice to handle certain types of cases for fees which accrue to the attorney and the firm with which a lawyer practices. Those designations are made on a long-term basis, usually over a period of years, and are very much sought after for the revenue they generate for an attorney and the firm. In what was a series of discussions over a couple of months, Jamie arranged to join a law firm in Oakland County and to bring with him such a designation from the Attorney General. The arrangement would allow him to campaign full-time and draw a small salary from the fees which the firm would acquire from the legal work done for the Attorney General. Jamie was not required to do the legal work himself, but the firm would pay him a percentage of the fees—similar to a finder's fee for the business he generated.

I remember the night he came home with this news. He had been to dinner with a partner in the firm and had reached agreement on the arrangement. Jamie was like a cat who had caught a canary and he was anxious to win my support for this proposal because it would allow him the time he needed to mount an effective campaign. The negative aspect of this arrangement meant that our income would be severely cut. He calculated that the arrangement would bring in enough to make the house payment, the car payment, our food and utilities and the bare necessities, but we would not have any disposable income for new clothes or miscellaneous expenses. We would have to charge those on our credit cards. Our financial situation would be precarious, to say the least. To add to it, Jamie had borrowed about $30,000 from his family to fund the campaign, which would have to be paid back—win or lose. The financial vise was tightening.

We talked for a long time and made a decision that evening. We decided we were young and had very little to lose which we couldn't recover in two or three years. We knew it would be harder and harder every year to take this kind of risk as we grew older, more settled, with more responsibilities and probably more children. We concluded that an opportunity like this doesn't present itself very often, and if we were going to do it we should do it in a way which would ensure the greatest chance of success. We decided to go for broke and take the arrangement.

Jamie left the Attorney General's office, but not before he applied for every credit card possible. With key supporters behind him, freedom to campaign full-time and a roof over his

family's head, the next milestone was the campaign announcement, slated for mid-March.

Jamie and his advisors decided to make the overriding issue
of the campaign a bread and butter one—inflation. Jamie
wanted to bring the issue home to the voters of the Eighteenth
and what better way to do that than from our front porch?
There are standard locations for campaign announcements like
hotel banquet rooms, steps of the Capitol, and press clubs, but
a front porch was a novel political launching pad.

But it fit. Jamie was positioning himself as the champion of
the average voter of the Eighteenth, who was a middle-class
worker and whose home was his castle. Bob Huber, the incumbent, was a wealthy Republican businessman who owned his
own business in Troy and rode around in a Cadillac arrogantly
smoking cigars. Huber was older and could be stereotyped as an
overweight, cigar-smoking politician. Jamie would contrast
that image with the portrait of a young, sincere, family-man
who had just bought his first home, and like his constituents,
was worried about the price of milk.

The family image was central to the Blanchard image in that
campaign and in all campaigns thereafter. We were a loving,
caring, supportive family with an all-American look. Jamie
could be positioned as a wholesome, honest, hard working family-man. He made the most of it, starting with the campaign
announcement on our front porch. We hoped the media might
actually be intrigued enough by the unique location to attend,
and Jamie could hold one-on-one interviews with the media in
our living room afterwards. We also planned a small reception
in our home following the announcement.

We needed to pull together a crowd to gather on the front
lawn to hear and witness the announcement, so I got on the
phone and called the neighbors to tell them Jamie was running
for Congress and to invite them to the announcement. The
reactions were interesting and predictable. Several were
stunned and couldn't imagine such an undertaking; many were
surprised but enthusiastic; and several were unimpressed. Many
of them showed up to stand outdoors on our front lawn on a
cold March morning to hear Jamie declare his candidacy. We

also invited a government class from an area high school, our parents, aunts and uncles, my cousin and her daughters, and family friends. All in all, we had a turnout of about fifty people.

Jamie delivered a ten-minute speech from our front porch under our address—Number One—in the winter cold. He wore no hat or coat but told me later his adrenalin was flowing so fast he didn't feel the cold. A journalist and photographer from the local paper attended to record the event. Jay and I stood among the crowd and listened proudly to Jamie's speech. Jay didn't understand what was going on but he responded to the excitement around him with his own. Afterwards, we greeted people and served coffee and donuts out in our small, as yet unrenovated kitchen while Jamie was, in fact, interviewed by the local media.

Our media strategy paid off. A picture of Jamie delivering his announcement speech before a diverse crowd ran on the front page of the local afternoon paper, above the fold, accompanied by a companion article. We were off and running, fueled by a successful launch!

Our first hurdle was the primary election which was hotly contested. Four candidates entered the race for the Democratic nomination, and Jamie was the third least known. The opponent who posed the greatest threat was Wilfred D. Webb, an extremely popular school superintendent from Hazel Park, who had the backing of a loyal army of administrators and school teachers. Luckily, he didn't have much experience in politics, because with the ranks he commanded he could have won easily—and almost did. The other serious threat was Adam E. Nowakowski, an elected official from Macomb County with his own loyal band of followers. Out of left field came Michael F. O'Connor, a Vietnam veteran who had never run for office before. Of the four candidates, the only previously elected office holder was Nowakowski. While he had never held office, Jamie was the most politically skilled of the four, and this paid off.

Our political war chest was the size of a cigar box, and money had to be spent very judiciously. One of the strategies was to demonstrate strength and money-raising capability at the outset. As soon as Jamie announced, billboards went up around the district, some limited radio advertisements were run and a couple of newspapers ads were placed. The point was to make it look as if this was a well-organized, well-funded campaign in order to intimidate other candidates and prevent others from entering the race. We implemented this strategy with borrowed money which would have to be repaid. One of our tactics was to employ targeted direct mail advertising. The challenge was to identify likely primary voters among registered voters and to mail literature to their homes and knock on their doors.

That's where I came in. We paid a computer company for a printout of all registered voters in the thirteen cities of the Eighteenth Congressional District. I organized and led a brigade of neighbors and friends—all women—to take those lists to city hall and begin to identify the names of primary voters. This was an extremely time-consuming and tedious task but an important one. It required us to request the voting books from the city clerk and to check the voting record of each registered voter. As you recall when you vote, the voting official turns to your voting record and stamps the date of the election in which you are voting. We had to look at each individual's record for the date of the previous primary election. If the date appeared, we identified that individual as a likely primary voter in this election. We then located and placed a check by that individual's name on our computer printout.

Voting records are public information and as such are open to viewing by anyone. Some of the city clerks were Republicans and weren't inclined to be cooperative. Most clerks, though, were extremely intrigued by this band of women and were helpful.

We couldn't remove the books from the premises so we had to work right in the clerk's office, in whatever space was available. Usually there were tables at which we could sit, but the chairs were hard and sometimes our working area was poorly lit. Sometimes we had to bring card tables and chairs to simply have a place to work. In the period of a couple of months, we looked at several hundred thousand individual voting records and checked-off several thousand likely primary voters.

We worked under difficult conditions, but we had a spirit of purpose and camaraderie which made it fun for all of us. I went on every trip to every city hall and usually found one or two women who were available to help me in this monumental task. They were my friends, neighbors, women from church, my aunt and even Jamie's mother.

Each day my first challenge was to find someone to babysit for Jay so I could organize a group to invade one of the eighteen city halls. Often, when one of these women couldn't go with me, she would offer instead to babysit for Jay. They gave willingly and unselfishly of their time doing a job which few people in the campaign organization understood or appreciated. Jamie, Sue Laird and Ron Thayer recognized the value of the work and always expressed their appreciation to these loyal volunteers whenever they had the chance. There was no free lunch for this band of loyal volunteers, but they persevered and produced an invaluable computer list which was worth its weight in gold. In fact, Sue Laird never let it out of her sight and took it home with her at night. We used it in two important ways. It identified which voters would receive mailings from our campaign and which voters would receive a knock on their front door.

Jamie estimated he walked over 500 miles, going door-to-door in that campaign, and he only went to the doors of likely primary voters. I walked with him and we worked out an effective routine. Entering a neighborhood together, armed with our list, Jamie would take one side of the street and I the other. We stayed in close proximity to each other because when I went to the door of a likely voter, I'd knock and say, "Hello, I'm Paula Blanchard and my husband is a candidate for U.S. Congress. If you'd like to meet him, he's right across the street." Then I'd gesture toward Jamie and the person would look. Jamie tried to keep his eye on me because if I waved, he would know the voter was looking at him and he'd wave back. Nine times out of ten, the voter was content just to look and wave but occasionally one would want to meet Jamie. If that was the case, I'd motion to Jamie to cross the street. We gave each person who came to the door a piece of campaign literature. If no one came to the door, Jamie would scribble a hand-written note on a brochure, indicating he'd paid a visit. He was the only one of the four candidates with such a systematic, organized and targeted campaign.

Eventually we were able to open up a campaign headquarters

in downtown Ferndale and much of the campaign activity was diverted from our house. Yet our home remained a focal point for important meetings and strategy sessions which pleased me because it made it easier for me to participate without having to leave Jay with a babysitter.

Jay and I spent a great deal of time at campaign headquarters that summer. I was enjoying the purpose and framework the campaign brought to my days, and I was eager to do anything that needed to be done. I organized the likely primary voter project, I walked door-to-door, stuffed envelopes, licked stamps, answered the phone, cleaned up after events and liked all of it. I discovered I liked the organizational tasks of a campaign, the process, the field work.

I also enjoyed accompanying Jamie on the campaign trail. He campaigned night and day and I went with him to many events. I never campaigned on my own or gave a speech. In fact, I made Jamie promise me two things when we agreed to enter the race for Congress: first, I'd never have to give a speech and second, we'd remodel the kitchen. Jamie faithfully kept both promises. I was still very shy and nervous in front of large groups and didn't even like to go on stage or to the front of the room to stand with Jamie to be introduced. Sam Fishman, a very powerful UAW kingmaker, once literally forced me to the front of the room for an introduction with Jamie, telling me, "You're his wife. You belong up there with him." But I was comfortable shaking hands and meeting people at an event with Jamie.

Through observation in the Sandy Levin and Frank Kelley campaigns, I learned how to circulate through a crowd and meet as many people as possible. I worked the room at Jamie's side, but I wasn't comfortable working the room on my own. It became second nature to me in later years, but in 1974, it seemed ridiculous. I thought to myself, "Why on earth would these people care who Paula Blanchard is? They don't even know yet who Jim Blanchard is." I thought it should be irrelevant to the voters what my views were or what I thought about anything. I did understand image and I knew I could reinforce Jamie's image as a nice, young, married, family man. At the time I readily accepted a place at Jamie's side and genuinely felt this is where I belonged. Given the demands of Jamie's schedule, at least this role gave us a chance to spend some time together.

Another family opportunity to campaign together arrived that summer with an array of campaign appearances. Parades are a wonderful means to obtain visibility with hundreds of people in a short period of time. The voters who see a candidate in a parade are also in a festive mood and the good feelings generated by the parade have a spillover effect on the candidate. In fact, people come away from the parade feeling as if they've met the candidate when in reality they have just exchanged a wave. Our polling data from later campaigns seemed to prove this point. In communities where Jamie appeared in parades, the percentage of people who responded affirmatively to having met Jamie was disproportionately high.

In fact, many parade spectators really did meet Jamie. Like most candidates, Jamie began parade appearances by riding on the back of a car with the convertible top down. Jay, who was only three and a half, and I usually rode with him. We'd try to determine which side of the parade route had the most spectators and Jamie would sit on that side. I'd sit on the other and Jay would ride in the middle.

We used to laugh about how ridiculous we felt sitting up there, waving to the crowd and smiling, like beauty queen imposters. Even at his young age, Jay said he felt stupid. It frustrated Jamie to ride by all those voters whose hands he wanted to shake, so frequently the urge would get the best of him and he'd leap from the back of the moving car to dash into the crowd to shake a few hands. He'd dart across the street to do the same on the other side. Then Jay and I and anybody else watching would hold our breath as Jamie executed a return leap back into the moving car. When he started doing this with regularity, we worked out a system. I'd watch and let the driver of our car know when he was ready to jump back in. The driver would stop for Jamie and then proceed once he was safely in. I used to plead with him not to do it because this was so dangerous. We solved the jumping back in, but the driver and I never knew when he was going to jump out. It also gave parade organizers fits!

The problem solved itself one day, as many problems do. Our

loyal next door neighbors, Ruth and Bob Greager, were campaign supporters. Their teenage son, whose name was also Jamie, parked his 1949 Pontiac Silver Streak in one side of our two-car garage and in return for that favor volunteered to let us use his car as our parade vehicle. He even offered to drive and dress up in period costume. We rode in a number of parades in that vehicle and were a real conversation piece.

Parade organizers insist participants be ready at least half-an-hour before the official starting time. Our neighbor Jamie wouldn't start his Silver Streak, however, until just before the parade began because he didn't want it to overheat. One hot parade day we had been waiting in parade formation for the parade to begin with the car started. The parade was delayed over and over and our neighbor Jamie was worried about his car overheating. Moments before the start, sure enough, steam spouted from the radiator. What to do?

We couldn't just drop out of the parade. This was a big parade, in a big city—Warren—with a big crowd, in the heart of Adam Nowakowki's base. We had to have a presence. I suggested we walk. All three of us liked that idea, Jay especially. We wouldn't feel embarrassed, Jamie could shake hands to his heart's content—without risking life and limb, and Jay wouldn't be bored. Only one problem remained. Without the car and its sign on the side, no one would know who we were. Jamie Greager proved to be a real trouper. He offered to walk ahead of us and carry the sign. And that he did. It was a good thing he was young and strong because it was an 80 degree day and his period costume consisted of wool pants, jacket, vest and cap. He also had on platform shoes which were more for effect than comfort. He walked the three-mile parade route, arms outstretched carrying the sign, in clothes and shoes totally unfit for the hike and did so without complaint.

Jamie Greager was only one example of the kind of person who cared, who gave time, who helped us win. We gave everybody who volunteered a job and recruited people who didn't realize they wanted to help until we made them aware they did.

The ultimate recruit was Jamie's mother. She helped finance the campaign, joined my likely voters identification brigade, stuffed envelopes, and signed up members of her church to help, too. As if that wasn't enough, we "volunteered" her to be the receptionist in the campaign headquarters. After a career as a social worker and administrator in Oakland County, she retired in June 1974. We were having a hard time finding a capable receptionist for the headquarters so I suggested Jamie's mother who is a natural born organizer. Jamie knew instantly she was the right person. She interacts extremely well with people; she is tactful and diplomatic. Her commitment, loyalty and dedication couldn't be questioned. The job we asked her to do was herculean—answer several lines of phones which were ringing off the hook, get the right messages to the right people in a timely way, keep volunteers busy, greet people who walked in and respond to their requests, and handle a thousand other miscellaneous things. She took the job reluctantly and she performed superbly. Her salary requirements were right, because she, too, was a volunteer.

Jamie was fond of saying after many other successful campaigns, that 1974 was a "textbook" campaign. He likes to recount that battle more than any other since. He left no stone unturned. The night before the election, he stood at the Dexter-Davison shopping center in Oak Park until the stores closed at 9:00 P.M. shaking hands. He knew it would be a very close election, and those last few voters might make the difference for him.

The campaign was my initiation into life as a political spouse. I was thrilled; I liked it. I was proud that I was good at it. I didn't mind being a decoration on the candidate's arm because that was where I was most comfortable. I also didn't mind because I made an important contribution behind the scenes in ways which Jamie recognized, complimented and appreciated.

I knew we would win. I also instinctively knew this was the first of many campaigns and a long career in politics. Jamie was a natural politician with an incredible memory for names and faces, the capacity for leadership, the skill for organization and strategy and the intelligence and integrity that could work for the public good. He even had an attractive and loving family. The elements were all there.

I knew we were only beginning our political lives, and I felt the need to document the campaign of 1974. I made two large

68

matching leather scrapbooks, one for the primary election and one for the general. In them I glued examples of all the literature, newspaper clippings, photographs and campaign memorabilia I could lay my hands on. I treasured them and kept them in good repair for fifteen years. They were the only campaign scrapbooks I ever made, and I made a present of them to Jamie when we were dividing up our property during our divorce. They chronicled the beginning of his lifetime political career, a career which I helped launch, but which would no longer define my life. They belonged with him.

The primary election in August was a cliff-hanger which we thought we lost all evening. Our campaign party was in the backyard of some dear friends and campaign workers, Steve and Judy Spiegel, who are divorced now, too. But in 1974, they lived in a big Tudor home in Pleasant Ridge. I had met Judy right after we moved in when I joined the Pleasant Ridge Garden Club. A family friend of Jamie's, Helen Fillmore, insisted I join as a way to meet people, and she sponsored my membership. Jamie and Steve met at the Garden Club's Men's Night soon after. The whole Spiegel family, all six of them, were "Blanchard Boosters." Steve worked as an engineer at the GM Tech Center and practiced his political avocation on evenings and weekends. He often was Jamie's advance man, campaign aide and driver. Judy worked in my brigade and volunteered in headquarters. Their four children were Jay's frequent babysitters. He loved to go over there because he was their darling and there was always so much happening at their house with four children in the family and a wide assortment of toys and pets. He only complained about going there once. When I walked with him up the steps to their front door on election night in November 1974, he cried. He was like the rest of us by that time. He'd had it.

But, we were still fresh as we gathered on the night of August 6, 1974, two days before Jamie's thirty-second birthday, at the Spiegel home to post the returns and celebrate the primary victory. It was long in coming. Wilfred Webb led all night and we just about gave up hope. At 1:30 A.M., Webb held a substantial lead and only the city of Oak Park had not reported its results. It would take an incredibly high vote total for Jamie in Oak Park to overcome Webb's lead. Most people didn't see how that could possibly happen, and many people left the party expressing their regret and disappointment over his loss.

Jamie asked me to take a walk down the street with him so we could talk privately. He explained to me how slim the prospects were for victory, and how we had to prepare ourselves for a loss. He practiced his concession speech with me on that walk and began to go over what the next steps would be. I was sympathetic, understanding and supportive, but I didn't believe we would lose and I told him that. I told him my instincts told me we would win and I discouraged him from making any announcement until we heard the Oak Park results. He was surprised, but pleased, by my optimism.

The Oak Park totals were posted about 2:00 A.M. His percentage was higher than we ever dared dream, giving him the victory he worked so hard for. Jamie beat Wilfred Webb by less than 1,500 votes. If anybody ever questions why Oak Park's former mayor and state representative, Joe Forbes, commands such fierce loyalty from Jim Blanchard, a look at the effort Joe put forth on Jamie's behalf in the summer of 1974 is the obvious answer.

The general election on November 5, 1974, was quite a different story. There was no suspense in that election, and we knew by 8:30 P.M. that Jamie had defeated the incumbent, Robert Huber. That election can be summed up simply: Huber never took Jamie's candidacy seriously. He wrote him off as a young, inexperienced whippersnapper. Only too late did he realize that Jim Blanchard was running circles around him and taking his seat right out from under him. Jamie beat Huber by over 25,000 votes.

We celebrated that victory in the Ferndale Fraternal Order of Police Hall. We were thrilled, exhausted, and in a daze. Several hundred people jammed the hall to celebrate with us. Campaign workers, volunteers, friends, neighbors, family, all the people who helped us put it together, were there to taste the sweetness of victory. A crowd of hundreds standing in front of us, shouting, hooting, whistling, singing, stomping, waving Blanchard signs and wearing Blanchard visors was a sight which brought tears of joy to my eyes as I stood on the platform next to Jamie as he announced his victory. People were standing on tops of chairs and tables to get a better view of the victor and everyone was smiling and grinning. All the people we had become so close to—the Blanchard campaign family—were there. It was wonderful they could share the moment with us and be as excited as we were. For the first time, I felt completely comfortable at Jamie's side in front of an audience and I basked in our success.

I saw my father standing on a table at the side of the room with my mother standing on the table next to him. I was surprised to see my mother crying. At first I thought she was crying, as I was, because she was happy. A second look, however, revealed she was overcome with sadness.

When the speeches were over, I went to her, and I asked her what was wrong. Apologizing, she said she didn't want to spoil the joy of the evening for me but she couldn't hide her concern. I insisted she tell me what was troubling her, and she gave me a long, loving look and said, "Paula, I'm afraid for you. Your life in Washington is going to be difficult and hard."

I couldn't believe it and didn't believe it. After all, what did my mother know of politics or Washington, D.C.? I dismissed her concern as typical of her tendency to worry. Too soon my mother's foresight would prove true.

Chapter Nine

W e flew to Washington the first week in December 1974, and stayed at the home of law school friends Kristin and Russ Anderson. They were living in the Washington suburb of Springfield, Virginia, about fifteen minutes from the Capitol. We'd kept in touch through Christmas cards and even spent a vacation with them touring Washington, D.C. in the summer of 1969. When they heard Jamie had won, they called immediately and offered us a place to stay which we accepted. The Andersons were wonderful hosts, eager to share all the exciting details of our adventures. They were also understanding when we were hardly there at all to talk to them. We went from early in the morning until late at night and the excitement of it all gave us energy to spare.

The newly-elected members of the 94th Congress had been invited to Washington for an orientation meeting, and what an exciting few days that visit was. This was our first opportunity to meet the other newly-elected members and their spouses, and they were a terrific group. Each new group is called a "class" and with over seventy newly-elected members this was historically one of the largest. Someone dubbed them the "Young Turks" because they rode into Washington on the wave of reform the voters demanded that election year following Richard Nixon's debacle.

We spent nearly a week attending a round of orientation meetings, receptions and parties. It was absolutely thrilling being in the capital, learning our way around, meeting other new members and "old" ones, too, sharing stories of our respective victories, anticipating the days, weeks and months ahead. We savored the sweet taste of victory and enjoyed every drop.

Jamie spent the days in briefing and orientation meetings and also started to give some thought to his staff and office requirements. Members of the U.S. House of Representatives are assigned an office in one of three House office buildings located across from the Capitol—the Rayburn Building, the Longworth Building and the Cannon Building. Office space is determined by seniority and senior members usually select an office in the Rayburn Building which is newer and where most of the House committees meet. There's also a subway from the Rayburn to the Capitol which is very handy when a member is rushing to make a roll call vote. A senior member might choose an office in one of the other two buildings if a view of the Capitol is available. But contrary to public belief, few offices boast such a view.

Jamie had a choice of an office in the Longworth Building or the Cannon building, and he chose the Cannon. It's the oldest one, the most beautiful and the most historic. In his eight years in Congress, he had two different offices in the Cannon Building and one in the Rayburn Building. When he moved to the Rayburn, he liked the convenience, but was always sentimentally attached to the Cannon. In addition to the Washington, D.C. office, Jamie also had to select a location for his office in the Eighteenth District and staff and organize that. During his eight years in Congress, his centrally-situated district office was located in an office building on Woodward Avenue in Huntington Woods near our Pleasant Ridge home. It was manned by a small and dedicated staff of former campaign workers and volunteers, most of whom were with him for all of those eight years.

I have three very vivid memories of that first visit to Washington. As we drove into the city on our first night there to attend a get-acquainted reception, we were awestruck at the beauty of the night skyline as we neared the city and the Capitol came into view. The lighted dome of the Capitol presides majestically over all other buildings and looking at it took on new significance and new meaning. This was now Jamie's place of employment! He was actually going to work there! Our route into the city took us past many of our nation's most famous landmarks such as the Washington Monument and the Jefferson Memorial which are artfully lit at night. Arriving at the foot of the Capitol on a clear, black night with the Capitol dome illuminated against the dark sky, inspired us and made the election victory a reality. We hugged each other in delight.

I thought back through the eight years of our marriage and was astonished at how far we'd come in such a short time. We were living the American dream. We were two middle-class people from a small city and a small town in the Midwest, and we were going to take our place in history. I never lost that sense of wonder in the eight years we spent in Washington. I went into the city every day, either to attend an event or to go to my office. I loved driving by the monuments and thinking about what they stood for and how important they were to our national heritage and pride. I reminded myself every day how lucky we were to have the opportunity to be a small part of the history being made there.

During our orientation visit, the Andersons loaned us the use of their second car which we appreciated. If we had stayed in a hotel near the Capitol, we could have walked to the meetings and events or taken taxis, but out in the suburbs we needed transportation. It was an older car, with holes in the floorboards, but it ran. Those holes weren't a problem when it was just Jamie and I in the car because the holes were in the floor in the backseat. It made the car cold, but the heater worked pretty well.

It did become a problem one evening when it rained heavily.

We were attending a reception at the National Democratic Club which was about a block from the Capitol, directly behind the Cannon Building. A number of us were invited to another party later that night at the home of one of the senior members of Congress. We were one of the few couples with our own transportation, so we offered to drive to the party and give two other couples a ride. Our destination was Potomac, Maryland, several miles outside the city. With map in hand, we set off on that dark, rainy night with six people in a leaky car.

None of us had any clear idea of where we were going. It was hard to see in the rain (the windshield wipers were old, too), the traffic was heavy and our backseat passengers were getting their feet wet. We drove for an hour and never even left the city. We made it as far as Georgetown, where the car began to sputter and spurt, protesting the bumper-high puddles we were driving through. Our passengers also protested the water which seeped through the floorboards in the backseat. We gave up and drove into a gas station to find out where we were and how far we had to go. When we saw we hadn't even left the city and had many more miles to travel, we turned right around and headed back to the Democratic Club—Jamie and I, that is. Our passengers called a cab and went back to their hotel to dry off!

We had another unexpected visit to Georgetown during that whirlwind visit. We received a last-minute invitation to a dinner party at the home of Rowland Evans, a nationally syndicated political columnist. The Evans have one of those beautiful Georgetown townhouses depicted in magazines. Their dinner parties were famous and an invitation to one was coveted.

When one of their invited couples was unable to make the party, the Evans began looking for substitute guests. They called us. Jamie had met Rowland Evans when he was in Michigan covering Sander Levin's race for governor a couple of months earlier. They talked then about Jamie's race, but Evans didn't cover it. Evans was aware the new members were in town and remembered Jamie. He thought it would be interesting to meet us and to hear politics discussed from the perspective of a new member.

We were thrilled to be invited and accepted as soon as we determined we had appropriate clothes to wear. Many of these dinner parties were black-tie and Jamie didn't have a tuxedo, but we didn't worry because Mrs. Evans said dress was informal. After multiple phone calls that day, I determined what informal in Washington, D.C. meant; I discovered it meant suits for men (even though some of the men did arrive in tuxedos) and cocktail dresses for women. My wardrobe at this point was minimal to say the least and what I had was worn to threads. We had tried to keep personal expenses to the minimum during the campaign so I didn't have much to choose from for a party like this. In fact, I had only one thing which was appropriate—a white evening polyester pantsuit which Jamie had just given me for my birthday. It was very dressy with a rhinestone design on the bodice. I loved it and even had appropriate shoes and bag to match. I didn't have the right coat so I just didn't wear one.

When we arrived at the party, we were lucky to find a parking place nearby so I didn't have to walk too far in the cold. We prayed that none of the other guests would observe the old car we arrived in. We were greeted at the door by a butler who raised his eyebrows at our coatless attire. He ushered us into the living room where cocktails were being served to a number of famous Washington personalities.

We drew in our breath as we entered the room. Among the notables who were chatting amiably were Art Buchwald and his wife, Tom Brokaw and his wife, Ben Bradlee and Sally Quinn, the ambassador from Iran, and Donald Rumsfeld who was President Ford's chief of staff.

The house, like the guests, was impressive. The living room was painted dark navy blue enamel with white trim and the whole color scheme was navy, black and white with red accents. A grand piano sat in the corner, lost in the scale of the room and the glitter of the guests.

Dinner was French service and took place in a garden in the back enclosed in a glass atrium and greenhouse. My dinner partner on one side was Tom Brokaw and on the other was the editor of the *Boston Globe*. Both men were friendly, kind, sincere, courteous and curious. They asked me several questions about Michigan, our district and the race we had just won. I had a wonderful time telling them about it all. Jamie sat at Mrs. Evans' table and was the object of curiosity himself. He sat next to Donald Rumsfeld who was very interested to know about Michigan, his boss's home state. We caught each other's eye during dinner and exchanged the same thought: Can you believe this?

We returned to the living room for after-dinner coffee and liqueurs, and I remember having a delightful conversation with Ben Bradlee. He sought me out, I think, because he had a reporter's curiosity and I was a face he didn't recognize. He asked me point-blank if all these famous people made me nervous. I answered no, which was true. I said my husband had worked for several years for Frank Kelley who was one of Michigan's most famous people, and I had learned that famous people are just like everybody else, except they like to be flattered more because their egos are bigger. He laughed heartily and we had a spirited conversation. Sally Quinn wandered over soon when she saw Ben and me in a lively discussion. They weren't married at the time, but were rumored to be lovers. She took his arm possessively and cast a chill over things when she asked me if pantsuits were still in style in Michigan, observing that people in Washington weren't wearing them much anymore. I was dumbstruck at her rudeness, but Ben saved me from a response by saying how nice it was to have met me and bowing gallantly and kissing my hand, by way of goodbye.

When it came time to leave, our hostess saw us to the door. She was alarmed when she saw we had no coats. All her other guests were leaving in fur or cashmere coats. "Are you crazy?" she said. "It's damned cold." We said we were from Michigan where it's even colder so we expected Washington to be warm by comparison and we left our coats at home. I don't think we fooled her, but she was gracious and wished us good night.

On our way back to the Andersons, I remarked that we were going to have to improve our wardrobes if this was what our social life was going to be like. Jamie smiled and said it would be a long time before we were invited to another Georgetown dinner party like that. He said it was a once-in-a-lifetime thing for a young Congressman to be invited to a party with that social set. Those invitations are usually reserved for people with much more power, money and influence. He was right. We never received another invitation like it until he was governor.

While Jamie was in meetings and briefings that week, I spent time with a real estate agent looking for housing in the Washington area. Martha Griffiths, who had retired from a twenty-year career in Congress in 1974, advised us to buy a home in Virginia, rather than Maryland. In her typical, forthright style, she said Maryland schools were overrated, property values in Maryland were inflated compared to Virginia, and tax laws in Virginia were more favorable. She also said commuting from Virginia was easier. Martha is not a person to doubt. She speaks with knowledge and authority and she's usually right. We took her advice.

She was right, but that didn't lessen the shock. Housing prices in the Washington area are about two and a half times what they are in the Detroit area. We discovered to our dismay that in order to buy a house comparable to our house in Pleasant Ridge, we would have to pay about $80,000. We simply couldn't afford it. We were in debt to credit card companies and to Jamie's family who had lent money to the campaign. We couldn't take on even more debt to finance a house which probably wouldn't be as nice or in as nice a neigbhorhood as the one we had. Most other new Congressional families experienced the same problem.

For families of modest means like ours, there was no good solution. Some families decided to pull up stakes in their home districts, sell their homes, and go further into debt to purchase a home in the D.C. area. Others decided to keep their homes in the district and rent a modest home in D.C. Still other families decided to remain at home in the district while the member commuted between D.C. and home on the weekends.

We chose the latter. It was a difficult choice and an imperfect solution, but it seemed the best arrangement at the time. Jamie had heard enough at the orientation meetings to know that he would have to spend almost every weekend in the district solidifying his support and serving his constituents. We also loved our Pleasant Ridge house, and the prospect of selling it was not appealing. We decided to stay put and live from weekend-to-weekend when Jamie would come home. His trusty aide, Ron Thayer, was moving to Washington to serve as one of Jamie's chief aides, so Jamie and Ron rented an apartment together in a Virginia suburb.

On New Year's Day, 1975, we gave a party at our home for about 100 of our key supporters, a band of wonderful people we called "Blanchard Boosters." This group had been the core of our support and over the years grew into the thousands. Two charter members were Nancy and Bernie Lennon who were invaluable in many ways, particularly in becoming a second family for Jay during our many campaigns. This party was the start of a tradition we maintained for many years until the number of boosters became too large for our small home to accommodate. It was our way of thanking those people like the Lennons who had given so much of themselves on our behalf. It was a joyful celebration for all our guests who shared in Jamie's excitement and anticipation of the term ahead. But for me it was a bittersweet party. I was one of the few at the party who knew he would be leaving the next morning for Washington and that Jay and I wouldn't be going. Our decision to stay behind made all kinds of sense, but it just didn't seem fair. I also knew we would miss each other, especially after we had been so close for the past year.

When the next morning dawned, Jamie was up early and so were Jay and I. The plan was for Sue Laird and Ron Thayer to arrive early with a U-Haul truck. Sue was moving to Washington, too, to be another of Jamie's chief aides. Jamie took only his clothes and enough furniture to outfit his bedroom in Ron's apartment.

An early start was important in order to load up and make the ten-hour drive to Washington. They arrived at 8:00 A.M. and were on the road by nine. Jay and I watched as they loaded the truck, all three of them nervous in anticipation of the drive and the work ahead.

Jamie and I said a tearful goodbye. Jay and I stood in the front window waving goodbye and watched the truck back out of the drive with Jamie behind them driving our car. When they were out of sight, I looked around me and my heart sank. The house was still a mess from the party the day before, it was dreadfully quiet, and Jay was already asking when Daddy was coming home. I looked at our darling little boy who wasn't going to see very much of his daddy for two years, and I went into our bedroom and sat on the edge of the our bed and cried. I cried for Jay and I cried for me.

Jay followed me in there and asked, "What's wrong Mommy?" which made me cry harder. He climbed up on the bed beside me and patted my shoulder. My four-year-old son consoled me, saying, "Don't worry Mommy. It will be all right." That brought me to my senses. A four-year old should not have to console a thirty-year old! Of course it should be the other way around. But Jay didn't need consoling. Thankfully, he was too young to understand, and home was where his mother was.

We tried the weekend commuting arrangement for three months and we hated it from the start. Jamie and I missed each other very much and were both lonesome. Jamie and Jay also missed each other. We talked on the phone every day, of course, but it wasn't the same as being together. Jamie wanted me in Washington to share his new adventure and the exciting things going on, and I wanted to be there to share it with him. We had both worked hard and sacrificed so much for him to be there. He also hated living in someone else's apartment and felt as if he had no home. He was working long, long hours in part because there was so much to do, and also because he had no one to go home to.

We had loving reunions on the weekends, but that time had to be shared with his Congressional responsibilities in the district. He usually went into his congressional office, attended town meetings, fundraisers, Democratic party events, and other gatherings to which his constituents invited him and expected him to attend. Dinner together often meant sitting beside each other at a head table talking to the people on either side of us.

In March, we decided to do what we could to find a satisfactory place for us to live as a family in the Washington area. We were determined to keep our house and home base in Pleasant Ridge where we could return for holidays and during the summers to escape the torrid Washington, D.C. heat. That meant we had to rent a modest place.

Jamie was disappointed we couldn't manage to buy a house. He felt strongly that a member of Congress should be able to live in his own home, in a nice neighborhood, not too far from the Capitol. He went over and over our finances, our monthly income and our budget, but the money for a home in Washington just wasn't there. He resigned himself to the reality of the situation, and we rented a two-bedroom condominium in a development called Fairlington in Arlington, Virginia.

We moved in there in April 1975, taking most of the furniture from our house in Pleasant Ridge, but leaving enough to make it liveable when we were returned. My parents also gave us some furniture which they weren't using which we moved into the Pleasant Ridge house. Since our condo had only a living room, dining room, kitchen and two bedrooms, we didn't need too much furniture. We had to purchase area rugs, dining room furniture and draperies. Between our house payment and our rent payment, we paid about $1,000 a month in housing expenses.

We never got out of debt while we were in Washington. The high cost and standard of living there, the need to maintain two residences, the travel expenses back and forth, campaigns every two years, and the need to maintain at least a decent wardrobe all conspired to create a perpetual cash flow problem. We were cash poor most of the time. Jamie continued to manage our finances and after he paid the monthly bills, we usually had little money left for the rest of the month.

Jamie always had the highest ethical standards and avoided both the appearance of a conflict of interest and the reality of a conflict. Consequently, we took only one Congressional trip in eight years and he accepted few speaking honoraria. Many members of Congress ease their financial pressures by accepting the maximum number of honoraria allowed by law. Jamie was never comfortable with that, preferring instead to take out personal loans from the House bank. It would take us a year in the Governor's Residence before we were out of debt.

Our move to Washington reunited us as husband and wife and as a family and we were happy and relieved to be embarking together on the new course our lives were taking. The move did not remedy, however, the underlying problems Jamie's new position presented, problems with which we would struggle for the next eight years.

Chapter Ten

Whose we moved to our condo in April of 1975, Jay was four and a half years old. He had been going to nursery school in Pleasant Ridge since the previous September and loved it. He was an extrovert and a very sociable person even at that young age. He loved being with people and adjusted very easily to the school setting. I didn't enroll him in a nursery school in Arlington, however, because the year was nearing a close and there were a number of children in our condo complex with whom he immediately made friends.

Jay and I did some extensive exploring together in those next few months. We learned our way around the Washington area and visited all the museums, the zoo, the monuments and his daddy's office. We spent almost every day and every weekend investigating our new surroundings, and we established our own routine. Weekday mornings, we'd all be up to have breakfast and see Daddy off to his office. I was still fixing Jamie eggs, toast, juice and coffee every morning. Bacon had been eliminated as a concession to cholesterol. He usually left the house about 9:00 or 9:30 to avoid early morning rush hour traffic and in time to make committee meetings which started at 10:00 A.M.

We took our Labrador retriever, Abby, to Washington with us, and she and Jay had a little game they played in the morning which all four of us loved. Jay and Abby loved to play, run, and chase one another around the living room and dining room which were really one big room. Jay would lead the chase and Abby would let him win. When Jay fell on the floor in a heap laughing, that was Abby's signal to grab hold of the feet of Jay's pajamas and try to pull them off. She would wrestle, snarl, growl and shake her head. Jay would scream with delight until he was tired of the game and then he would pretend to cry. That was Abby's signal to stop. Then she would stop and sit beside him, panting with excitement and eyeing us for approval. Jay would stop crying and egg her on again. That, along with breakfast and the *Washington Post*, was the beginning of the day of the Congressman from Michigan's Eighteenth Congressional District.

Once Jamie left, Jay and I would dress and head out for a morning of sightseeing. We usually drove into the city and went to a museum. Jay's favorite was the Natural History Museum where the dinosaur skeletons were displayed. We came home for lunch and an afternoon nap. When Jay awoke from his nap, his neighborhood friends were home from school and he would go out to play or they would come over to our house to play.

About 6:00, they all went home for dinner, and I started feeding Jay apples and cheese to hold him off for our dinner. We never ate before 7:30 or 8:00 because Jamie was never home before then. Congress was usually in session until 6:00 or 6:30, after which Jamie returned to his office to deal with stacks of materials to read, phone calls to return, and correspondence to read and sign. Jamie just couldn't get home any earlier, and when he did arrive he knew Jay and I were impatiently waiting. He usually came home with a stack of work to do after dinner.

I still hated having dinner so late but couldn't find any way around it. With Jamie back in Michigan nearly every weekend, we had only four nights for family time—Monday through

83

Thursday—so I felt it was important for us to sit down together and have dinner as a family. I was doing my best to maintain some semblance of a "normal" family life. Our family time was even more limited by the endless round of receptions, parties and events to which Congressmen were invited during the week. Jamie would accept one or two of these invitations a week and I usually accompanied him. I would drive to his office at the Cannon building, park in the Cannon garage and meet him in his office so we could go to the event together. That meant, of course, that we drove home separately. Most Congressional wives did the same thing because there wasn't enough time for our husbands to drive home, pick us up and return to the capital for the event.

On weekends when Jamie was back in the district—usually two or three weekends a month—Jay and I entertained ourselves with more sightseeing, visiting other congressional wives and their kids who were also "batching" it, going to movies and playing board games. My most frequent companion during those eight congressional years was my young son. I also spent time sewing and doing needlework. I was still making many of my own clothes, Christmas presents and decorative items for our home.

When Jay started kindergarten in September of 1975, I was more than ready for a pursuit of my own. After four and a half years of devoting my life completely to my son and my husband, I was eager for my own challenge. Jamie and I talked about some feasible options, and at this stage in my life I basically did what he told me. It was his advice that I enter graduate school and pursue a master's degree in business administration. He had earned an MBA from Michigan State University before law school, and he had found it an extremely useful degree. He also is a student of trends and predicted that women with business degrees would be very much in demand. He said I would have my pick of some very desirable and lucrative jobs when I finished.

I had always enjoyed school and had done well. I also hoped I could arrange a schedule of classes which would accommodate my need to be home afternoons and evenings so I wouldn't have to hire a babysitter for Jay. I researched colleges and universities in the area and was accepted in the MBA program at American University in Washington, D.C. It was one of the few programs which didn't require an undergraduate background in business. I hadn't taken even one business course at Michigan State when I majored in education.

Excitedly, I went to register, but my hopes were soon dashed. All MBA courses were offered in the evenings because the majority of students in the program were working at full-time jobs. I was bitterly disappointed. I realized then how much I was counting on this opportunity, and knew I had to find a way to make it work in spite of this difficulty. The program was designed to take three years if you took a minimum of two or three courses a term. That required students to be on campus two or three nights a week. I registered for a schedule of classes which met two nights a week. I discussed this turn of events with Jamie. I proposed that for those two nights, Jamie take responsibility for Jay. I suggested I could either take Jay to his office, or Jamie could promise to be home in time for me to get to class. I remember Jamie looked at me in a way which made chills run up my spine and I recall his words, "If you think I got elected to Congress so I can babysit while you go to school, you're crazy." There have been very few times when I've felt as alone as I did then. He said he would pay my tuition, but I had to figure out a way to make the schedule happen. And I did.

I had found a terrific babysitter—a nice, responsible young high school student, whom Jay liked very much, and I hired her to babysit for Jay those two nights while I went to school. I packed Jay in the car, picked Jill up about 6:00, took both of them home, organized their dinner, drove to school, attended classes, drove home about 10:00 P.M., got Jay out of bed and into the car, took Jill home, drove home, put Jay back in bed and went to bed about 11:00. I suggested a compromise and asked Jamie if he could help by coming home early enough to take Jill home so I wouldn't have to wake Jay up, take him with me to drive Jill home, and put him to bed again. He said he would try. Instead, he used those two nights to work late and in my recollection, he never came home in time to drive Jill home.

In fact, I usually was asleep by the time he walked in the door. I resented his lack of cooperation very much, but when I tried discussing it with him, he made it clear I was on my own.

I studied in the masters program for one year and earned a straight 4.0 average. Friends and constituents in the district used to tell me how proudly Jamie talked about my studies and how well I was doing, and they often asked about me about my courses and my plans.

After a year, I dropped out of the program for a variety of reasons. First, I didn't like the course of study even though I was doing well. It wasn't challenging, I didn't like the material, the professors were mediocre, and it appeared to be the kind of degree anyone could get if you paid the tuition. Second, the tuition was expensive and it further depleted our already precarious budget. Third, it was too much of a strain on our family life—what there was of it—and on me. I felt worried and guilty that Jay was spending too much time in the hands of a babysitter. Finally, to make the investment in tuition pay off I would have to go to work full-time after I completed the degree. I knew that wasn't feasible, considering Jamie's workload, his schedule, and his attitude toward sharing responsibility for Jay's care.

In June of 1976, after three terms in the MBA program, I closed the door on a business career. Jay and I went home to Pleasant Ridge to enjoy a pleasant summer. Jay spent his days swimming in the community pool across the street from our house and I relaxed there with him, mentally exploring what other opportunities might lay ahead for me.

Chapter Eleven

T he fall of 1976 was a very busy one.
Jamie was up for re-election even though it seemed like
he had just been elected. Members of the House of Representatives must run every two years which means they are
campaigning all the time. After they've been in D.C. for a while
and are secure in their seats, they can spend the first year of
their term serving and the second year campaigning. But when
they are new and most vulnerable to a challenge, they have to
campaign virtually all the time. That's why most congressmen,
especially newly-elected ones, spend most of their weekends
attending events and meeting constituents in their districts.

Jamie took his re-election very seriously and beat his opponent, John "Jack" Olsen, handily by a margin of two-to-one. His
strategy of spending a great deal of time in his district those
first two years worked well. He established a good reputation for
constitutent service, his name recognition and approval rating
steadily improved, and no serious candidate of either party

stepped forward to challenge him. He survived his first re-election, the most dangerous one, and went on to win re-election two more times by even wider margins.

We also moved that fall. We had been trying to figure out a way to buy into the real estate market in Washington, D.C. and still keep our house in Pleasant Ridge. Appreciation on real estate in the D.C. area was exceedingly good, astonishing in fact, and it didn't make economic sense to live there and pay rent if there was a way to buy. I spent some time looking for houses in a price range we could afford, and and all I found were dismal prospects. The bare fact was that there was really no way we could buy a decent house in Washington and keep our house in Michigan. Jamie was determined to find a way and felt if we, actually I, just kept looking long enough something would materialize. So I looked. And I found nothing we'd be proud to call home that we could afford.

I was convinced the best way for us to get into the market was to purchase a townhouse in the development in which we were already living. It made all kinds of sense, especially since it would be minimally dislocating for all of us, particularly Jay. Moving expenses would be manageable because we wouldn't be moving very far. And all of our draperies, floor coverings, and other household accessories would fit.

After several months of looking for houses and finding nothing suitable, one of the most attractive and desirable townhouses in the development went on the market. The owners had made some improvements to it and it was in one of the best locations. Located on a corner with windows on three sides instead of just front and back, I was enthusiastic about buying it but it took some real persuasion to convince Jamie. He didn't like townhouse living and wanted us to have a home of our own befitting a Congressman. I convinced him that buying this townhouse was a manageable way into the market and would allow us to build up some equity which we could use to purchase a home in two or three years. He grudgingly agreed and we were able to buy it. We moved in November 1976. I calculated that this was our eleventh move in ten years of marriage. It was an easy one, however, because we literally were able to transplant everything from one townhouse to the other, and we were settled in about a week.

It was an important time for Jay, too. He started first grade that September at a magnet school in the Arlington school system. He had attended kindergarten the year before at Fairlington Elementary School, the neighborhood school which served our townhouse development. In fact, the townhouse development and the school shared the same name. The development was large enough that a whole elementary school was devoted to the school population. I wasn't particularly pleased with Jay's experience at Fairlington and was looking for another educational opportunity for him as he started first grade.

I had become acquainted with the mother of his best friend David Broughton. The Broughton family lived directly behind us at our first townhouse location in Fairlington. Doris was the librarian at Fairlington School, but her two children did not attend there. She had enrolled them instead at Drew Model Elementary School, a short bus ride away. Drew Model was established by the Arlington school system as a means of integrating the system. Its population came from all over the district and was a modified open classroom approach to education. Jay's friend David and his sister Leslie loved it there and did well.

I investigated the school further and decided to enroll Jay there. The teachers and the administration used a much more progressive and enlightened approach to education than was used at Fairlington and the school population was much more integrated. In fact, a visit there was like going to the United Nations. The D.C. area is very international, of course, and Drew reflected that. There were students enrolled of every race, color, creed and nationality.

Both Jamie and I believed in public school education and never seriously considered private schools for Jay. We wanted him to have the broadening experience that a public, integrated school would offer him. We wanted him schooled in the ways of the world and the ways of the street, as well as the ways of the intellect. We felt it was essential for him to emerge from his educational career having experienced the mainstream, not the elite. We felt he should be able to relate to and get along with all types of people, not just those like himself. We wanted him to have as normal a childhood as possible, not a privileged one. We believed his social education was at least as important as his academic education.

It was the right decision. Jay entered Drew Model Elementary School as a first grader and remained there through the fifth grade. It was an exceptional experience for him, and he did well academically and socially. His first friend, besides David Broughton, was a student named Roosevelt Russell, whom he proudly introduced to us at Back-To-School night shortly after school started, and we were pleased to see the friendships he was making with students from different backgrounds.

Jay loved school and always looked forward to going. There he expanded his intellectual and social skills and was popular with teachers and students.

His first grade teacher told me a funny story during the first parent teacher conference that fall. The children were asked to describe what work their parents did. When it was Jay's turn he announced proudly that his father was a Congressman, and he described fairly accurately what his dad did. He then proceeded to describe my work. He told the class that his mother was a waitress in a Mexican restaurant. At the conference, his teacher discreetly inquired if that was truly my occupation. I laughed and told her no, I had never been a waitress in a Mexican restaurant. I said I'd been a waitress for a summer during college, but that was the extent of my waitressing career. We wondered and laughed together about how Jay came up with that!

Later at home, I asked him why he told the class that. He said he felt he needed to give me some kind of job. Since Dad had one, and so many of his friends were telling about their mothers' jobs, he wanted me to have one too, so he just made that one up. I asked him why he picked that particular one to give me. He said it was just the first thing he thought of and it sounded like fun! It was the perfect time for me to tell him that I was, in fact, planning to get a job.

Most Congressional wives did not work in 1976. They raised their families, waited on their kids and husbands, and joined civic, volunteer and social organizations. Some worked, but they were in the minority. A number sold real estate and several worked in a volunteer capacity in their husbands' offices. Like most of the other wives, I raised my child, waited on both him and Jamie and joined a number of organizations. But it wasn't enough. I wanted a pursuit and niche of my own, separate and apart from Congress and politics.

I had tried graduate school, but that didn't fit the Congressional schedule and our lifestyle. I thought the perfect arrangement would be a part-time job which would give me the outlet I needed, but also give me enough time to meet Jay's and Jamie's needs and keep things on track at home.

As soon as I settled our new townhouse after our move in November, I began searching the want ads in the Washington Post under part-time work. I answered only one ad, was offered the job, and took it. I was hired as the secretary to the Director for Government Affairs at the Animal Health Institute (AHI), a trade association in Washington, D.C. It represented companies which manufactured food and drug products for animals and its work was comprised of providing information and lobbying support for its members.

My boss, Fritz Kessinger, told me after I was hired that he had held only two reservations about me. I was over-qualified for the job, so he was afraid either I wouldn't stay very long or would want an immediate promotion. He also asked during my interview what my husband did. I refused to tell him, indicating that my husband's career or position had no bearing on my qualifications or aptitude for the job. He didn't insist or challenge me. Instead, he did a little research and discovered on his own that my husband was a Congressman.

He was very candid about his detective work when he offered me the job. He told me he knew what my husband did, and he was curious why I wanted a part-time job. I told him I wanted the outlet and we needed the money. He understood both and hired me.

Jamie and I were concerned about a potential conflict of interest in the event the Animal Health Institute took a position in opposition to his own on an issue or a piece of legislation. We also had to make sure that I would not be required to do any lobbying for the Institute or its members. We researched the

91

committees with which the Institute dealt and satisfied ourselves that it was unlikely legislation in its interest would come up before any of Jamie's committees. We also obtained a commitment from AHI that I would never be required to lobby the Congress in any way. We were very sensitive to any real or perceived conflict of interest. After taking these precautions, I worked for AHI for nearly five years and a conflict never arose.

I made Fritz promise not to tell my fellow co-workers that I was the wife of a Congressman. I wanted to work there for a while and be accepted as a "regular" person. I wanted to be appreciated for my skills, my aptitudes and my "pitch-in" attitude first. I wanted to be accepted and respected on my own merits, not on the basis of what my husband did. I also didn't want anybody thinking I was hired because of his position and not because of my own abilities.

Jamie and I were discovering that once people realized he was a Congressman, a position of power and prestige, they immediately began treating both of us differently. People expected that a Congressman or a Congressman's spouse would have money, maids, fancy houses and a full social schedule of fancy Georgetown dinner parties. They thought Congressional members and their spouses were invited to the White House all the time. People believed we regularly hobnobbed with all the important people they read about in the *Washington Post*. They invariably invested us with more power, influence, prestige and money than we really had. Those people in Washington who tried to perpetuate that false image often fell into trouble doing so. Jamie and I were too well grounded in reality and good Midwestern values to be caught in that trap. We lived modestly, as close to within our means as possible, and remembered that the power and influence accrues to the position, not the person. At any rate, I eventually did disclose to my co-workers the "other side" of my life and they were pleasantly surprised and discreetly curious.

Finding that job was a stroke of luck because it turned out to be perfect. My hours were Monday through Friday, from 9:30 A.M. to 1:00 P.M. I was able to see Jay safely off to school before going to work, and I was back by the time he came home. I had time to keep my life organized, the home fires burning and met

Jamie's and Jay's needs. I also had time to keep up my memberships in several organizations and become acquainted with other Congressional wives.

My co-workers were a wonderful group. In fact, the President of AHI, Fred Holt, was from Michigan, and soon I was promoted to the position of his administrative assistant. He is still AHI president and a friend. It turned out that his family owned a place on Mackinac Island, and I used to get together with Fred and his wife, Fran, when I spent summers on the island at the Governor's Residence.

The summer of 1977 presented a challenge. I was working at a job I enjoyed and didn't want to give up. But I also wanted to go back to Michigan with Jay for the summer. Summers in D.C. are notoriously miserable with excessive heat and humidity, and the one summer we spent there in 1975 was more than enough.

My employer was most understanding of my desire to return to Michigan and arranged to give me the summer off and to hire a temporary replacement for me. This became the pattern for the duration of my employment there. AHI met my need for flexibility so Jay and I could return to Pleasant Ridge for summers, the three of us could celebrate holidays in the home where our hearts were and I could return to campaign with Jamie during the fall of election years. In return, I believe I was a loyal, valuable and effective employee, and I missed my work and my fellow workers a great deal when Jay and I left Washington in 1981.

That's getting ahead of the story, however. We had many eventful years in Washington between the time I went to work at AHI in November 1976 and when we came back to Michigan in 1981.

There were four milestones.

Chapter Twelve

The first milestone was a trip that made history. We took only one Congressional trip and it was one that made the history books. In November of 1977, we joined a group of Congressmen and their wives for a trip to Israel, Egypt, Spain and Portugal. It was another instance of being in the right place at the right time.

Jamie and I hadn't traveled much at all, and we'd never been to Europe. We eagerly anticipated this trip and we weren't disappointed. Jamie's mother came to stay with Jay for the ten days we were gone so we went with peace of mind and didn't have to worry about the homefront.

Our trip started off in Spain where we visited Madrid and Toledo, two beautiful and historic Spanish cities. Our delegation spent two days in Spain in a round of meetings, receptions and a bit of sightseeing. We were hosted and greeted by the ambassador at his residence, by the president in his palace and by various other officials and dignitaries.

Our next stop was Egypt where history began to unfold. We visited Luxor, the Pyramids, the Sphinx, and King Tut's tomb, and ancient history came to life. It was modern history, however, which was awe-inspiring. Our delegation had an audience with Anwar Sadat who announced to our group, and through us to the world, that he was willing to make an historic journey to Israel to meet with Israeli Prime Minister Begin to talk face-to-face about peace in the Middle East. This was enormously significant because President Carter was trying desperately to bring peace to the Middle East, and Sadat's announcement was a major advance toward that effort.

It was doubly significant because our group was scheduled to visit Israel next, and Sadat knew the leaders of our delegation would carry that message to our meeting with Begin. We did. He accepted Sadat's invitation to visit and called on him to come immediately. The members of Congress, including Jim Blanchard, were seated around the table with Begin at this meeting. Guests, including spouses, were in chairs grouped behind the participants at the table. I had my movie camera with me and was allowed to take it into the meeting room. I was lucky enough to secure a seat where I could capture Begin full-face in my camera lens. I recorded him accepting Sadat's invitation to visit. Unfortunately, movie cameras in those days were sans sound. No doubt, a lip-reader could verify the truth of this story.

Sadat came within days while our delegation was still in Jerusalem. We were staying at the city's finest hotel, The King David, and that posed a real problem for the Israeli government. They wanted to put Sadat in the same hotel, and for security purposes the hotel had to be vacated. Pandemonium broke out in the hotel as guests were hastily and unceremoniously ushered out the door. Our group, fortunately, was allowed to remain, and thus we witnessed more history in the making.

The world's eyes were focused on Jerusalem, and we were in the center of all the momentous happenings. Leaders and journalists converged on the city and the hotel. Elaborate security measures were set up and soldiers with very large guns were stationed at doors, elevators, and in all the public areas. We were issued special passes which allowed us to enter and exit the hotel. I remember witnessing Walter Cronkite having difficulty getting past an armed guard at the door of the hotel. When he succeeded in getting through, I went up and introduced myself to him. He was suitably impressed because I was already in the hotel.

Sadat arrived at the hotel in the evening under extremely heavy security and without much fanfare. We were given a general idea of the time of his arrival. I stood for hours on a chair in the hotel lobby because I wanted to witness his arrival and record it with my movie camera. Jamie thought I was crazy. At the time, he was embarrassed that I had the nerve to record Begin during the meeting and the nerve to attract attention by standing on a chair in the lobby. I recorded a confident, glowing and handsome Sadat on his historic arrival. When we returned home and watched the movies of Begin and Sadat, Jamie changed his tune and was happy that I had had the determination to record history in the making.

The members of Congress in our group were invited to see and hear Sadat at the Knesset when he addressed the Israeli parliament. And when President Carter held a news conference in the East Room of the White House to welcome Sadat and Begin to Washington for the signing of the Camp David accord, Jamie was invited. He was in Michigan when I got the call in Virginia inviting him to attend. I spent hours tracking him down because I knew he would want to be there. I finally got in touch with him, and he caught the next plane out of Michigan. He arrived at the news conference in time to witness that historic event. Jamie calculates that he is the only living person in the world who was present at each of those four events. He was the only member of Congress to attend the news conference who was also in Egypt, Israel and at the Knesset.

The second milestone resulted in the only major disappointment in my life, with the exception of the end of our marriage.

In November 1978, Jay and I and Abby were on a plane to Michigan to return for a week of campaigning before the November election when I became very ill. This was Jamie's second re-election and we expected and won a clear victory. What we didn't expect was that I would spend that election day in the hospital.

96

I had been having some severe undiagnosed medical problems which culminated in surgery and coincided with the 1978 election. When Jay and I and Abby, our Lab, arrived at Detroit's Metro airport from Washington, D.C., I was bent over double in pain because my abdominal area was causing me extreme discomfort. I thought it was the flu or something temporary. Jamie had picked us up at the airport and we went out to dinner on our way home, thinking it was something which would pass. I was in too much pain to sit at the table so I left the restaurant and lay in the backseat of our car while Jamie and Jay ate dinner.

I went straight to bed when we reached home, and Jamie took Jay along with him to a campaign event he was scheduled for. He mentioned to one of our long-time friends that I was home ill when she inquired where I was. She immediately called me and upon speaking to me came right over. She took one look at me and insisted on taking me to the hospital.

After several hours in the emergency room and several doctors and diagnoses, I was taken into surgery for an appendectomy. Upon inspection, however, doctors discovered they were dealing with a severe case of endometriosis. They promptly sewed me back up and scheduled a hysterectomy for several days later.

Jamie and I were alarmed. We had been hoping to have another child and had been puzzled why that hadn't occurred, especially after my first pregnancy happened so easily. We spent many hours in consultation with my gynecologist, who was also my surgeon, about what my alternatives were. Unfortunately, there weren't any. The endometriosis was very advanced and would continue to cause me many medical problems. The only long-term solution was a hysterectomy. This explained why I hadn't become pregnant: endometriosis caused sterility. We had to come to terms with the realization that our family of three was now complete. I wouldn't have any more children. Jay wouldn't have any brothers and sisters.

I recovered well from the surgery and have experienced excellent health ever since. I never completely lost the desire for at least one more child, nor have I ever completely dismissed the disappointment.

The third milestone was the purchase, finally, of our own home in the Washington area. We decided to stay in Arlington so Jay wouldn't have to change schools. As long as we were in Arlington county, he could continue to attend Drew Model School. He was doing well there and enjoying it, and we didn't want to disrupt that. We had already asked him to make so many changes at such a young age that we couldn't bring ourselves to require another when we didn't have to. Although we would have preferred to live in historic Alexandria, Arlington was closer to the Capitol and more within our price range. But staying in the same school district for Jay was the overriding reason.

Our townhouse development was part of a hot real estate market in the early winter of 1979. We saw how rapidly the values were rising and we felt this was our chance to sell our condominium, realize a sizeable profit and gain enough equity to make a down payment on the kind of house we had always wanted. We knew we'd be stretching things financially, but we saw an opportunity to make the move and we were out of patience with condo living. We wanted more space, inside and out. We wanted a garage for our two cars. We wanted to be able to let our dog out in the yard without all the neighbors complaining. We wanted room for guests to park outside our house. We wanted more privacy than our condo afforded.

It was customary that when the desired house was found, the prospective buyer was expected to bid on it immediately and offer a bid which met or exceeded the asking price. The demand was so intense for moderately-priced homes that buyers were always in competition with many others for the same piece of property.

After a couple months of looking in Arlington neighborhoods at houses in the price range we could afford, we found what seemed to be a remarkable buy. It had all the features we were looking for in a nice neighborhood and it was only $10,000 over the price we had targeted. We received a call from our realtor who demanded we come right out to see it. She said it had just entered the market that afternoon and hadn't been been multi-listed yet. She said when it was we would be out of luck, because it was priced below the market and as soon as other realtors had

98

wind of it, there'd be a plenty of buyers willing to pay much more than the asking price.

I called Jamie at his office. Luckily, it was Friday night and the House was not in session. He came right home, and the three of us went out to see the house in the dark. We looked it over carefully and could tell it had enormous potential. It was a two-story, red brick, Georgian colonial on a corner, tree-filled lot. It had a central entrance and stairway, a living room, dining room, den, kitchen, breakfast room, downstairs bath, finished basement, three bedrooms, two baths upstairs, a screened-in porch, a slate patio and two-car detached garage. It was our dream!

We made an offer on the spot for full price—with two contingencies—a full inspection within two days and approval of a mortgage. The seller was a widow who was unable to maintain the house, and she was happy to sell it for full price within hours after she listed it to a nice young Congressman and his family. She accepted our offer.

We went back the next day to see it again—in the daylight. Only then did we sense what we'd gotten ourselves into. We could tell the house had once been a beautiful place. We could also tell it needed a substantial amount of repair and redecoration. We were also surprised to see that it was on a very busy corner, a bus route in fact. When we had seen it the night before the traffic had slowed for the evening, but on this day, Saturday, cars and buses were roaring by. We certainly had second thoughts, because we knew we would be hard pressed to come up with the money needed to restore the place to the shape we'd want it. We also knew we'd have to do most of the work ourselves to save money. The busy street also worried us with Jay.

We debated for a short time about withdrawing our offer and sacrificing the earnest money we'd put down the night before. In the end, we couldn't resist the house. When it was renovated, it certainly would be the nicest house of all the houses we'd looked at in our price range. We knew we could look long and hard and not find another buy like this one. So we went through with it and bought it.

Buying this house was one of the few mistakes I think we made in our married life. It's one of the things I would not do all over again if I could repeat those years. We became slaves to the house. It required all of our spare time to restore it, redecorate it and keep it up. Every room had to be repaired, scraped, painted or wallpapered. It required new carpeting, curtains and drapes. New kitchen counters were needed as well as a new kitchen floor. The outside trim required reglazing and repainting. The lawn needed a great deal of work and the twenty-six trees on our lot demanded constant maintenance.

The traffic noise drove me crazy. It made the slate patio and the screened-in porch places to look at and store furniture—not places to sit and relax. Occasionally, Jamie and I would sit out on the porch late on warm spring evenings when the traffic died down while he smoked his late-night cigar. I did that only to keep him company and fool myself that the porch was actually a pleasant place.

It was not good for Jay either. He missed his friends from Fairlington, especially his best friend, David Broughton, and there weren't any children his age in our immediate neighborhood. If he rode his bike about a mile across another busy street, he could play with a couple of friends from Drew Model School. Since he was only in the third grade when we moved there, I was reluctant to let him do that. Consequently, I frequently drove him to friends' houses and his friends to our house so Jay would have companions. Our yard was not suitable for playing in either. The backyard consisted entirely of the slate patio, the side yards were completely treed, and the front yard was planted with ground cover and newly seeded grass. There were no sidewalks, and our house sat up high on this busy corner so balls and other playthings were always rolling into the street.

Jay and I missed our townhouse. I had liked it because it was in good repair when we bought it and required hardly any redecoration or work. Admittedly, parking was a problem and some people tried to mind everybody else's business, but in retrospect, it was a very manageable situation. In light of the fact that Jamie was not home much, I felt comfortable in our townhouse which I could handle on my own. Jay, too, missed the townhouse where the sidewalks were ideal for bike riding,

100

and there were parks for playing ball and other games with his friends. It was also a friendlier environment because houses were closer together and the residents were also out and about. In our new neighborhood, the houses were larger and farther apart, and many of our neighbors were older and tended to stay indoors. We had a great deal more privacy but were much more insulated and isolated, too.

Our new home also further strained our budget. In fact, I temporarily extended my work hours from 9:30 to 3:30 to supplement our income. I soon returned to four hours a day, however, because I wanted to be home when Jay arrived from school, and I needed the time to maintain the house which was much larger than our townhouse, and required a great deal more maintenance. For a while, I hired a cleaning woman who came every other week, but soon had to give her up because we couldn't afford her services.

Our weekends were totally devoted to working around the house. When Jamie was not in Michigan, he painted, did minor repairs, replaced floor moldings, and completely restored the front yard. I cleaned, gardened, and painted and wallpapered. Once in a while, when our guilt overcame us, we would take a Saturday or Sunday if Jamie stayed in Washington and spend a "family" day. We often let Jay pick the activity and he usually chose one of the museums downtown, more than likely the Natural History museum.

We moved into the house at the end of April 1979, and in the space of a year, we completely refurbished the house. Every room was freshly painted and wallpapered. New carpet and floors were laid and the exterior was reglazed and painted. The garage was repaired and the landscaping was redesigned. It was beautiful and we were very proud of it and proud of our accomplishments and improvements. We were proud to own and live in such a lovely place. I had ambivalent feelings about the house, however. I didn't like the location, and I didn't like the way it swallowed our time and money. I didn't like being a slave to a piece of property, especially one which wasn't particularly well-suited to Jay and his needs. My grandmother Beardslee always said that things work out for the best. I've come to believe that things happen for a reason. The reason for this house, I believe, was that it turned out to be great therapy for Jamie during our fourth milestone.

That event was the Chrysler loan guarantee in Congress. It was through this work that Jamie made his mark in Congress. He believes, and I agree, that the loan guarantee legislation he helped craft and navigate through the shark and shoal-infested waters of Congress was his greatest legislative achievement. It also charted his way to the governorship. The Chrysler saga began in the summer of 1979. We were on vacation in Canada, at a cottage in Grand Bend, Ontario, on Lake Huron. Jamie had been alerted to the desperate situation of the Chrysler Corporation before we left on vacation. The company was in danger of going bankrupt and laying off thousands of workers. Many of those workers were in Jamie's district. As their representative and as a member of the House Banking Committee, Jamie had a dual responsibility to attempt to avert the crisis.

The House Banking Committee was where the New York City rescue package originated, and Jamie had worked actively in support of that legislation. Consequently, he had a working knowledge of loan guarantee legislation and immediately recognized that Chrysler would require the same type of assistance New York had received. He spent hours on the telephone during that vacation, calling members of Congress to alert them to the situation, to explain it to them, to enlist their support for a loan guarantee, and where that failed, to neutralize their opposition. And that was only the beginning. For the next year and a half, Jamie worked night and day on this rescue mission—on top of his other Congressional responsibilities.

It took blood, guts, sweat and tears and without Jamie, it wouldn't have happened. True, it took many influential people to put it together, including Lee Iaccoca, President Carter, and hundreds of others. But Jamie was the glue that held it all together. Jamie invested his resourcefulness, energy, skills, negotiating talents and ability to compromise to this endeavor. For over a year, Jamie came home about the time I was going to bed almost every night. What time he spent at home was devoted largely to phoning members of Congress, his staff, people at Chrysler, people at the White House, people at the Department of Treasury, bankers in New York—literally hundreds of people.

He was so often the liaison, the bridge, the catalyst for reaching agreements and compromises. Many times the agreements were fragile and would immediately break apart. Jamie always had the stamina, patience and wherewithal to put them back together again. It required enormous patience, maturity and leadership from him. He drafted the legislation and created the common ground to enable disparate interests to come together to agree to disagree, agree or compromise. It completely occupied and preoccupied him for eighteen months. It consumed him like nothing had ever consumed him before. He gave it everything, he gave it his all, and he succeeded.

To Jay and me, he became an absent husband and father, because even when he was there he really wasn't. If he was home, he was on the phone. During those rare times he wasn't on the phone at home, he was reading or preparing materials or working on the diary he kept throughout this period.

His one outlet during this whole time was our house, especially the yard. It gave him physical activity to engage in as he hauled gravel, mulch, and topsoil. He seeded, fertilized, planted ground cover, raked, and mowed. While he strained his muscles, joints and body, his mind raced. He ruminated on the Chrysler situation endlessly, plotted and planned ceaselessly, inspected every angle, anticipated every question and objection, and gave it his heart and soul. He never cared about anything more. To this day, I think he still might consider it his proudest accomplishment. He has done remarkable things as governor, but I venture to say the Chrysler loan guarantee legislation still tops the list. Chrysler was saved, our yard bloomed, and our house was beautiful.

Our marriage, however, was in trouble.

Chapter Thirteen

This kind of pressure was a terrible strain on our marriage. During our congressional years prior to 1980, Jamie and I were trying our best to meet each other's needs and we were managing, but just barely. I felt continually torn between Jay's need for a normal, stable family life and Jamie's need for love and support from a family willing to accommodate a totally erratic schedule. I valued routine, predictability, and control of our family time. To his credit, Jamie did his best to meet my needs within the context of a profession which allows for none of them.

There is virtually no way to bring routine or predictability to the lives of congressional members and their families. When Jamie left our home in the morning, he never knew how long the House would be in session that day or what issues, crises or phone calls he'd have to deal with during the day or after the House adjourned. The House rarely adjourned before 6:30 and was often in session later, sometimes much later.

A representative votes on legislation when the House is in session, but consideration of issues and preparation of legislation is handled in numerous House committees. Ordinarily, a representative is a member of several committees and subcommittees which require meetings and preparation. Members are also duty-bound to attend receptions in the evening hosted by constituents or colleagues, to meet with constituents who visit Washington, to meet with lobbyists who represent the interests of constituents, to provide constituent service, and to correspond with constituents and colleagues by mail and by telephone.

It was always difficult for us to make any plans in advance. Just when I'd make plans for the evening, the House would be in session late and our plans would go awry. Just when we were sure the House would be in recess for Christmas or another holiday on a certain day, business would remain unfinished and the House would stay in session into the night or for several more days. We could never really count on going on flights, trips or vacations as we'd planned. We lived at the mercy of the schedule of the House of Representatives.

The time demands and pressures were horrendous. The emotional and physical demands were extraordinary. It took a superhuman being to do a good job. Once the job was done, there was very little left for anything or anybody else in terms of time, energy or emotional strength. It is a job which is almost too much to ask of anyone.

I think I could have accepted the little time we had together as a family during the week more easily if I could have counted on having the weekends together. But Jamie was so conscientious about staying in touch with constituents and spending time in the district attending events and providing constituent service that two or three out of every four weekends he went home to Michigan.

Jay and I didn't travel back and forth with him very much because he usually flew. Congressional budgets pay for a congressional representative to make a designated number of flights back to the district every year. Those budgets don't include airfare for families to fly along. We were too strapped financially to be able to afford to pay for very many flights for

Jay and me. In fact, when we returned to Michigan as a family for holidays or recesses, we usually drove.

The one-way 520 mile trip by car took us fourteen hours. It was a very long trip for all of us, especially Jay and our dog, Abby. We always did it in one day because we had Abby along and we wanted to save on overnight expenses. We had some very anxious and stressful trips during those years when we traveled at Christmas. The Pennsylvania turnpike was a treacherous stretch, even in good weather. Under snowy or icy conditions, it was a nightmare. One particular trip took us eighteen hours as we crawled through Pennsylvania in the dark at about thirty miles per hour on a sheet of ice.

Consequently, Jay and I spent half or two-thirds of our weekends without Jamie. He would leave on Friday night for Washington National Airport right from his office and return Sunday night either about 7:00 P.M. or 10:00 P.M., depending on which flight he caught from Detroit Metro Airport. I have some wonderful recollections of the enjoyable times Jay and I spent together on weekends. We went sightseeing, out to dinner, shopping, to museums, ice skating and did a host of other entertaining things. We played board games and cards and watched television. My son, however, couldn't fill the void left by Jamie's frequent absences, and I was very lonely.

And I resented the situation very much. I did my best to be understanding of the demands, but I never liked them, and as the years went by I had less and less patience for them. Jamie understood my need for control of family time, and consequently, he left the family and our home in my hands. He didn't really have time to manage that aspect of our lives, anyway, so this arrangement worked well. Of course, my frustration and resentment mounted as there was so little family time to manage and control. Jamie had a need for a supportive, understanding and accommodating wife. I was able to fulfill that need most of the time—when I could keep my resentment of our political lifestyle under control.

The Chrysler loan guarantee crisis added more pressure than my patience could bear. In the middle of the Chrysler crisis came the 1980 election and Jamie's fourth try for office. At this point, my resentment went out of control.

106

Six months old.
*(Benjamin H. Craine,
Detroit)*

I felt very grown-up with Mother but needed a hand from Dad on my first day of school.

Kindergarten
five years old.

Ready for the Junior
Prom in May 1961.

Three generations at Christmas in 1964. With
me are my mother and Grandmother Beardslee.

Jamie and I as seniors in college. *(Photo of Paula by Lawrence Tomita, East Lansing)*

Arriving home from Chaska, Minnesota in 1968 with one of our many U-Haul trailers in tow to spend the summer with my parents while Jamie studied for the bar exam.

Jamie and I walk back down the aisle as man and wife. *(Richard Frye, Pontiac)*

Our social life centered around politics as early as 1969 when we attended a testimonial dinner for Secretary of State James Hare with friends Steve and Mary Pat Byrnes.

Jay kept me going through the worst of times.

Seated beside Jay, Jamie instructs our dog Abby to face the camera.

In Jamie's office in the Cannon Building the day he was sworn in as a member of the Ninety-Fourth Congress of the United States in January 1975.

April 6, 1975

To Paula,

Our big venture worked out well. Thanks for making it happen. You did only what a great wife and friend can do ---- understand and then make the difference.

Love, Jamie

Jamie's inscription in my copy of the Ninety-Fourth Congressional Directory.

Jay flags down a bus for Mother and me across the street from our second townhouse, pictured on the corner, in Arlington, Virginia.

Our last house in Arlington, Virginia, before Jamie reseeded the front lawn during the Chrysler loan guarantee crisis.

With President Carter at a reception on the South Lawn of the
White House.

Jay and I visited Fort
Michilimackinac in Mackinac City
during the summer of 1979.

In one of only two speeches I gave
while Jamie was in the U.S.
Congress, I nervously accepted the
Ida Nudel Award for work with
Congressional Wives for Soviet Jewry
in May 1980.

The family Christmas card in
1982 with our suitcases marks
the end of eight years in
Washington, D.C. and the start of
Jamie's first gubernatorial term
(in Michigan).

After voting on November 2,
1982, Jamie and I are greeted on
the front porch of our home in
Pleasant Ridge by our dog Abby.
(UPI)

On the inaugural podium enjoying Jamie's inauguration as Michigan's
45th governor on January 1, 1983. Pictured with us are Jay, Lt. Governor
Martha Griffiths and her husband Hicks.

Jay tries out the governor's
chair on Inaugural Day 1983.

Jamie enjoys a victory cigar on
inaugural night in 1983.
Pictured with him are two of
our inaugural hosts Sonny
Eliot and Mort Crim.

We barely had managed to have two or three family dinners a week at 7:30 or 8:00 P.M. prior to the Chrysler issue. I had no patience when we had to eliminate those few dinners altogether because Jamie was arriving home every night between 10 P.M. and 2 A.M. during the Chrysler situation. I was barely satisified with spending one or two weekends a month with Jamie, and losing him the other weekends to Michigan. I had no patience when I lost him every weekend—either to the campaign or to Chrysler. I had no patience when he spent what little time he had at home on the telephone. I had no patience when all he wanted to talk about was the Chrysler situation. I became angry when he looked at me with preoccupied, glazed eyes when I tried to talk because he didn't really hear anything I said.

I also became angry when I felt guilty because I had matters I wanted and needed to talk over with him. I resented the fact that he was so overburdened by his work that I didn't feel I could justify troubling him with what seemed to be petty concerns, as if Jay and I and our family could be described as such. But somehow, in the scheme of things, they seemed to be at the time and I resented it.

The lack of time, my lack of patience and my building resentment and anger caused a nearly complete breakdown in communication between us. We lived in the same house but we spoke less and less. We stopped sharing and we stopped listening. But we didn't stop feeling. Instead of love, intimacy and fondness, however, we felt hurt, disppointment, and abandonment. I retreated into silence, distance, anger. Jamie retreated to Michigan, spending every weekend there.

In June 1980, our marriage reached the crisis stage. I was a bitter, disappointed, angry and resentful wife. He was a preoccupied, distant and absent husband. One early Sunday morning in June, as I was about to take Jay to one more baseball game by myself and sit with other mothers and fathers as we watched our children's teams play, I couldn't take being alone anymore. I telephoned Jamie at our Pleasant Ridge home. In tears, I choked on my own words as I told him I was afraid our marriage had come to an end. He was quiet for a minute, and then said, "I'll catch the next flight to D.C. and we'll talk about it when I get back."

And talk we did. The crux of my concern about our marriage was Jamie's commitment and ability to bring as much fidelity to the marriage as he did to politics which was a demanding mistress. For the rest of the summer, we talked about marriage, our feelings and our ourselves every spare minute we could steal together. We discussed separation and divorce and couldn't bear the prospect of either. We rediscovered how much we loved each other and wanted to stay together. I began to think of Jamie's needs as well as my own. Jamie promised to be at home as much as possible, and leave his work—mentally, physically and emotionally—at the office as much as possible. He made a commitment to try to bring balance to his time and give Jay and me as much time as he could. I asked him to make Jay and me at least as important, if not more, than his work, and to demonstrate that by his actions. He promised to try. For my part, I promised to try to be more understanding, more patient, more loving and less resentful of the demands of his career. Our marriage was completely rejuvenated. We recommitted ourselves to each other, our life together, and our mutual goals.

Eventually, one mutual goal became the quest for the governorship. And until the demands of that position became all-consuming, our promises to each other were kept.

Chapter Fourteen

Jamie was easily re-elected in 1980 and felt that his seat was quite secure. He could foresee spending many more years in Congress. As a reward for his triumph with the loan guarantee legislation, he was named chairman of the Economic Stabilization Subcommittee of the House Banking Committee. He realized if he stayed in Congress, he would continue to gain influence and seniority. By doing so, more plums would come his way in terms of committee assignments and chairmanships. He had many exciting ideas for the subcommittee and began the decade of the '80s full of enthusiasm.

Ronald Reagan, however, got in the way. Reagan was elected to his first term as President in 1980 and immediately began to make his mark on the budget and on Washington, D.C. This was not good news for Democrats. It didn't take Jamie long to see the handwriting on the wall. The brick wall. It was a wall he and other Democrats immediately began running into in 1981 as they tried to move the Democratic agenda forward in Reagan's

Washington. Jamie's political instincts told him that Reagan would serve a full eight years as President and those years would be long, cold hard ones for Democrats. He foresaw much disappointment and frustration as subcommittee chairman. He realized his good ideas would receive an icy reception from Reagan Republicans and he would have to pull a very large elephant up a very steep hill.

He began to consider alternatives. Talk already was abroad in Michigan about who the Democratic candidate for governor would be in 1982. The current governor, William Milliken, would complete fourteen years in that office in 1982 and odds were against him running for another four-year term. Jamie had established himself as an energetic, smart, skillful, charismatic, and electable legislator in his six years in Washington. His reputation was solidified and significantly enhanced by his triumph with the Chrysler loan legislation. With the Chrysler success under his belt, he clearly pulled away from the pack of other Michigan Democrats who were considered viable candidates for the office of governor. Democrats, politicians, observers, columnists, reporters and others began placing his name at the top of the list of possible candidates in 1982.

Two of those "others" were Ron Thayer and myself. For more than a few years, Ron had believed Jamie's destiny was to be governor of Michigan. Ron continued to be one of Jamie's closest advisors, if not his closest. Following his service in the Washington office for a couple of years as his executive assistant, he headed Jamie's district office in Royal Oak. Throughout Jamie's career, Ron conceived, directed and implemented all of Jamie's fundraising efforts, and he continues to serve in that key role today.

Both Ron and I believed Jamie was the right man, at the right time and in the right place. Ron and I had a code word for the governor's race—we called it "the big picture." Jamie knew Ron and I had been talking about it since about 1978 when Milliken won his third full term as governor and people began speculating that it was his last. Jamie wouldn't let us discuss it openly because he wasn't interested in it, and he didn't want people to think he had higher ambitions when he didn't.

In early 1981, however, Jamie began to give it serious con-

110

sideration himself and started hearing Ron and me out. After considerable thought and discussion, Jamie identified four compelling reasons to do it:

1. He didn't like the prospect of serving eight years in Washington under Ronald Reagan.

2. The governor's race was winnable, especially if Milliken didn't run again, and winnable even if he did.

3. The challenge of pulling Michigan away from the brink of financial disaster was compelling.

4. I wanted him to do it.

He was very interested in why I favored this decision, and we spent hours together discussing it. It was very simple. I knew there was nobody else in Michigan who could do a better job or who would care more about doing the right thing. I had observed first-hand what he accomplished for Chrysler against enormous odds, and I knew he was the kind of leader Michigan needed. I had observed his frustration with the legislative process, and I felt he might be more fulfilled in an executive position.

That all sounds like campaign rhetoric—but sometimes rhetoric is real. We also agreed it would probably be good for our marriage and our family. In 1981, our marriage was in good shape after surviving a rocky 1980. We also knew, however, it would continue to be vulnerable to the same pressures which nearly destroyed it. We both naively agreed that returning to Michigan, to family and friends, to weekends together and to a position which would would allow more control over the schedule would be a healthy thing for our family and our marriage.

It was a decision which did not come easily for Jamie. He offered five reasons for not entering the race:

1. Serving in Congress was the fulfillment of a lifetime dream for him. Giving up a dream was not easy—especially when he liked living the dream.

2. He would have to relinquish his seat in Congress in 1982 to run a risky race for governor, and he would have nothing if he lost.

3. He was good at his job and relished it.

4. He was fond of his colleagues in Congress and would miss them. He would have forty-nine colleagues as governor, none of

whom would be in Michigan, none of whom he knew, none of whom he'd worked with.

5. We loved Washington, D.C. It's a great place to live. We both loved the city, its beauty, its headiness, its culture, its international scope and its power.

He talked to many people before he made his decision and opinion was divided. Nearly everyone agreed he could probably win it if he wanted it badly enough. But most people couldn't figure out why he'd want it, including his mother. His star was clearly rising in Congress and he had a secure seat—a politician's dream. They wondered why he would risk that for the governorship of a state in very bad economic and financial shape. Why would he want the headaches, the heartaches, the risk?

In 1981, Michigan had the highest unemployment rate in the nation. Executive budget cuts had decimated education and social services. The auto industry, the heart of Michigan's economy, was in deep trouble. The state was in debt to Japanese bankers to meet its payroll. The picture in Michigan was grim, to say the least.

In Jamie's mind, all those reasons made it worth doing, made it worth the risk. It gave him another purpose, another goal, another challenge, and he had my full support and encouragement.

Chapter Fifteen

The campaign was fourteen months long, and it was a turning point for me. In my previous seven years as a political spouse, I had stayed very much in the background. I listened and offered counsel, advice and assistance to Jamie in a supportive, secondary role. I enhanced his image as a good family man by appearing on campaign literature and Christmas cards. I accompanied him to a limited number of appearances and events in the district. I campaigned with him, but never without him. I gave only two speeches which I can remember in those years. Both were dreadful and made me a nervous wreck.

But as a potential First Lady, expectations of me were significantly different. Michigan had a history of contemporary first ladies who were visible and active in their own right—Nancy Williams and Helen Milliken, to name two of the pacesetters. I understood that I would be expected to stand in Jamie's stead as well as at his side.

I knew drastic action was required to prepare me for the role of governor's spouse. I knew, also, that I didn't have a choice. Moreover, I recognized Jamie would never have decided to run if he didn't think he could win. In my heart I believed he was destined to be the next governor and I the next First Lady.

To get ready, I decided to jump into the campaign with both feet. I resigned from my job at the Animal Health Institute which I had held from December 1976 until June 1981. I had enjoyed every day of it, but I was ready to move on.

As was the case in all the previous summers dating back to 1976, Jay and I returned to spend the summer months of 1981 at our home in Pleasant Ridge. Only this year was different. When we left our Arlington home in June, I knew we would be returning only to move out. When we moved into Pleasant Ridge for the summer, I knew we'd be there until we moved to Lansing and the Governor's Résidence in January 1983. So we settled in. I went to work for the campaign as a volunteer, and in September Jay entered the sixth grade at Roosevelt Elementary School, our neigborhood school and the school Jamie attended.

By September, an exploratory committee had been formed and we opened up a Blanchard for Governor office in rented space in Royal Oak. I served for a couple of months as the receptionist. When we first began, there were three of us in that office: Nancy Lennon, who managed the office and administered the funds we raised, Shirley Gray, who handled Jamie's schedule and I who handled the phone.

Jamie didn't announce his formal candidacy until March 1982. Once again he selected a familiar location for the announcement—the Pleasant Ridge Community Center across the street from our house, One Woodside. By this time, the campaign was in full swing and the field of candidates in the primary was awesome. Jamie was up against a large field of opponents, including Bill Fitzgerald who had run unsuccessfully against Bill Milliken in 1978. The Republicans fielded Jim Brickley and Richard Headlee among others. Bill Milliken retired, just as Jamie had predicted, so it was a wide open race.

Jamie had the advantage and disadvantage of holding office in Washington, D.C. He had his congressional responsibilities to

114

fulfill during the week and consequently had only weekends and holiday recesses to campaign for governor. That allowed him to distance himself from the other candidates and stay somewhat above the fray. People understood when he couldn't attend an event, a candidates' night or the multitude of other things candidates are expected to do because they knew he had to be in Washington. He was able to let the other candidates slug it out and bloody themselves while he served with distinction in Washington. Critics called it a "Rose Garden" strategy, but it worked.

Meanwhile, I remained in Michigan with Jay and mentally prepared myself for an active role in the campaign, not in the campaign office, but out on the campaign trail. I started attending more and more events with Jamie and conscientiously began to improve my political and campaign skills.

I already knew how to work a room at Jamie's side. I now started to work crowds independently. Jamie would take one half of the room and I would take the other—sometimes we had time to switch, sometimes not. If not, my side of the room met only me. But this time, it made sense. Where people didn't really seem to care much what their representative's wife looked like or said or thought, they were interested in meeting a woman who might be the next First Lady of their fair state.

I also listened very attentively when Jamie spoke to crowds. The audience probably thought I was just an admiring wife, which I was. As always, I was genuinely proud of Jamie. What onlookers didn't know was that I was memorizing his messages, his key phrases, his themes—in preparation for the time I would have to deliver them.

My initiation came unexpectedly. It was a Sunday afternoon in April. Jamie was scheduled for appearances in Bay City that afternoon in Congressman Bob Traxler's district. Traxler's chief staff person, Gary Bachula, had set up two events. I was planning on going with Jamie because I hadn't visited that area yet. The strategy was for me to accompany Jamie to as many key areas as possible so that I could return to campaign on my own, having established my identity as his wife.

We were still in bed on that Sunday morning when Traxler called from Washington, D.C. Congress was in session that weekend, but Jamie had returned to Michigan to campaign because no one expected any crucial votes to be called until Monday. Traxler warned Jamie that an important vote would be coming up later in the morning or early afternoon and he had better return to Washington to be present to vote. Traxler said he would have someone at National Airport to pick him up when he got to Washington.

We called the airport to book a flight that would get Jamie to Washington in time. We looked at the clock and calculated the odds of making it. He had to dress, put things together and drive forty-five minutes to the airport to catch the only plane which would fly him to D.C. in time for a vote. The plane was scheduled to leave in about one hour. Odds were against making it, but we decided to try. We threw on clothes (it's one of the few times in his life Jamie left the house without a shower and a shave first) and jumped in the car. He didn't pack his bags.

I drove so he wouldn't have to take time parking the car. It was early Sunday morning and there was very little traffic. I exceeded the legal speed limit, but I don't know by how much. I was afraid to look at the speedometer. I slowed down at red lights but ran them if there was no traffic. On the way, Jamie and I talked about how to handle Bay City.

He talked me into going and making my first campaign appearance on my own. He used his best persuasive arguments: the crowds would be small and friendly, Gary Bachula would be there to introduce me to people and warm the crowd up for my speech, the crowd would be very disappointed if neither of us showed up when they were expecting both of us, and this was a good opportunity to try my wings. I decided to do it. It was the beginning of my successful battle in conquering my fifteen-year fear of public speaking.

I dropped Jamie off at the terminal and followed him inside to make sure he made the plane. He ran like hell, but he made it. I drove home, already working my remarks out in my mind. I wouldn't be nervous meeting people one-on-one by myself, but I knew I would be nervous speaking in front of them.

I called Gary Bachula when I got home. Traxler had already called him to alert him to the situation. Gary was secretly hoping Jamie would miss his plane so he'd be able to make Bay City,

116

but when I told him Jamie had made the plane, Gary was relieved to know at least I would be coming.

I think someone drove me to Bay City but I can't remember who because I was in a pretty thick fog of dread. I was earnestly regretting my decision to be brave. My hands were like ice, I was in a cold sweat, and my mind was a blank.

All that changed, however, when I met Gary at a local restaurant beforehand. He was so pleased and excited I was there and seemed so sure that my appearance would be successful that I immediately gained confidence from him. He gave me some ideas about what to say and I actually felt enthusiastic about doing it. When the time came to go to the first event, I was ready.

When we arrived at the the hall, it was nearly full. There were probably about 100 people in attendance. Gary seemed to know everybody there and we went around meeting them all. Many asked where Jim was, and Gary and I explained that he was called to Washington by Traxler for an important vote. They were impressed. Traxler was a hero to this crowd and the fact that Traxler himself had called Jamie back to Washington carried weight with them. They also were impressed that I came anyway.

While I was traveling to Bay City, Gary had arranged for Bob and Jamie to speak to both groups by speakerphone. We agreed that I should give a short speech first and then introduce them to speak from the "squawk box." When it was time, Gary walked with me to the front of the hall and put a handheld microphone in my hands. There was no podium and at first I felt naked standing up there all alone without anything between me and the crowd.

But when I looked at the smiling, expectant faces of the people before me, and Gary who was cheering me on silently, I relaxed. They seemed sincerely glad I was there. I smiled and started speaking. I was surprised by how strong my voice sounded over the loud speakers. I was actually astonished because I had always had trouble just catching my breath when called upon to read or speak in front of people. I gained confidence when I heard my own voice and told the group how sorry Jamie was that he couldn't be there. I explained why and I

117

explained how pleased I was to be there anyway—which by that point was true! They applauded when I said that, and I was home free!

That day marked the emergence of Paula Blanchard as a public person. It also marked the first time I had enjoyed giving a speech or being in front of people since I was in the sixth grade. I have no idea what I went on to say, but it wasn't important. The important thing was I did it, I liked it, and knew I could improve. Public speaking is still something I enjoy especially as I improve with practice.

I went on to do more and more campaign appearances on my own. In the general election I had my own staff person who arranged my attendance at events and drove me there. I maintained an active pace standing by Jamie's side, and more frequently standing in his stead. It was great training for my position as First Lady.

The primary was in August, and Blanchard and Headlee were the victors. It was an intense, hard-fought battle, and we were overjoyed that Headlee had won the Republican nomination. We were expecting Jim Brickley to win, and he would have been a formidable opponent. He had a similar style to that of the popular Bill Milliken, and was moderate, credible, reasonable and capable of attracting Democratic voters. In fact, he and Jamie had some things in common in terms of stands on issues, image and style. It would have been difficult for Jamie to draw the sharp distinction between himself and his opponent the way he could with Headlee.

Headlee and Jamie couldn't have been more dissimilar, which worked to Jamie's advantage. Headlee was rash where Jamie was cautious and controlled. Headlee was unseasoned as a candidate where Jamie was extremely experienced. On occasion, Headlee displayed his anger while Jamie remained calm. Headlee became desperate as Jamie grew more confident. The contrast sharpened daily and much in Jamie's favor.

One of the areas where the distinction was most dramatic was in the area of women's rights. Headlee and his wife were staunch right-to-lifers and against the ERA. Jamie believed strongly in a woman's right to choose what to do with her own body, and he was solidly behind the ERA. We saw tremendous potential for support among women voters. To mobilize and solidify the women's vote, Jamie considered asking a woman to join him on the ticket as lieutenant governor.

After the primary, we convened a meeting of Jamie's "kitchen cabinet" and his members of his campaign staff in our living room in Pleasant Ridge to determine who would be invited to join Jamie on the ticket. It was a large group, and we sat around on the furniture, on folding chairs and on the floor. I attended the meeting and thought about the full circle we were completing, remembering the many, many campaign meetings which had been held in that room when the goal had been Washington, D.C. Now we were back in Michigan and the goal was Lansing.

We developed an "A" list and a "B" list. The A list consisted of our preferred choices but was comprised of people who were unlikely to accept. The B list were individuals who were less politically desirable, but were more likely to accept. At the top of the A list was Martha Griffiths. All evening long we kept returning to her name as the perfect choice. The problem was nobody believed she would accept. We went round and round about how she had retired from Congress in 1974, nearly eight years ago, and was out of politics. She was practicing law, serving on several corporate boards, and earning a substantial income. She and Hicks, her husband, also an attorney, were living on a farm which they loved. Nobody believed she would want to return to politics. Besides, as Morley Winograd pointed out, she'd been asked to run as lieutenant governor by other candidates and had turned them down cold.

I listened to this debate silently, but finally spoke up. I said I believed Martha had a very high regard for Jamie which was evidenced in a couple of ways. When Jamie was a newly-elected member of Congress in 1974 and she was retiring, she made a special effort to impart to him some of the wisdom she had gained in her twenty years in Congress. He took much of her advice to heart, and it served him well during his eight years in Washington. He often mentioned how much he regretted not having the opportunity to serve with her as fellow members of the Michigan congressional delegation. She had also asked him to be one of the signators of her will, along with her very close friends, Joe Forbes and Phil Power. In fact, she had invited Jamie and me out to the farm the previous summer with the Forbes and Powers for brunch and a signing ceremony. Instinctively, I knew she favored Jamie very much and I said so at this meeting. I said I didn't think she had a very high regard for the men who had asked her to run with them before, but it would be different in Jamie's case. I also pointed out to the group that we were making assumptions on her behalf which might not be fair to her, and that before we went any further I suggested that Jamie ask her. The worse she could do was say no. You could have heard a pin drop when I finished. Then everyone talked at once, expressing their agreement that she should be asked.

The next morning Jamie invited her and Hicks to dinner. He called me right away to make sure I could go, too. He was ecstatic that she hadn't turned him down cold and was willing to listen to us make the case. Jamie felt it was important that I be there and express my enthusiasm. He knew Martha wouldn't want to accept his offer if I didn't support her wholeheartedly. He didn't want her to suspect any territorial concerns on my part and, of course, there weren't any.

We took Martha and Hicks to dinner at Chuck Joseph's in Berkley, and true to Martha's style she immediately went to the heart of the issue. Almost as soon as we sat down, she asked why he wanted her on the ticket. He said simply, "I know I can win if you run with me. Without you, I'm not sure."

She asked if she would have a car and a driver. Jamie said he'd get her whatever she needed. She laughed and said, "In that case, you've got a deal." Within fifteen minutes of sitting down, the deal was done. We went on to have one of the most enjoyable dinners of our political career. Martha and Hicks love to tell political war stories. They had a captive and adoring audience in the two of us, and they made the most of it!

We had the same group awaiting us in our Pleasant Ridge living room as we had when we convened to assemble the "A" and "B" lists. We had decided they should be ready to propose other names in the event that Martha declined (and most were sure she would). On our way back home, Jamie and I decided to play a little trick on the group which was surely waiting impatiently. We decided to walk into the house silently, with long, sad, disappointed faces and announce that . . . Martha had accepted! We even pulled it off without laughing and fooled them all. The rest as they say is history, or as Martha herself might say, herstory.

Martha was an enormous boost to the campaign and Democrats were unanimous that selecting her was a stroke of genius. Throughout the fall we grew increasingly optimistic that Jamie would win by a very impressive and favorable margin. Fundraising and organizational efforts were going extremely well and this was reflected in the polls. All went well until about a week before the election when Headlee began his strategy of negative advertising.

He had run a despicable campaign, but it didn't seem to be influencing voters in his favor. In fact, it had the opposite effect. For instance, he attempted to counter his image as a man who was anti-women. He feebly tried to make the case that he liked women more than Jamie did because he and his wife had more children than we did. That was one of his cheapest shots and the only one which really hurt me. I was still suffering from a dull ache deep inside me caused by the fact I couldn't have any more children, and to have it thrown in my face in such a callous way was hideous. I didn't have to express my outrage. Others did it for me, and the newspapers crucified Headlee for days about that remark. I've never forgiven him for putting a knife in a wound which was barely healed.

Toward the end of the campaign with just days remaining, Headlee struck a negative chord with the voters which seemed to catch on. He decided to capitalize on the polarization which exists between Detroit and the rest of the state. He began making very negative statements about the city and its mayor and implied Jamie had a cozy relationship with both.

We were extremely alarmed when polls showed that this message was hitting home with voters. With just days to go before the election, Headlee began gaining ground on Jamie. All of us were in agreement that we shouldn't overreact and should stay the course of our established strategy which was to emphasize Jamie's experience, his twenty-point program for addressing Michigan's economic woes, and his optimistic belief in Michigan, its people and its future. It was rough sledding for the last

121

few days. It was hard not to lose heart when the polls indicated that people were responding to negatives when Jamie was trying to emphasize the positive.

I vividly remember the Saturday prior to the Tuesday election. Jamie left the house for a round of campaign appearances, Jay was off playing with friends and I was left alone at home. I didn't have anything scheduled for that day, thinking I'd want the weekend to catch my breath, catch up on things around the house, and gain some perspective on what was ahead for us in a few short days. That was a mistake.

I found I couldn't bear to be alone. For the first time in those thirteen months I had doubts about our ability to pull this off. I was extremely worried that Headlee might gain just enough steam in the last few days to win by a thin margin. I paced around the house and couldn't stand the tension that was building up inside me.

I looked out my kitchen window and saw that my dear friends and neighbors were home, puttering around their kitchen, which faced mine. I bolted out of the house, ran around the fence and straight into Ruth Greager's kitchen. She took one look at me and put her arms around me. I broke down and sobbed. She and her husband Bob listened for two hours while I shared my worries, fears, anxieties, hopes and dreams. They saved me. I pulled myself together and was able to get through the election with faith in the future intact.

Our fate was sealed for the next four years on Tuesday, November 2, 1982. Jamie and I got up that morning, dressed and went across the street to cast our votes. Our polling place was the Pleasant Ridge Community Center which was kitty-korner from our house on Woodside. It was the same place where Jay and I had spent hours during many summers at the community swimming pool, where Jay attended nursery school, and I went to garden club meetings and met several Pleasant Ridge friends. We cast our votes amid smiling faces of poll workers, other voters and a crowd of reporters asking questions and snapping photos in the same community room where Jamie had announced his candidacy for governor.

I knew that day would be a long one so I made some special plans for it. I made arrangements to go to a local spa with

Jamie's sister Suzanne. She and her family were visiting from Canada for the election and were staying with us. Our families were very close. Her three boys were like brothers to Jay, and we were like sisters.

After Jamie and I voted, I returned home, put on some sweat clothes, and Suzanne and I went off to pamper ourselves. It was the first time in my life for a massage, a facial, a pedicure, a manicure and a professional make-up job. We had a ball. We laughed and relaxed. In fact, we were late arriving home to prepare for the election-night results and festivities.

Jamie spent the day making morning rounds to several polling places, having a long relaxing lunch and an afternoon at an exercise club with some of his friends.

We arranged our election night festivities and celebration at a local hotel, preceded by a dinner with family and close friends in our hotel suite. During the evening we watched the election returns on the television with the same group of family and friends. Jamie met continually all evening with campaign advisors to assess the returns, and key supporters and contributors drifted in and out of our suite of rooms. Jamie and I also made the rounds to the suites of other candidates and elected officials up for re-election.

The news media was clamoring for a victory statement and we were all fairly confident of the outcome, although returns from some areas of the state gave us cause for concern. Jamie and his advisors decided to make a statement in time for the 11:00 P.M. news so we gathered the entourage together and went down to the hotel ballroom for a cautious victory statement.

Following that, we went into some dark hours of a long night. Some of Jamie's key areas where he expected, and needed, to do well weren't looking very good. He and his key aides were very worried that the results were about to turn in Headlee's favor. Several very quiet, depressing meetings were held in our suite around midnight and into the early hours of the morning.

Finally, I couldn't take the worry, uncertainty or suspense. About 2:00 A.M. I said goodnight to Jamie. I expressed my optimism and my certainty he would win, but said I couldn't take the interim. He understood. I'm blessed with the ability to fall asleep as soon as my head hits the pillow and sleep I did. I didn't wake up until Jamie came to bed about 5:30. I awoke and asked him if he'd won. He said yes and I said, "I knew you would." I went back to sleep with a pleasant sense of anticipation at the prospect of the exciting times ahead.

We awoke when the phone rang about 8:00 A.M. Jamie had stopped answering the phone long ago so I picked up the receiver. It was Richard Headlee calling to congratulate Jamie. He said, "Tell Jim he'd better get up. He's got a hell of a mess to fix in this state."

124

Chapter Sixteen

J amie wasted no time in starting the repair.
After the election, Jamie, Jay and I took a short vacation to
the Bahamas with Jamie's sister Suzanne, her husband
Bob, their son Rob, and a friend of Jay's. We had about eight
days to recharge our batteries during which time Jamie tried to
relax and not think too much about the awesome task ahead of
him. He was a good sport and fulfilled his promise to take Jay
and me on a vacation after the election, but most of the time his
thoughts were thousands of miles away, back in Michigan.

And no wonder. There was an enormous amount of work to
be done to get ready to assume the governorship. By the time
we returned from vacation, only a little over six weeks remained
before his inauguration as Michigan's 45th governor on January
1, 1983. Those vacation days he spent with us were very precious in light of the little time left when we arrived home.

This is what he faced: Michigan was in the depths of a depression, with an unemployment rate of 17.5 percent, the high-

est in the nation. The state was facing an enormous deficit and payless paydays by February if something were not done immediately. Repairing a state that was hemorrhaging financially was the most urgent part of his responsibilities, but only a part.

There was a transition from one administration to another to accomplish, which was compounded and complicated by the fact that his predecessor had been in office for fourteen years—the longest term of any Michigan governor in history. It was, therefore, an administration which was very firmly entrenched and made the disengagement process very difficult for many people who had served long and hard.

Jamie had six weeks to identify, contact, interview and choose nineteen cabinet members, key members of his executive office staff, and other members of his administration all of whom needed to be in place by January 1. There was also an inauguration to plan, Thanksgiving and Christmas to celebrate, and a state budget for 1984 to prepare by year's end, 1982. Some time was also required to sleep and eat.

It could be likened to taking over a multi-million dollar corporation which was facing bankruptcy in six weeks. Strategies, plans, programs, budgets, and personnel all had to be in place by January 1. A celebration to mark the take-over was expected on top of it. Holidays had to be squeezed in there somewhere as well. We also had to plan our move from Pleasant Ridge to the Governor's Residence in Lansing.

Fortunately, we had many, many good staff members to assist in these efforts. Some of the campaign staff became members of the transistion team to assist in the awesome task and help select and hire new people to join the effort. It couldn't have been accomplished without them, but in the final analysis the responsibility and the final decisions rested with Jamie.

I tried to share as much of the burden as I appropriately could, and from the beginning I took my position as First Lady seriously. I viewed it as an opportunity to champion causes, work on issues and enlarge my professional skills. I wanted to get right down to business quickly so I asked for and received money to hire two staff people of my own to assist in the transistion, help me design my agenda of activities as First Lady, plan the inaugural, assist with our move to Lansing and the myriad of other things to be done.

I also needed a place where I could work and I requested and received an office in Jamie's transition office which was located in the Detroit Plaza Building in Detroit. Actually, because space was so tight, I shared an office with Martha Griffiths. One of my staff members, Carlene Bonner (now Carlene Carey), also was allocated space there so we were able to maximize those six weeks and have the benefit of working with other members of the transition team in coordinating activities.

Activities like the inaugural. Jamie really wanted to have a hand in planning the inaugural activities, but the demands on his time were so severe and he was so consumed with more urgent matters that he left the planning to a committee organized expressly for that purpose. He asked me to participate actively in the committee's work because he trusted me to know what he would want, like and feel comfortable with.

In light of the financial stress the state was under, we felt it wouldn't be appropriate to have any lavish galas or affairs. On the other hand, there was a great deal of pent-up demand on the part of Democrats around the state to celebrate. After all, it had been twenty years since the Democrats had held the governor's office. We tried to balance a great many factors and concerns and created a number of understated, tasteful and festive activities.

Events were held in Lansing and Detroit, beginning with a prayer breakfast in Cobo Hall. That was a joyful songfest, led by the magnificent St. James choir from Detroit. Events moved between Detroit and Lansing, and consisted of rounds of receptions, some hosted by us and others hosted by groups, organizations and individuals, to toast and congratulate the new governor and his family and wish them well.

We celebrated New Year's Eve at several events in Lansing, including a reception at the Hilton Hotel on the west side of town. At that event Michigan Supreme Court Chief Justice G. Mennen "Soapy" Williams and his wife Nancy invited us to come up to their suite in the Hilton before we left to return to our own hotel, the Harley, on the other side of town. Soapy would be swearing in Jamie the next morning, and we assumed he wanted to talk for a little while about the ceremonies the next day. And that he did. Soapy was a brilliant man and proved it to us that night. He knew Michigan law like the back of his hand and had realized that constitutionally Jamie took office at the stroke of midnight on January 1. Well, the stroke of midnight had just passed and Soapy was worried that Jamie wasn't properly sworn in yet—and wouldn't be for another twelve hours! So he arranged a simple, private swearing-in ceremony right there in his suite, with Nancy and me as witnesses. He was also a very religious man and didn't feel right doing it without a Bible, so he went right to the nightstand beside the bed and pulled out a Gideon's Bible. He used it to deliver the oath of office to Jamie and inscribed it afterwards. It's one of Jamie's most treasured possessions.

Everything culminated in the events of January 1, 1983. The day dawned very cold but bright and sunny. The swearing-in ceremony took place as tradition demanded—outdoors on the steps of the Capitol in Lansing.

The ceremonies began at noon with a fly-over by planes in formation from the National Guard. We missed that because we were up in the governor's office chatting with Soapy Williams and outgoing governor William Milliken and their wives Nancy and Helen. We were having such a pleasant conversation we lost track of time and had to be hurried out of there and downstairs to begin the swearing-in. The master of ceremonies was Dr. John Hannah who was president of Michigan State University when Jamie and I were students there. I suggested him to the committee for that role, and I was proud when he did a masterful job as I knew he would. He opened the ceremonies and introduced Ortheia Barnes who sang the national anthem so movingly and meaningfully that it brought tears to the eyes of a great many of us.

Next on the program was our son, Jay. He was twelve at the time but very poised. He led the audience in the Pledge of Allegience. Again, he was my suggestion to the inaugural committee who concurred enthusiastically. Watching him stand so proud and tall at the podium and lead the pledge in his strong but boyish voice was one of my proudest moments.

128

We planned the program to move along at a sprightly pace because we knew it would probably be bitterly cold. There was more to do that day than swear in the next governor. Other constitutional officers of the state needed to be dutifully sworn, including members of the boards governing state universities, judges, the secretary of state, the attorney general and the lieutenant governor. They all took their cues well and were sworn in in the first twenty minutes of the program. Our goal was to have the entire ceremony over in forty-five minutes before we had to start treating people for frost-bite.

At just about 12:20 P.M. on January 1, 1983—for the second time that day—James Johnston Blanchard was sworn in as Michigan's 45th governor. Administering the oath was Chief Justice of the Supreme Court, G. Mennen Williams—for the second time that day! I stood beside Jamie and held a family Bible, provided and inscribed by Jamie's mother for the occasion, as he took the oath.

Photographs from the occasion show all of us looking very calm and poised. They don't reveal the barely contained excitement and pride during that ceremony. My heart felt as if it would pound itself out of my chest. I wanted to jump and shriek for joy. I felt none of the bitter cold—my whole body was infused with warmth and love—for Jamie first and foremost, but also for our family, friends and loyal supporters who helped us achieve our goal, many of whom were present that day to witness the event. I was nearly overwhelmed with the scope of what Jamie and I had accomplished and achieved as man and wife and political partners. In our sixteen years together, we had navigated our ship of marriage through calm sunny waters and dark stormy seas and it had been a wonderful voyage. On January 1, 1983, we were riding the crest of a great wave triumphantly. It was one of the greatest moments of our marriage.

The ceremony concluded with Jamie's inaugural address. He delivered that twenty-minute speech in about fifteen minutes. It was windy as well as cold that day, and he felt the wind chill as he stood at the podium to address the audience. He was very cognizant of the fact we'd all been out there over half an hour, so he moved it right along. It was a speech he was proud of and had worked very hard on, on top of everything else he had to do.

129

In reality, it was a shame he had to deliver it outdoors. The wind seemed to take his words and whisk them away before they reached the audience. It was never fully appreciated as the great speech it was.

Everything proceeded on time and according to plan, with only a slight hitch. I was in such a euphoric state I didn't even realize what was going on, even though it happened right beside me. Our seats were arranged on the podium so that Jamie sat on the aisle, I sat next to him, and Jay sat on my other side, beside the Millikens. Several members of the governor's security detail were sprinkled around the podium and in the audience, including the head of the detail, Gene Hoekwater. He sat immediately behind Jamie. When Jamie rose to deliver his address, Gene slipped into the seat beside me. Gene was in a constant state of readiness throughout the ceremony, his eyes and head moving constantly, scanning the audience and the Capitol grounds for anything alarming or out of the ordinary. About half way through Jamie's speech, Gene suddenly leaned forward and appeared poised to leap out of his seat at any moment. I sensed the change but didn't realize the cause.

Gene told me later than he came within about one second of tackling the new governor and throwing him to the floor of the platform in midspeech! Gene had observed a window being raised in the Olds Hotel across the street from the Capitol soon after Jamie rose to speak. He also observed a man in the space of that open window. He was somehow able to telegraph a silent alarm to one of his fellow members of the detail who bolted over to the hotel to check it out. It was an innocent resident of the hotel who had raised the window to hear the ceremonies taking place across the street. Gene was within a second of throwing the governor out of harm's way when he received the all-clear signal from his fellow officer. Jamie had no sense of any of this, thank goodness, nor did Jay and I.

The ceremonies concluded with a 21-gun salute and Jamie descending the podium to review troops from Michigan's National Guard. Jay and I were standing at the rostrum to witness this part of the ceremony and Jay leaned over to whisper that he thought this was the best part of the whole thing. He hadn't realized his dad would be the commander of troops, nor had I!

130

We were thrilled when the outdoor ceremony concluded for several reasons. Jamie was "officially" governor, the ceremony had gone smoothly and well, and we could go inside and warm up. We went to Jamie's new office, just recently vacated by Bill Milliken, for a photography session with Martha and Hicks, other constitutional officers and our families. Following that, we spent a few minutes catching our breath and relaxing before the start of a reception and receiving line in the executive office suite. Members of the swearing-in audience and the general public had been invited to greet and congratulate the new governor, his family, and other dignitaries in a receiving line outside the governor's office, and enjoy musical and dance entertainment by Michigan artists in the Capitol Rotunda.

We were overwhelmed by the response. Literally hundreds of people responded to the invitation, and some waited in line for as long as two hours to file through the receiving line. I shook hands and greeted people at Jamie's side for two hours. Jay was a good trouper for about half an hour, and then went to sit at his dad's desk to draw. Martha, Frank Kelley, Dick Austin and various top staff members rotated in and out of the receiving line. Only Jamie went the entire distance. For three and a half hours he stood there and shook every hand that was offered.

We were late—by about two hours—to an inaugural lunch at the Civic Center, but as long as there were people who wanted to see him, Jamie stood there and was unfailing in his handshake, his friendliness and his genuine delight at their good wishes. We returned to our hotel room about 5:00 P.M. following the lunch, just in time to catch a hot bath, have a private dinner in our hotel suite and dress for two inaugural balls that evening.

The inaugural committee, at my urging, had decided to hold one ball in Lansing and another in Detroit. This was again in response to the pent-up demand for Democrats to celebrate the governor's victory. The Lansing ball would be the site most convenient for people from around the state to attend. The Detroit site would accommodate guests from southeastern Michigan. We also planned a third ball in Marquette for people in Michigan's upper peninsula so they wouldn't be required to travel all the way to Lansing or Detroit during Michigan's

131

snowy, slippery winter. That ball was held about two weeks later at Northern Michigan University.

Our first stop was the Lansing ball, held in the Civic Center where Jamie and I had one dance together. One of my favorite things is dancing, and I naively hoped we would have several dances. We couldn't have known how the evening would turn out. First, Jamie began experiencing back problems, which was very unusual. I can't remember him having back problems, ever, before that night. We decided it was probably the result of tension, sitting and standing in the cold for nearly an hour earlier that day, and then being on his feet all afternoon in the receiving line and greeting people at the inaugural lunch. Whatever the reason, dancing was very uncomfortable for him that night.

We also discovered he was fair game on the dance floor. Women were not the least hesitant about cutting in on us while we were dancing to have a dance with the governor. He enjoyed dancing with me but was uncomfortable dancing with unfamiliar partners. So as long as we stayed off the dance floor, he was safe. That was true for the remainder of our marriage and was disappointing. We attended a great many black tie affairs and dinner dances but if we danced at all, it was one dance and Jamie was usually a reluctant partner. So that evening, we spent most of our time as we had earlier in the day—shaking hands, greeting people and accepting good wishes. I did have a couple of dances, however, which were special. My dad, a polished dancer, was one of my partners that evening, as was my son, Jay.

Jay handled himself throughout all the inaugural activities with a maturity well beyond his twelve years. He was an unfailing good sport and participated enthusiastically in what were essentially adult activities. Like Jamie and me, he was adjusting to the spotlight and trying to find his place, his niche, and figure out how he fit into all of this. He didn't become upset or complain once, that I recall. Unlike Jamie and me, he didn't have the benefit of an adult perspective or our years of experience. He did have our love, our patient support, our understanding, our example and his unfailing pride in his dad to sustain him. He did beautifully, and even consented to dance with his mom without complaint!

After about two hours at the Lansing ball, we gathered our entourage together for the trip to Detroit. It included the three of us, Martha and Hicks, Frank and Nancy Kelley, Dick and Ida Austin, and a number of security people. We flew out of Lansing's Capital City Airport in one of the state's official airplanes and landed at City Airport in Detroit. Only after a rough landing did it dawn on Jamie that we had all the state's constitutional officers in one plane. He decided that would never happen again.

The Detroit ball was at the Westin Hotel and was mobbed. By the time we arrived, it was about 11:00 P.M. and the party was well underway. As in Lansing, the three of us went up on the stage to greet the crowd. Our hosts in Lansing were Mort Crim, senior anchorman at WDIV-TV in Detroit, and Tim Stout, popular sportscaster at WILX-TV in Lansing. Serving in that role in Detroit were Sonny Eliot, well-known TV personality and weatherman, and Diana Lewis, top anchorwoman at WXYZ-TV in Detroit. We were given enthusiastic and warm introductions by our hosts and rousing, foot-stomping, cheering, whistling welcomes from our audiences at both balls. It was thrilling and exciting and fun.

We stayed at the Detroit ball for about an hour and a half, again dancing only one dance together and greeting well-wishers. About 12:30 A.M. we excused ourselves to go upstairs to our suite where we hosted a small, private reception for a few close friends, supporters and staff.

Here we finally put our feet up, let our hair down and celebrated. We had drinks and cocktails, a midnight buffet—with coney island hot dogs from across the street—and cigars all around. Jamie gave up a pack-a-day cigarette habit in 1978 for two cigars a day, both of which he savored. And he certainly savored one that night.

We had an absolutely wonderful time. It was the celebration of victory, triumph and relief. The transition had been accomplished, the cabinet and key administration people were in place, the 1984 budget was completed, the financial recovery was underway, Thanksgiving and Christmas had been duly celebrated, and a successful, stirring inaugural capped the campaign victory and months of feverish activity.

It was amazing what had been accomplished in less than two short months since the election. We were thrilled, euphoric, and anything seemed possible and within our grasp. We didn't want the day or night to end, so we fought our exhaustion with our last reserves of energy until we collapsed in bed just before dawn.

For me, that day was a high point of our marriage and our political partnership. It seemed to be the culmination of all the years that had gone before, the reason for the difficult choices and sacrifices we'd made, the justification of our marriage and the rationalization for the trials and tribulations. The achievement of our joint goal made it all worthwhile. We were proud of each other, how far we'd come together and how much we'd done for each other along the way. Nothing quite equaled that day in our marriage, ever again.

Chapter Seventeen

I caught a very bad cold on inaugural day and woke up the next morning barely able to get out of bed and dress. I think it was my body's way of forcing me to rest. The three of us were planning to drive to Lansing that day to see the Governor's Residence, our home for the next four years, and plan our move there. I hadn't been there since Helen Milliken invited me to lunch shortly after the election and took me on a short tour. I wasn't comfortable at that time looking into every nook and cranny of the place. Bill Milliken hosted the same kind of lunch for Jamie, and he'd had the same kind of tour. Jay also had a quick visit one day when he was in Lansing visiting his new school. So all three of us had had a peek but not a really good look.

I was too ill to go to Lansing and Jamie and Jay didn't want to go without me, so we left the Westin Hotel and headed straight for Pleasant Ridge. I was sick for the next week which was especially frustrating because I was itching to get our move to Lansing organized and begin my official duties as First Lady.

Jamie was engrossed in engineering and directing Michigan's financial rescue and preparing his first State of the State speech which followed on the heels of the inaugural by about two weeks. He needed to stay on top of things in Lansing, so he moved into the Governor's Residence immediately, taking only a few personal possessions and his clothes.

Jay and I remained in Pleasant Ridge for about three weeks to allow Jay to complete his first semester of seventh grade at Best Junior High School in Ferndale before transferring to Dwight Rich Middle School in Lansing. Jamie and I were staunch believers in the value and importance of a public school education, so we enrolled Jay in the neighborhood school serving the area around the Governor's Residence.

When I visited the Governor's Residence for the first time at Helen's invitation, she made me feel immediately at home with her welcoming comment, "Paula, thank goodness it's you." This type of remark was typical of Helen who is a warm, gracious and intelligent woman. On that first visit I was surprised, as were most visitors, that the Governor's Residence was a very unassuming dwelling for such a distinction. It was designed by a prominent Michigan architect, Wallace Frost of Birmingham, for a Lansing businessman, Howard Sober, who had lived there with his wife for about ten years before giving it to the state in 1969 for use as the Governor's Residence. It's essentially a one-story, long, low, contemporary stone structure with a low fence and circular drive. Set in a country-club neighborhood, the Governor's Residence is overshadowed by many more stately and expensive homes. When you approach it from the street, you're really looking at the back of the house. There is no sign indicating it's the home of the governor, and your only clues are a locked entrance gate and a flag pole in the front which flies the U.S. and Michigan flags.

Once inside the front door the visitor is greeted with a breath-taking surprise. The combined foyer and living room open up magnificently on a spectacular view of the gardens and backyard through floor-to-ceiling room-sized windows. The living room is large enough in square footage to accommodate our

136

entire Pleasant Ridge house. It also has a dining room which seats twelve, a library, a garden room, kitchen, three bedrooms, eight bathrooms and a three-car garage. There are also maid's quarters off the kitchen which we turned into the Residence Manager's office, and cook's quarters over the garage which for a time I used as my office at the Residence and which later became Jay's room. The Residence is fully furnished in a very contemporary, oriental style with furniture the state purchased from the Sobers when he made the home a gift to the state.

When we moved in, it was badly in need of redecoration and repair. Helen Milliken is a master gardener and concentrated her early efforts on the gardens and grounds which are magnificent. She told me they were ready to begin on the inside of the home, starting with renovation of the 1950s kitchen, when the recession flattened Michigan economically and those expenses couldn't be justified.

We certainly found ourselves in the same predicament. The state didn't have a dime to spare—in fact it was in hock to Japanese bankers in 1982—so we had to find sources of private money to redecorate, refurnish and repair the Residence.

In the spring of 1984, I founded and organized the Friends of the Governor's Residence with the help of several prominent Lansing citizens who spearheaded a fund-raising drive to raise money to restore the Residence. We raised $100,000 and were able to bring both the Lansing and Mackinac Residences up to a standard of which we and our thousands of guests were proud.

But, I'm getting ahead of my story.

In January 1983, the Blanchard family—Jamie, Jay, our dog Abby, our cat Scooter, and I—moved into a house which had the potential to be spectacular but which was worn, tired and not our own. We remedied the situation temporarily by giving it a fresh coat of paint inside, a good cleaning and a feeling of home with some of our own things. Photographs here, a chair there and mementos everywhere.

Living there was a difficult adjustment for all of us. Only Abby and Scooter settled in quickly because home to them was where the three of us were. It's a grand home on a grand scale and one anyone would be honored to live in. We were certainly proud to be there, but several things made the adjustment difficult.

137

First, the house and the lovely things in it didn't belong to us. It was like living in a luxury hotel on a four-year lease. It never felt like home to me and we never called it that. We called it the Governor's Residence or the Residence. I would talk to Jay or Jamie about what time they'd be "home", but I meant it in a generic sense. Our home was in Pleasant Ridge, but since we seldom had time to go there and our needs had outgrown it, that too lost its meaning as "home." I tried to remedy that over the years, but that homeless feeling contributed greatly to my eventual discontent.

Second, the Residence wasn't homey or cozy. Even after we refurnished it, it never had a lived-in feeling. The rooms were beautiful and dramatic and very large, with high ceilings. When we raised the money to refurbish it, I felt we should remain true to the original design, tone and feeling of the house as it was when it was donated to the state. I didn't feel a governor or his family should imprint their own taste on the house but should preserve and protect its original character and style. The Michigan Governor's Residence is considered one of the premier examples in the United States of 1950's American architecture and design. I felt obliged to honor that. Hence, we restored it to its original beauty rather to our own liking.

Third, the floor plan made privacy in the home difficult to achieve. The bedrooms are in one wing and the kitchen is in the other, on opposite sides of the house from each other. Going from the bedrooms to the kitchen required us to walk right past the front door and through the foyer, in full view of the living room, library and dining room. It necessitated that we be fully dressed in street attire when we went to breakfast in the morning—at least during the week. Jamie often held meetings in the library, the living room, the dining room and the garden room—in every room except the bedrooms and the kitchen. I used the Residence for meetings occasionally, too. Consequently, we had to be presentable—Jay included—when we walked through the house because we never knew who we might see. One of the reasons Jay moved into the cook's quarters above the kitchen was so that he could move easily from his room to the kitchen and outside without going through the rest of the house. One day I was in the back hall by the kitchen talking to the housekeeper. I ran face to face into Jack Valenti, president of the Motion Picture Association of America, who had been mistakenly brought in the house through the back door. Luckily I recognized him immediately, even though I wasn't aware he was expected at the Residence. I introduced myself to him over several piles of laundry, and he was quite relieved to have me escort him out of the laundry room and into the living room for his meeting with the governor.

More than once I sneaked in and out of the house through the outside door from the master bedroom. If I wanted to go to the kitchen or leave the house without being seen in the main part of the Residence, I had to exit or enter our bedroom through a patio door which accessed the backyard. I then circled around the house to the front and walked past the front door on the outside and into the garage, from which I could go into the kitchen or climb into the car. I had to do this around the front—in full view of the street—because the backyard was completely exposed to the inside of the house through all those beautiful floor-to-ceiling windows. Thus, I would have been in full view of anyone inside. I had to time these excursions carefully to avoid running into people either leaving or arriving at the Residence for a meeting or a reception. Occasionally, I misjudged my timing and ran into someone. I stopped and greeted the puzzled person as if I always left the Residence in such a manner. This arrangement, needless to say, made me feel like a captive—or a fugitive—in this house more than once.

Our privacy was also limited by the presence of our Residence staff and security personnel. Someone besides us was always there and likely to enter the public areas of the house. The staff had the weekends off, but security was there 24 hours a day, 365 days a year. The staff was headed by our Residence Manager, Carolyn Simmons. She was the second person I hired after Carlene Bonner and she's still there in that capacity. It also included a housekeeper, a chef, a maintenance man/grounds-keeper, and a secretary. In the spring and summer months, Hank Newhouse, who had tended the Residence gardens for years, joined the staff to supervise the summer garden plantings and their care.

With Carolyn's assistance, all our staff were hired after our arrival. I personally interviewed and selected all of them, with the exception of Hank. For a while we retained Wellington, the chef who had worked for the Millikens, but he couldn't adjust to our hectic and ever-changing schedule, and after he threw a chair at me in a fit of rage I discharged him. The chef's position was the hardest position to fill and manage. After Wellington left, we hired a chef with his own set of idiosyncracies, including a propensity to treat his so-called "diabetes" with a daily six-pack of beer. He lasted less than a year. Carolyn finally found Forrest Waldo II, a nineteen-year-old chef who could prepare anything from hors d'oeuvres for 400 to a six-course dinner for twelve, to macaroni and cheese for Jay. He was at the Residence from November 1983 until about a year after I left.

Carolyn also recommended our housekeeper, Jeanette Morrison, who was a miracle worker. She was hired almost immediately and is still there. Dan Crow was our full-time groundskeeper, maintenance man and jack-of-all trades. He and Jeanette were indispensable. The staff was friendly, loyal, hardworking, and discreet. They made our hectic life manageable. While we weren't living a life of ease by any means, they made our life much easier. We couldn't have done all that we did without them. I became very fond of each of them, and I still hear from some of them on different occasions during the year.

Nevertheless, they limited our privacy by their need to be in and about the house to do their jobs. They were headquartered in the kitchen area and the back hall, just outside Carolyn's office, the former maid's quarters. We also had office space in the basement which was reached from the back hall. Every time we went to the kitchen we could expect to see and talk with one or more of them, and they became like part of our extended family. They were people we liked, enjoyed and depended on more and more as the years went by.

The only room completely off-limits was the master bedroom. Only Jeanette entered our room to clean and change linens, either when we were away from the Residence or with my permission if I was there.

We never answered our own telephone. It was answered either by Carolyn, the secretary or a security guard. We had phones in every room and calls were either transferred to us in the house by in-house phone lines or by messages hand-delivered by Carolyn or security. When we were home, we used the library a great deal. It was the coziest room in the house because it was the smallest and had the lowest ceiling. Jamie had a desk in the library and usually worked there in the evenings and on weekends. I'd keep him company and watch television, read or work on some needlepoint. It was located in the "private" wing of the house with the bedrooms and had to be approached from the opposite wing—the kitchen wing or the garage where security were headquartered—by crossing the foyer. The foyer had a marble floor so we could always hear Carolyn or a security person approaching by the sound of footsteps across the floor. That was sometimes our only warning that someone was delivering messages, papers or bills for the governor's signature.

Both Jamie and I associated the Residence with work. He often worked mornings and almost every evening at his desk in the library. I maintained an office at the Residence where I took care of the correspondence I received there and directed household activities, including the entertainment schedule for the Lansing and Mackinac Island residences. The Lansing residence was in constant use as a site for meetings and entertaining. Carolyn developed a terrific system of record-keeping for the entertaining we did and the count when I left in June of 1987 was nearly 30,000 people who had been entertained at dinner parties or receptions in the four and one-half years I was First Lady. That number reflects only people who were entertained and does not include the hundreds of people who were there to attend meetings.

After we moved in and began looking at opportunities for official entertaining, we were astonished to find out how many people—prominent and otherwise—had never been to the Governor's Residence. Foremost among those were thousands of active Michigan Democrats who had worked hard for Jamie's election. There hadn't been a Governor's Residence when the last Democratic governor, John B. Swainson, had served in the 1960s, so we faced pent-up demand on this front, too. We sincerely wanted to share the rewards of office with the people who helped put us there so we began a round of receptions which were still going on when I left.

There was usually at least one reception a week at the Residence and more often than not, two and sometimes three, especially during the Christmas season. They were usually held on Tuesday, Wednesday or Thursday evenings from 6:00 until 7:30 P.M. I would stand at the front door and greet people as they arrived. Often Jamie would be late arriving from the office or an event, so his chief of staff greeted with me or I would greet guests by myself. Carolyn sometimes did the greeting, too. When Jamie arrived, he dove right into the middle of the party and started shaking hands. When most of the guests had arrived, I would mix and mingle too, but rarely at Jamie's side. Frequently, we never even had the chance to say hello until the guests had left. Occasionally, the press of people upon me became claustrophobic and stifling, and I would slip away from the party after greeting everyone at the door to retire to the bedroom until guests began to leave. I then would rejoin the party to say goodby.

I had ambivalent feelings about these receptions as I did about so many things in our life. I derived great pleasure from sharing the Residence with our guests and seeing their joy and delight at being there and meeting us. Their appreciation was genuine as were their good wishes and encouragement of the good job most thought we were doing. On the other hand, it was difficult to maintain a high level of enthusiasm for an activity which became so repetitious. The faces blurred together, the conversations—by the very nature of a cocktail party—revolved around small talk and it was hard on the feet. People used to ask me if my hand tired, but truthfully, it was my feet. The marble foyer of the Residence had absolutely no give. And, most importantly, if an evening was devoted to a reception, that meant one less evening for quiet, private, family time.

My favorite type of occasions were the small dinner parties we hosted. The dining room was not large and the table seated a maximum of twelve. That is in contrast to many governor's residences which have massive dining rooms with tables which

142

seat twenty-five or thirty. We hosted a number of these special evenings, and I was particular about the way they were planned.

We usually invited ten to twelve people. Jamie and I or the staff and I would work out the invitation list and find a date on the calendar. Then Carolyn would go to work phoning our guests, often working with their secretaries, to determine if they would be able to attend. If so, a formal invitation, done in calligraphic style, embossed on white with the state seal in gold, would follow. Once we knew who our guests were going to be, Forrest and I would sit down and develop the menu.

In order to give Jamie a chance to arrive at the Residence before our guests and give him time to freshen-up, our dinner parties began at 7:00 P.M. He usually beat our guests through the front door, but I remember a few times hosting the cocktail hour solo. Guests were greeted at the door by a staff person, who took their coats and asked them what they would like to drink. Jamie and I were either in the living room, seated around the fireplace, or in the backyard patio, depending on the season. We would have cocktails until 7:45 or 8:00, after which dinner was served. A pianist provided background music on the Residence's grand piano.

Dinner usually began with appetizer or soup. Jamie preferred soup, so soup it usually was. Although I am not especially fond of this course, Forrest was a master of delicious homemade soups and even I became partial to his lobster bisque. The next course was a salad, served with homemade rolls. Many hostesses prefer the European way of serving salad after the entree, but I never have an appetite for it then so it was served before the main course. Since Jamie doesn't like fish, the entree was usually veal or beef. It was accompanied by a vegetable and a potato or rice dish.

The pièce de resistance was always dessert, Forrest's real specialty. Every dessert was a masterpiece. Organizers of spring fairs at the schools Jay attended always called to ask us to provide a cake for the cakewalk. We did and Forrest's was always the first cake to go. We usually remained at the table through coffee, but we liked to adjourn to the living room for after-dinner drinks. There Jamie would offer his male guests cigars, and we would relax with after-dinner entertainment which I arranged. My favorite choice, if he was available, was Jerry Klickstein, a classical guitarist from Michigan State University. For about fifteen minutes, he would play several short selections which he preceded by a short commentary about the piece and the composer. This was delightful. We usually hosted our dinner parties during the week so our guests departed about 10:30 or 11:00. If they were people we knew well and they didn't have far to travel to reach home, our evenings were often much later than that.

One of the most memorable dinner parties we hosted was in honor of Henry Ford II and his wife, Kate. Jamie discovered in talking to Henry that he had never been invited to the Governor's Residence. In fact, Henry had never even been in Lansing! It didn't take Jamie long to rectify that and in no time, Henry Ford and Kate were our guests of honor. Several other prominent Michigan people joined us that evening. The dinner was shortly after we hired the cook with the purported "diabetes" problem and it was his first dinner party as our chef. It's a good thing the company was spectacular because the food and service left much to be desired.

Our invitation to Henry and Kate was returned by their invitation to us. They hosted a small dinner party in our honor in their Grosse Pointe home. Protocol seated me on Henry's left as the female guest of honor. How glad I was for protocol because Henry was a charming dinner companion. He was a great storyteller and I'm a very good listener so we got on in grand fashion. He also loved to charm the ladies and he set about charming me. He complimented me on this and that all evening and as the hour grew later and later, he was well into his cups, as they say. He rather lost track of what he had complimented me on and began to repeat himself. Before we rose from the dinner table, he told me at least five times what beautiful teeth I had.

I remember well one other thing he said because I was so surprised by it. He was regaling me with stories of presidents he'd known so I asked him which president he liked best of all. Thinking I knew his political persuasion fairly well, I expected

144

him to name a Republican. Without hesitation, Henry proclaimed LBJ his favorite.

"Why?" I asked in an inquisitive tone.

"Because LBJ was a man's man. He'd invite me to his Texas ranch and we'd ride around in his jeep—drinking, smoking, cussing and talking about women." Henry replied.

Three seasons out of four we entertained in Lansing. In the summer, we entertained at the Mackinac Island Governor's Residence. Its beauty, majesty, elegance and comfort cast a magic spell over me whenever I was there. Every time I left this house I hated to leave and couldn't wait to return. It's one of the few things I miss about life as the governor's wife.

The Mackinac Residence commands the best view of the Straits of Mackinac and the Mackinac Bridge of any place on the island, and I spent hours sitting on the front porch reading, chatting with friends, doing needlework, playing scrabble, napping in the hammock and just drinking in the view. It positively restores the soul to be there. Each year I moved up there for the summer as soon as school was out for Jay and didn't return to Lansing until Labor Day when school resumed. The Island Residence has a living room, dining room, sunroom, kitchen, butler's pantry and back sitting room on the main floor. The front porch spans the whole front of the house, running in front of the living room, dining room and sunroom. Upstairs is the large master bedroom suite which commands a spectacular view of the Straits and the Bridge through a bay window and from a private sundeck where I spent many hours on sunny days. There are ten other bedrooms and seven bathrooms. The grounds are beautiful because of the years of loving care and tending furnished by Rollie Hill, who has been the gardener there for years. The house was built in 1909 and was owned privately by two families before it fell into disrepair and was purchased by the State of Michigan in 1949 for the original construction price of $15,000.

Jay spent two complete summers up there with me before high school friends and activities made him reluctant to leave Lansing for the whole summer. Jamie came up nearly every weekend. He'd arrive Friday night after a day in Lansing or on the road, and if nothing was scheduled we'd have a late dinner at the residence. If it was warm, we'd sit on the front porch after dinner looking out over the Straits and the Mackinac Bridge while he smoked a cigar. He usually spent Saturday on the Grand Hotel golf course. Sometimes I played with him but he really preferred to golf with Jay, male staff members, or friends and talk politics. Saturday evenings we often entertained friends for dinner or went to one of the Island restaurants. If I could talk him into it, we'd wrap up Saturday evening playing cards, scrabble or charades with our friends and guests. His favorite entertainment, however, was to take a seat on the front porch where he could smoke his cigar, take in the great view and talk more politics.

As with the Lansing residence, the Mackinac residence was a joy to share with friends, family and other guests. We rarely had overnight guests in Lansing, except for family members, but on Mackinac we hosted several weekend parties each summer. Our guests for the weekend would arrive Friday evening and stay through Sunday afternoon. Over the course of my four summers there, some of the guests we entertained for weekends were Great Lakes governors and spouses, Midwest governors and spouses, Washington friends, Democratic party officials, several groups of personal friends and our families. Mary Nelson, our housekeeper there, made everyone feel right at home, including the three of us. She was very popular with our guests, and upon their arrival, returning guests often went directly to the kitchen to give their regards to Mary. She was a marvelous cook, specializing in good, old-fashioned home cooking, and she had several specialties which became our favorites. She also became a good friend. She and I had great fun working jigsaw puzzles together and talking about her kids and grandchildren. We played game after game of double solitare in the small room off the kitchen and Mary almost always won. Sometimes the governor's security person would join our games and Mary still won. Every once in a while Mary used to forget and call me Mrs. Milliken. We'd laugh and she'd tell some favorite stories about the Millikens, of whom she was very fond. I loved her stories. If she slips and forgets now, she needn't worry—the last name is the same!

I've had several delightful visits to the island in the last three summers. My friend, Michigan's premier hotelier and Grand Hotel owner, Dan Musser, always sees to it that I have a room with a view at his wonderful establishment. On occasion my room has overlooked the Governor's Residence, and it tugged at my heartstrings to see it because I remember the special people and times I spent there. When I'm on the island, I place a telephone call to Mary to say hello.

With Mary's help, we usually hosted a Sunday brunch at the Island Residence from 11:30 until 1:30. These brunches were catered by the Grand Hotel and were absolutely elegant. About 9:30 on Sunday morning, the Grand Hotel dray, pulled by its team of horses, would wind its way up the hill from the hotel to the Residence loaded down with gourmet food, silver trays and service, glassware and linen. Keeping it all balanced were the young men and women in their fine Grand Hotel service uniforms who would set it all up in the dining room and on the porch and serve it to our guests. Invitations to these summer garden party affairs were very much coveted and, as was the case with the Lansing Residence, thousands of people had never received an invitation. We were blessed, almost without exception on these Sundays, with the most glorious weather and our guests could enjoy the spectacular view from the porch or a stroll through the colorful, old-English gardens. Men and women came in their best Sunday, summer finery and it was like a scene from another century. It took a brunch every Sunday to meet the demand for invitations.

We chose to serve brunches because it gave people time to drive up to Mackinac City from anywhere in the state, catch the boat across to the island, and arrive by noon. They could then complete their return trip in the same day, if necessary. Many of our guests chose to make a weekend of it and stayed at one of the island hotels. Many more of our guests, however, couldn't afford that kind of expense and we needed to accommodate their need to make the trip up and back in one day. Jamie, too, could take in an afternoon of golf on Sunday after brunch before heading back down to Lansing Sunday night or Monday morning. Our parties, I think, were catalysts in the rapid increase in tourism on the island after we arrived!

Through the years, we entertained Democrats, Republicans, independents, business leaders, labor leaders, governors, mayors, other elected officials, religious leaders, judges, friends, neighbors, family—the list goes into the thousands. I was disturbed by the fact that there were still so many people we couldn't invite whom I knew would like to see the Island Residence. And I wanted to find a way to share the uniqueness of the residence and the breath-taking view of the Straits and the Bridge with the many tourists who came to the island. All they could do was stand outside the white picket fence around the Island Residence and imagine what it was like inside.

So I came up with the idea of public tours. Tours of either governor's residences were very few and far between. Helen Milliken had granted them occasionally to garden clubs and other worthy organizations, as did I during my tenure. Tours of the Lansing residence weren't very feasible because the place was in constant use for working meetings and official entertaining, and the floor plan made it difficult for us to go about our business if public groups were touring. After some thought, I realized tours would be feasible on the Island. Because Jay's room and the master bedroom had a back stairway which led directly to the kitchen and outdoors, I realized all of us would have access to all the private rooms of the residence while tours were conducted in the public areas.

I talked it over with Jamie who thought it was a great idea, so Carolyn and I worked up a plan. We approached members of the Mackinac Island Park Commission, which has jurisdiction over the residence, and secured their support for the project. In June of 1983, our first summer there, we began our weekly tours on Wednesday mornings from 9:30 to 12:00. It was a first for Michigan and gave visitors a tour of the living room, dining room, sunroom and a walk along the total length of the front porch. At the suggestion of my friend, Kathy Lewand, I invited women who were cottage owners on the island and who knew island history to be tour guides. The Boy Scouts and Girl Scouts had troups visiting the scout barracks weekly and they assisted, as well. The Park Commission set up the tours each Wednesday morning and distributed free tickets at the Visitors Center and

148

Fort Mackinac. We asked each guest to sign our guest book on the front porch, and we gave them a color brochure with pictures and a description of the Island Residence. Each week several hundred people enjoyed the chance to see the Island Residence they've provided for their governor and his family since 1946. I think instituting the tours is one of the best things I did as First Lady.

I didn't greet people myself while they were taking the tours. I went about my business upstairs and sometimes would come and go from the house while the tours were taking place. If someone recognized me, I'd stop to chat for a minute and sign an autograph and have a picture taken, if they liked. As rewarding as it was to share both Governor's Residences and ourselves with our thousands of guests, one can well imagine how demanding it was. It consumed not only time, but it drew on reserves of physical and emotional energy. And our entertaining was not in place of other responsibilities. Evening receptions in Lansing came after a day already ten to twelve hours long. Our weekend entertaining was added on to the end of a sixty hour week. Understandably, there was not much time or energy left over for leisure, relaxed conversation, simple togetherness or reflection. We enjoyed many luxuries, but the luxury of time without political purpose was rare.

For Jamie, this state of affairs was not a matter of concern. He loved being in the middle of our thousands of guests and wasn't happy unless he talked to each one personally and shook each hand. He thrived on the challenge and demands of his work, which included the vigorous entertainment schedule, and it charged his batteries. It drained mine. I needed uninterrupted, undistracted personal, private, family time—time by myself, time alone with Jamie, and time for the three of us as a family—to restore my energy. Ironically, that kind of time drained his. It made him anxious if he didn't have a schedule to keep, phone calls to make or someone to meet with. If he had open time on his daily schedule, he would arrange meetings, make phone calls, do paperwork or clean out his briefcase. His favorite vocation and avocation was politics and work. Even golf games reflected that. If he had open time on weekends, he would arrange a golf game with someone who would play golf and talk politics. For myself, I can honestly say I miss many of the people . . . but only a few of the parties.

Living in both Governor's Residences created a profound sense of isolation. I felt very much buffered from the world and out of the mainstream. We had a twenty-four-hour security detail on duty, and when guests arrived at either residence, they were stopped and checked by security, either at the gate or at the front door. Guests and visitors were required to state their names, and logs on arrivals and departures were kept by security around the clock. Even family, friends and staff were checked in and out.

Both residences are fenced in and elaborate security systems with cameras and monitors track everything that goes on. I felt like I was living under a very watchful eye, which I was. With these kinds of safeguards, people didn't just drop in, and the ebb and flow of my interaction with people became more formal, less spontaneous and certainly more restricted.

As I mentioned before, we never answered our own phone nor did we hear it ring. All our calls were screened before we received them. It was not a matter of convenience for us that calls were handled in that fashion, but a matter of absolute necessity because daily phone calls sometimes numbered in the hundreds. No matter who called—the White House or my mother—their call was answered by Carolyn, a secretary or a security guard. The call was either put through to us if we were there and available to take it, or a message was taken. One day it dawned on me that while this system of handling the phone was a necessity for Jamie and me, it was far from necessary or "normal" for a teenager to have his calls screened by a secretary and callers identified. Jay never complained about it but I decided, again in the interest of normalcy, to have a separate line installed in Jay's room so that he could receive calls from his friends directly.

I didn't realize how much distance this telephone system put between us and other people until I moved out of the Residence and started answering my own phone again. I was excited to hear it ring, anticipate who might be calling and answer it myself. I have a phone answering machine but I never put it on when I'm home because I like to answer calls myself. When

Jamie and I were married, I resented the telephone a great deal because it was an intrusion into the little time he had at home. It would begin ringing for him as soon as he walked in the door and he took most of the calls. Even if he didn't take the call, it was an interruption and the message would usually cause him to become preoccupied with the call or the caller.

When we left the Residence, the governor's security detail preferred, and expected, us to be accompanied by at least one of them and sometimes two or more depending on where we were going and what we planned to do. Members of the governor's security detail are the cream of the crop of the Michigan State Police. I found them to be extremely likeable, capable, sensitive, discreet, intelligent, fine men. They were great to be around and their assistance was indispensable. They were responsible for getting us safely to our destination on time and assisting with arrangements once we arrived. They do a very difficult job extremely well.

But their very presence had the effect of setting us apart from the people around us. They were a psychological barrier between us and other people and could become, if necessary, a physical barrier as well. They were most comfortable if they had us in sight or at least knew where we were at all times. The physical safety of the governor and his family is their job, twenty-four hours a day. That's a heavy responsibility.

I know I caused them a few gray hairs. While I enjoyed and appreciated the safety, assistance and convenience the security provided for us, I didn't feel comfortable being chauffeured around all the time. I'm a down-to-earth person and I didn't want any of us—Jamie or Jay or me—to become too removed from a normal life. A normal life to me meant one being led by "normal," average, middle-class people living in neighborhoods like the ones Jamie and I had grown up in. I wanted us to remember our roots, our values and the life we'd return to when we left the Governor's Residence. I didn't want our heads to be turned by living a lifestyle we could never afford were it not for Jamie's position. Consequently, I always tried to minimize the role of security in our everyday life. I wanted them with Jay or with me only when necessary.

I felt strongly about this where it concerned Jay. Jamie

agreed with me and both of us worked hard to make Jay's environment as normal as possible in spite of the fact we were living an unusual life. For this reason, I took Helen Milliken's advice and got my own car. That way I could run personal errands, go to the beauty parlor, go shopping, visit friends and take Jay places without the presence of security. I had security with me whenever I was conducting official duties and of course when I was with Jamie, but with my own car I achieved a degree of personal privacy and freedom. I don't think the security detail ever felt comfortable with this degree of independence, but I compromised by letting them know where I was going when I left the Residence and estimating when I thought I'd return. It was kind of like checking in and out of the house with your parents or your housemother at the sorority house at college, but it was still better than taking a security man into the lingerie department at Hudson's!

It was just this sort of circumstance which made me determined to have my own transportation. I had some personal shopping to do one day and as was customary, I contacted the member of the security detail assigned to me that day to indicate I planned to go out. He arrived and we set off for Hudson's in the Lansing Mall. As was also customary, he accompanied me on my shopping rounds, staying a discreet distance from me but always keeping me in sight. This wasn't a problem if I was in the shoe department, or housewares or the men's or boy's department. It was a problem, however, when I dropped by lingerie. Our security people usually tried to make themselves as inconspicuous as possible in these situations by browsing and looking at merchandise as if they were shopping. But this was tough to do in lingerie! It was compounded on this day by the fact that he did not see me go into the dressing room to try some things on and became alarmed when he lost sight of me. He told me later that the sales personnel in the department became suspicious of his roamings and curiosity about the whereabouts of a particular customer and called store security personnel to question his behavior. He was called upon to explain who he was and who I was—something security personnel try not to divulge. When none of the sales people recalled seeing me, he became alarmed. He left lingerie to canvass the store and was not around when I emerged from the dressing room. I was surprised when I didn't see him because security had always stayed within sight. I made my purchases in a hurry and was about to set out on a search for him when he reappeared in lingerie and sagged with obvious relief upon catching sight of me at the lingerie counter. I decided then and there not to put anybody through that again, myself included, and in December 1983, I became the owner of a Chevrolet Cavalier convertible.

Having my own car also allowed me to have some private outings with Jay. These were quite frequent, at least until Jay got his driver's license and his own car, because Jamie was often out of town or tied up with work. Jay and I could go by ourselves to get some dinner, do shopping, go to the movies or I could drive him to a friend's house—the kinds of things normal mothers do with their sons. If you think about it, a car offers a haven—at least it used to before mobile phones—from the distractions of television and telephones, and it is a place where couples, families, and parents and children can have some together time, some talk time. Jay and I had some heart-to-heart talks in that Chevrolet.

Jamie and I lost that haven. We never had any privacy in the car or any mode of transportation anywhere. When we traveled together by car there was always at least one security person, usually two, in the car with us. The security person assigned to Jamie for the day would drive and the person assigned to me would ride in the front passenger seat. Jamie and I would ride in the back seat. If Jay was with us, he'd either ride in the middle in the back or in the front passenger seat. In that case, the rest of the security detail would follow in another car. We traveled in state-owned cars. Jamie's was a Lincoln Town Car and mine was an Oldsmobile Ninety-Eight. Jay was driven back and forth to school each day and insisted on traveling in the oldest, most modest car in the fleet. The state doesn't own, doesn't want to own and can't afford limousines, and even if they had been available, we would have refused to ride around in them. The only advantage would have been that Jamie and I could have put a window up between our security people and us to have privacy in our conversations. As it was, every word

Jamie and I said to each other or to Jay, if he was with us, was heard by our security people. Consequently, the car became a place for casual conversations only, and another place for business where Jamie made phone calls by mobile phone, read the paper or did paperwork.

Our security people accompanied us on vacations, too, facilitating our travel arrangements and driving us around in rented cars. I finally put my foot down on one of the last vacations Jamie and I took together and insisted he rent a car for our own private use. Reluctantly, he did so and actually ended up enjoying the driving. It was a vacation to the Cayman Islands in January 1987 where driving is done on the "wrong" side of the road. It was quite an adventure for both of us since the last time Jamie had driven was on a vacation out West in August 1984 following the Democratic National Convention in San Francisco. On this trip to the Cayman Islands he not only had the challenge of boning up on his driving, but he had to do it on the wrong side of the road. He did very well—he's a good driver— and it was so much fun to be in the car by ourselves. I had the same feeling I had as a teenager going for a drive with a boyfriend for some privacy away from the prying eyes of parents. Jamie even started to feel comfortable enough on that trip to leave security behind when we went out to eat in the evening. That might have boded well for more privacy in the future, but we were already discussing divorce by then.

Another significant adjustment I had to make while living in the Governor's Residence was to the total lack of routine. It should be clear that I'm a person who needs structure, control and predictability in my life. There was plenty of organizational structure in terms of procedures and the organization of our various staffs, and the bureaucracy of state government is certainly a structure within which we operated. There was also structure in terms of daily, weekly and monthly schedules to be met, and both Jamie and I had our own schedules assembled by our staffs. These organizational structures were an attempt to manage an enormously demanding, complex, problem-beset job which changed minute-by-minute. The most carefully crafted schedule could be, and usually was, thrown off daily by developing events. That didn't happen with my schedule very often because I wasn't dealing with the crises, the problems, the legislature, the courts, New York bankers, the jobless, the homeless, and the never-ending list of decisions to be made and executed. But Jamie was—just as he should have been. His best-laid plans were always subject to change by events of the day, and change was the only constant. Because of his school schedule, Jay was the only one of us with any semblance of routine in his life. And even he learned at a very early age that there was little predictability about what the evening would hold when he walked in the door after school.

Jamie's schedule was developed on a weekly and monthly basis. Commitments and activities were planned several months in advance. I tried my best to bring some order to my life by working with and around his schedule to plan my calendar of First Lady activities and our activities as a couple and family. I tried to plan one or two family dinners for the three of us each week, leisure activities for the weekend (if there was any spare time on the schedule), family celebrations, time for participation in Jay's school activities, vacations and other things ordinary couples and families do together. To his credit, Jamie did his best to accommodate my need for control and predictability.

The difficulty was that it just wasn't possible to plan very well around a schedule which could change drastically with just one phone call. Because of his total commitment to his work and his responsibilities, Jamie gave those matters top priority. With few exceptions, other plans came second and were subject to immediate and constant change. I tried my best to accommodate this situation, but instead of resigning myself to it and accepting it, my resentment and frustration over my lack of control grew steadily as the years went by.

If I had been willing for us live essentially two different lives, planning my priorities, activities and time completely apart from Jamie's, I could have achieved the control, predictability and routine I desired. I wasn't willing to do that because that wasn't my idea of a marriage or a family. I believed, and still do, that quality, undistracted and devoted time together is required for a healthy marriage and a healthy family. I held on as long as I could to the hope that we could achieve that kind of time together in the context of the position which Jamie held.

While trying to achieve some balance in our personal lives, I undertook the professional challenges of being Michigan's First Lady.

Chapter Eighteen

Adjusting to life in the Governor's Residence certainly had its difficulties, and there were many adjustments I never made. But I didn't have any difficulty assuming the position of First Lady. I never liked the title, but from January 1, 1983 until December 21, 1987, the day of our divorce, I certainly enjoyed the position. I borrowed a favorite quote from a fellow First Lady, Dagmar Celeste of Ohio, who said, "I'm too much of a Democrat to be called first and I'm too much of a woman to be called lady." I often opened up my speeches with that line following an introduction as "Paula Blanchard, Michigan's First Lady" and it always drew a big laugh. Jamie enjoyed it, too, and frequently introduced me as the "First Woman of Michigan."

I loved the opportunity for advocacy my new role provided. I valued my position for the chance it afforded for personal and professional growth, and the opportunity it gave me to use power to advance causes I believed in.

As a First Lady, I was placed in an uncommon situation since there are only about fifty individuals in the country who hold this position at any one time. Because I was married to someone who happened to be our state's governor, I had the privilege and advantage of a very valuable tool: derivative power. And I was determined to make the most of it.

This was new-found influence and it required a new approach. In my previous professional positions as a teacher, and as an administrative assistant in Washington, as well as in my work as a civic volunteer, any influence I had was based on my own experience and expertise. Suddenly my opinions and participation were important, because I was married to the governor. Using derivative power was exciting and challenging, but there were no guidelines for its use. Moreover, no job description existed for the position of First Lady. Jamie and I never sat down and discussed this formally, but I had an instinctive understanding of it. I decided I wanted to put this influence to serious and good use for work on critical issues and programs which would benefit a state in dire need of repair.

I knew, however, that I would always have to be mindful of the fact that whatever I did and said would reflect, for better or worse, upon Jamie. He knew I understood that crucial reality. He also knew that he could trust my instincts and good judgment. I don't think I ever failed him in that. Motivating my decision about the best use of my position was my deep love for the beauty and bounty of this state and its people. I wanted to share my pride in Michigan with others in an effort to generate pride among all citizens. Michigan was badly in need of some psychological mending as well as economic healing. I also believed that the state's psychological recovery was a key element in an economic recovery. I wanted to prove to all, skeptics and supporters alike, that pride was an integral component to economic development.

Economic development programs and policies were directed by Jamie and his new Commerce Department director, Ralph Gerson, an original Blanchard supporter from our Washington days. I knew Ralph and was elated when he accepted the appointment because he had an impressive set of credentials, and he did a superb job in his two years in that position.

158

Ralph was excited about my interest in participating in the activities of the Commerce Department, and I had his support when I indicated I wanted to establish an office there. At first it was viewed as more than a little unorthodox when I moved in, becoming the only governor's spouse in the nation who had an office in a state department and who worked directly on department goals and initiatives. Department personnel and staff were skeptical about my role and my intentions initially, but as weeks and months went by, I believe I earned their support for my efforts. They saw that I was taking my chosen reponsibilities seriously, without fanfare, and seemed pleased when I chose to exercise my energies on behalf of their particular projects and programs.

I have always craved work and with the exception of Jay's early years and the gubernatorial campaign, I had held a job since high school. With Jay busy with school and related activities and a household staff to relieve me of duties at home, I had an ideal opportunity to seize the challenge, the work and the outlet I craved. I yearned to make the most of it. For the next four years I devoted a full-time effort to my chosen activities— full-time, that is, as a volunteer. I was never offered, nor did I take, a penny for the work I did or the speeches I gave. Political spouses who work side-by-side with their elected mates are the best Yankee bargain voters will ever get.

I could easily have been consumed by the full-time responsibilities of running two governor's residences, especially with the active schedule of renovations, meetings and entertaining we undertook. With Carolyn Simmons' able assistance at the Residence, I was able to devote about a quarter of my time to my reponsibilities there and three-quarters of my time to my work in the Commerce Department.

After several enthusiastic discussions, Ralph and I worked out a role for me—Special Advisor to the Department of Commerce—and I went about setting up shop. Carlene Bonner, whom I hired to assist me during the transition, stayed with me and became my executive assistant. I was also allocated a secretary and two offices, one for me and one for Carlene. I wanted a regulation size office with standard issue government furniture because I didn't want anyone to think I was in this for the sake of a fancy office, because I wasn't. The form of what I was doing mattered not in the least; it was the substance I cared about.

I was excited at the prospect of being part of the Commerce Department team, despite some raised eyebrows. I knew I could bring something to the table which no one else could—derivative power. My co-workers realized that and learned to use it to advance our efforts. They brought their own experience, insight, knowledge and skills to the table and together we made a great combination.

I decided during the campaign that when (not if) Jamie was elected, I would concentrate at least some of my efforts on Michigan product promotion. I was amazed to learn during my travels on the campaign trail that Michigan grew and produced a wide variety of products. The whole world knows we make cars. What the whole world doesn't know is that we grow fifty major crops and manufacture a host of other products known worldwide: Hush Puppy shoes, Lazyboy chairs, Simplicity Patterns, Baker furniture and many others. I knew Michiganders would be as proud and surprised to learn about this bounty as I was. In my mind, product promotion could be a key element in the psychological recovery I believed in so strongly and an effective business retention tool in keeping existing Michigan businesses here permanently. Ralph, Carlene and I agreed this would be my first order of business.

Our efforts were temporarily delayed. We had a parade to save first. In December, after the election, sponsors of the annual Detroit Thanksgiving Day Parade announced they could not continue sponsorship of the parade after 1982. That meant this revered Detroit holiday tradition that brought Santa Claus to town would be dead and gone. Television, radio and newspapers announced the bad news and people went up in arms. Citizens called their legislators in Lansing who prevailed upon the new governor to save the parade. He turned to his new Commerce Director who turned to me.

I remember answering the telephone at home in Pleasant Ridge in December 1982 to hear Ralph explaining the situation to me. We both agreed Detroit and Michigan could not afford any more bad news. If the Thanksgiving parade failed, a parade

160

which had been sponsored for over half a century by J. L. Hudson's and then by Detroit Renaissance, Inc., and had marched proudly across television screens around the world in the company of the Macy's parade in New York, the story would be picked up nationally and would be one more piece of evidence that Detroit and Michigan were on the skids.

Ralph's idea was to appeal to Detroit Renaissance for time to try and raise money before they started selling off parade assets like floats, costumes, and equipment. He asked me if I would be willing to help by signing some fundraising letters to the CEO's of Michigan's largest corporations. He thought if we could raise enough money quickly we could buy time to put a long-term strategy for the parade in place. I knew in my heart it was a big undertaking—one with only a slim chance of success—and that I would end up doing much more than signing a few fundraising letters. But I agreed because I had always watched the parade on Thanksgiving and felt it was a tradition which probably couldn't be resurrected once it were lost. I also knew that losing the parade would be one more piece of evidence used to demonstrate that Detroit was a dying city, a perception I believed to be false.

Our first mission was to convince Detroit Renaissance to give us two or three weeks to raise money before burying the parade for good. Ralph was able to have our names added to the agenda of the January 1983 meeting—quite a feat in itself—so he and I could make our plea. This was only about three weeks into Jamie's new term, and I had no idea the kind of high-powered meeting I was walking into. That was a good thing because I would have been intimidated if I'd known. Carlene and Ralph knew, but they were smart enough not to tell me. The members of Detroit Renaissance are the CEO's of Michigan's largest and most powerful corporations—men like Roger Smith, Max Fisher, Joe Hudson, Walter McCarthy and Alan Schwartz. It is one of the most powerful and prestigious group of business people in the world with a mission of fostering growth and economic development in the Detroit area. This was the group which took the parade over when J. L. Hudson's dropped its parade sponsorship of over fifty years and the same group which had decided the parade wasn't viable. To say these men were

161

skeptical of our endeavor was an understatement. On top of that, most of them were Republicans, and we were perceived as not only new in town but of the wrong political persuasion. Two strikes against us! All this is hindsight, however, because my naivete was total.

Ralph, Carlene and I were invited into the meeting and greeted with a puzzled silence. The chairman at the time was Dave Easlick, Chairman of Michigan Bell, and he was warm and gracious. The other members, of which there was only one woman, couldn't figure out why the devil we were there. In a five-minute opening statement, I emphasized the symbolic importance of the parade and the economic development benefits of preserving it. I delivered it with conviction and sincerity. When Ralph spoke, he explained what we wanted to do. After we finished, there was a moment of stunned silence. After what seemed an eternity, Roger Smith, Chairman of General Motors, spoke up. He said he felt the group should give us a chance to see what we could do because the parade was an institution worth saving. And his words were our saving grace because members took their cues from Roger. Others added their support and we walked out with a short two weeks to raise about $500,000.

The press, including Detroit television, had caught wind of our attendance at the meeting and were waiting for us when we emerged. I wasn't expecting them, nor was Ralph. We didn't have any time to collect our thoughts or prepare our response. I wasn't used to being the point-person yet, and I expected the press to question Ralph. Surprise! They wanted to interview me. Instinctively, I remained noncommittal and low-key. Ralph confirmed that by whispering in my ear, "Don't make any promises!" I told the media that Detroit Renaissance had given us the time we asked for and that we were hopeful we could raise enough money for the parade for at least one more year. From there, I said, we'd have to take it one step at a time. They weren't quite satisfied and pressed me for more. I stood my ground and didn't budge from that response. They turned to Ralph and tried to pry something more from him, but he said basically the same thing as I did, giving it a little more "spin."

With only three weeks under my belt as First Lady, I had an

unusual trial by fire, but I was pleased I had been able to handle it professionally and confidently. I was on my way!

Ralph and I were successful in our fundraising efforts. I had my first chance to use the derivative power of my last name to involve people in this project above and beyond their normal level of interest. Our calls and letters to the CEO's of Michigan's corporate community were in most cases the Blanchard administration's first contact with them since the inauguration, and by and large they were anxious to cooperate.

Walter McCarthy, Chairman of Detroit Edison, and Alan E. Schwartz, a prominent attorney and civic leader, were two of the first to become involved in a major way. They assisted greatly with the establishment of the Michigan Thanksgiving Parade Foundation to fund, sponsor and stage the parade. Along with Roger Smith, they helped me persuade Thomas B. Adams, Chairman of Campbell-Ewald, to chair the foundation. Tom had been at the meeting when Ralph and I spoke, and he had voiced his support then. Tom, Walter, Alan, Carlene, and I formed the nucleus of the foundation and worked diligently to bring the parade to the people of Michigan each Thanksgiving. Tom retired as chairman of the foundation in 1989 and during those seven years he saved the parade many, many times with his savvy, his expertise, his charm and his persistence. Nearly a million spectators have lined the streets to enjoy the parade each year, and television viewers all over the world have seen Detroit looking its best in its holiday finest—a city of happy families and smiling survivors—and proud of it.

Carlene and I spent most of the spring of 1983 securing parade funding, organizing the foundation, and initiating other programs and projects.

First among those was the Michigan product promotion program. With Ralph's enthusiastic support, and the able assistance of Rick Cole, Deputy Commerce Director, and others in the department, we established the Office of Michigan Products Promotion to design, direct and implement the promotion campaign.

We kicked it off during Michigan Week in May 1983. Each year, two weeks are designated in May for the celebration of the great things about our state. A day is designated for the cele-

163

bration of a particular aspect of state achievement in education, government, commerce, religion, and so forth. We decided that Commerce Day was perfect for the announcement of our product promotion program. The Greater Michigan Foundation sponsors Michigan Week, and when we approached a number of its board members with the idea they were enthusiastic. They invited me to join the foundation board and serve as their special "Michigan Week Ambassador."

My first official Michigan Week had me on the road for a statewide swing promoting Michigan products. From Lansing we headed north to Calumet in the Upper Peninsula, showing off the beautiful work of local artists. Next we moved south to Grayling on the Au Sable River to showcase our recreational products. In Bay City, the heart of Michigan's breadbasket, agricultural products were our focus, visiting farms and hosting hearty lunches of Michigan products. The engine of Michigan— our auto industry—was our focus in Flint as we toured plants and factories. We topped off our whirlwind tour of Michigan's finest in Rockville with a visit to the home of Hush Puppy shoes. The new Michigan product logo, designed to help consumers identify Michigan products, was unveiled during that first Michigan Week trip.

That week, and every other Michigan Week for the next four years, was filled with an array of activities, all designed to bring Michigan products into the eyes and minds of Michigan consumers. I gave speeches, held news conferences, talked to reporters, smiled for the cameras, held meetings with local business people and community leaders, and toured factories of internationally known companies like Steelcase and small cottage industries of companies like Cameron Balloons. At every stop, I promoted Michigan's people, places, products and pride. And I had a fabulous time!

Over the next four years, I devoted a significant portion of my time to these activities. In 1984 Kelly Rossman came on board as director of the Office of Products Promotion. With a diverse background that included stints at two Detroit television stations, experience in both the Michigan House of Representatives and the Senate, she had most recently served as director of the Michigan Youth Corps. Our program grew dramatically as

164

we brought together my commitment to Michigan products with Kelly's enthusiasm and energy. Together we conceived some of the most exciting ways to promote what was made and grown here, criss-crossing the state and marveling at our newest product discoveries.

Our favorite project was one which truly struck a chord with Michigan citizens. It was the Michigan Gift Guide, a four-color publication filled with photos and descriptions of more than 100 toys and games, gourmet foods, clocks, furniture and designer clothing. We took a big risk with the first gift guide. We trusted our instincts and knew in our hearts that people would buy Michigan products if only they knew what they were and where to buy them. And that's exactly what the gift guide did. Our first printing of 10,000 guides was snapped up in less than three weeks. Our toll-free number for requesting guides rang off the hook. We had a winner!

One of our greatest finds while working on the gift guide had been the gourmet and specialty foods that were being made and grown here. We followed our initial success later that year with the Michigan Specialty Food Guide, introducing the new publication to food writers and editors from around the state at a reception at the Governor's Residence where we served only those foods which appeared in the guide. Our guests munched on smoked whitefish, free-range pheasant, fresh basil, gourmet cheeses, rich chocolates, sparkling wines and juices, jams and breads, mustards and sauces and those writers have raved about Michigan's great specialty foods ever since.

I didn't limit my product promotion efforts to Michigan. In fact, I even took our campaign overseas to Japan and China in June of 1984 when Jamie and I traveled there to visit the State of Michigan trade office in Tokyo and the province of Sichuan in China with which we have a sister-state relationship. With the assistance of Erica Ward, Ralph's wife, who lived for several years in Japan and was on the trip with us, I met with Japanese and Chinese government officials and businessmen to identify and arrange opportunities to introduce Michigan products to those markets. I returned in November of that year as the head of a state delegation, accompanied by Ralph and others from the Commerce Department, to launch a major exposition and sale

165

of Michigan products in Tokyo's largest department store. It was thrilling to give the Japanese a glimpse of Michigan beyond the one thing they knew about us—our cars. Their favorites were our food products and our handcrafted gift items. They recognized quality and our exposition was a great success.

Our program became the model for product promotion. Economic development officials from other states began calling to find out what we were doing and how we were doing it. They heard about our program from their First Ladies at meetings of the National Governors' Association where we had shared with one another the activities we were undertaking in our respective states. Michigan had gained the reputation of having the most aggressive and successful product promotion program in the country.

I expanded my promotion efforts into the area of travel and tourism. It went hand-in-hand with product promotion and complemented my theme of pride in Michigan's people, places and products and my love of her beauty and bounty. I loved singing Michigan's praises, and travel and tourism became my second verse.

Ralph wanted to organize an annual Governor's Conference on Tourism to focus attention on one very healthy segment of Michigan's economy. Travel and tourism in Michigan were growing steadily each year, employing more people and bringing increased revenues to the state's economy. It was important to give the industry its proper credit and for the state to assist, where appropriate, in maximizing the growth potential.

Ralph asked me if I would co-chair the first conference. I agreed on the condition of being a working, not honorary, co-chair. I wanted to take an active role in planning, shaping and participating in it. Again, Ralph was enthusiastic, and I embarked on another exciting and rewarding endeavor. I was a working co-chair of four annual conferences—1984 in Flint, 1985 in Belaire, 1986 in Kalamazoo and 1987 in Detroit. I attended and participated in planning meetings, conferred with the Travel Bureau staff on plans and arrangements, and attended each conference. I addressed the participants at various times during the three days of the conference and often introduced the main speaker. Once I even introduced a keynote

166

speaker by the name of Governor Jim Blanchard. In between the annual conferences, I hosted and spoke at mini-conferences around the state, worked with the Commerce staff and its ad agency on television and radio commercials and printed promotional materials. Along with Jamie, I was the state's cheerleader.

Working in travel promotion led me into another area which I also became interested in pursuing. After speaking in the spring of 1984 at a meeting of the Michigan Parks and Recreation Association about the economic potential of the travel industry, I was approached by a young woman who offered me an interesting item of information. She worked with individuals who were physically challenged and wanted me to know that Michigan was a very popular state with handicapped travelers. Our approach to accessibility and our laws to accommodate the needs of handicapped people were much more enlightened than in most states. She saw a great opportunity for Michigan to take advantage of that and promote itself as a destination for handicapped travelers and their families. I was delighted to hear that Michigan was sensitive to these needs and a leader in doing something positive about them. I agreed wholeheartedly with her, and that conversation was the beginning of my involvement with the community of physically-challenged individuals.

After we saved the parade in 1983, the hard work of putting the foundation together, organizing staff, and planning and staging the parade was assumed by Carlene. She commuted daily to Detroit where the parade is headquartered to direct operations there. She also continued to serve as my executive assistant in the Commerce Department and so performed double duty in these capacities for me for over a year. It was a tremendous amount to ask of anyone, and Carlene was able to do both jobs successfully because of her energy, creativity, resourcefulness, intelligence, skill and dedication. After a year, it became too much even for someone of her talent. She managed all of it successfully but at a great sacrifice to her personal life and her time with her son, Lincoln. After a year of this, we both agreed it was too much for one person to manage and she decided to join the parade as its full-time director. She is still with the parade as president of The Parade Company and a

167

member of the executive committee of the foundation. She has done a remarkable job in keeping that important tradition alive. She assisted me in the selection of my next executive assistant, Steve Thomas. I met Steve during the spring of 1983 when I was co-chairing the involvement of state government departments in the Lansing Food Bank Drive. Steve was executive assistant to the Director of the Department of Mental Health, Pat Babcock, and coordinated my visits to various state departments to encourage state employees to participate in the food drive. He had worked in several state departments over his distinguished public service career, including commerce and mental health. He had extensive knowledge of the people and workings of state government which became invaluable to me. He had excellent organizational, planning and analytic abilities. We were great colleagues and disagreed on only one thing—he is an ardent University of Michigan fan and I'm an equally ardent Michigan State University fan. We worked together from 1984 until 1987, and I credit Steve with a large portion of any success I had during those years. I was the only First Lady with a male assistant, and there were many times when it was extremely helpful in business dealings to have him there. The fact that he was a male added credibility to our work and our positions. That's a chauvinist thing to say, but a reality.

He had an enormous bank of knowledge of the human service and social service areas from his work in mental health. When I indicated an interest in working with the handicapped to promote travel opportunities for them in Michigan, he knew exactly who we should involve. When word circulated I was taking an interest in these issues, people working in that area encouraged me to go beyond travel promotion and devote additional time to some of their other concerns such as entrepreneurial opportunities and adequate representation on boards and commissions appointed by the governor. I accepted this challenge and worked with the governor's Director of Personnel, Greg Morris, to suggest names of physically-challenged individuals for gubernatorial appointments. I hosted for the first time—and keynoted—a conference which brought leaders of the travel industry and handicapped communities together to discuss common concerns and opportunities. I facilitated the organization of a conference which I keynoted that brought handicapped entrepreneurs and state officials together to explore and discuss business opportunities. Working as an advocate for the handicapped and focusing efforts on their behalf is an area which I would have expanded had I remained First Lady. There is an enormous amount of work yet to be done, and the people I worked with were extremely dedicated, motivated and tireless. They were an inspiration to me, and working with them was very satisfying and rewarding.

Another highlight of my years as First Lady was the state's sesquicentennial celebration. Jamie asked me to be his representative on the Sesquicentennial Commission, a statewide group appointed by him to plan a year of festivities to mark this important milestone in the state's history, her 150 years of statehood.

It was an enormous undertaking but an exciting one. The activity in which I took a direct interest was the 150 First Lady Award Program. It was an idea I conceived and helped to plan and implement. It was also my last official act as First Lady. I wanted to identify and recognize 150 women from all over the state for outstanding contributions to their communities and the citizens who lived in those communities. We put together a plan to search systematically and extensively Michigan's eighty-three counties to find the women who were the unsung heroines, the women everyone else in the community counted on, the women who were previously unrecognized, the women who were quietly making a significant difference in the lives of those around them. The Michigan Women's Commission sponsored the program and solicited nominations for those women from citizens around the state. We organized a distinguished panel of judges—men and women—to review the nominations and select the 150 women we would honor.

At a luncheon in Lansing in November 1987, after Jamie and I had announced our divorce and I had moved out of the governor's residence, we honored these outstanding women. Over a thousand people attended from all over the state to pay tribute to our 150 First Ladies. The award ceremony lasted three hours. As each woman was announced by name and a short synopsis of her efforts was read, she proceeded from her seat to a platform in front of the dais where I presented each woman—all 150 of them individually—with an award certificate inscribed with her name. Her picture was taken as I handed her the award. Sustained applause greeted each woman and few people left during that three-hour program. I was delighted to meet and greet each woman, and I was astonished by the breadth and depth of the volunteer work these women were doing. It was a humbling and joyful experience for all of us. It was sad and bittersweet, too, because I knew that this occasion was my last official one as Michigan's First Lady.

Throughout my years as First Lady, I was always tremendously honored and grateful to have the opportunity to serve in that capacity. In contemporary society, a First Lady is much more than the belle of the Inaugural Ball or the governor's hostess. The day Jamie was inaugurated as Michigan's forty-fifth governor, I got the best job—albeit nonpaying—in state government. As First Lady, I had a blank page on which to write a job description and a world of choices to make.

Like every First Lady before me, I adopted some of the conventional roles—like hostess, confidante and trusted advisor. At the same time, I attempted to carve out my own niche and my own unique role. No two first ladies have chosen the same path and no two first ladies have pursued the same goals and activities. As I look back, I'm satisfied that I used the opportunity and responsibility of the position well. I know I experienced tremendous personal and professional growth during those years. I'm very glad I seized the opportunity to make the most of my position. If I hadn't, no one would have regretted it more than I.

Chapter Nineteen

In carrying out my chosen professional and official activities as First Lady, I had complete and total independence. Jamie rarely became involved in my work in the Commerce Department. In fact, he visited my office there only once. I wanted him to see it very much and invited him several times, but I'd been there about two years before he saw it. We were out shopping together one Saturday afternoon in Lansing, and I had to drop by my office to pick up something. He went up to my office with me, and I had a chance to show him where I worked.

Occasionally we did joint travel and tourism promotion work, including events like the Thanksgiving Day Parade and the Detroit Grand Prix, but he never became involved in other areas. He was willing to brainstorm ideas with me and offer his counsel if I asked, but he rarely inquired about what I was doing or how things were going.

The same was true regarding most of what went on at the Residence. He left the running of the Residence, the administration of the staff, the restoration and maintenance of the house and property, and the activities of the Friends of the Governor's Residence to me. He participated more directly and actively in the entertainment and meeting schedule in terms of determining whom we would host and when.

He also left the affairs of the family to me—Jay's daily activities and arrangements, holiday celebrations, cards and gifts, personal shopping, vacations—all the family needs were attended to by me. The only exception to this was managing the family finances. Jamie continued to handle the checkbook, pay the bills, and take care of insurance, taxes and the like.

He took the time—if I asked him—to talk about personal or professional concerns of mine. But he was so busy and his reponsibilities so monumental that I was often reluctant to bother him with what often seemed minor concerns in comparison. Time was the crux of the matter. Time became our most precious commodity and managing it became the greatest challenge. I believe the choices one makes in how to spend time is how one defines priorities in life. Jamie and I had had differences for nineteen years over how to spend our time, and we had reached uneasy compromises which held up, more or less well, for those nineteen years. But time pressures became more intense than ever as the demands upon each of us, especially Jamie, increased.

Jamie worked with his staff to maximize his time during the hours from 9:00 A.M. to 11:00 P.M., Monday through Friday, and often Saturday and Sunday, too. During those hours, he would hold meetings, make appearances and speeches, review materials and papers, and place and receive telephone calls—typical activities for the CEO of a large organization, a good analogy for the position of governor. Also typical is the amount of work which came home at night, especially paperwork and phone calls which weren't accomplished during the day. Saturdays and Sundays were catch-up days, too, for making phone calls, reviewing briefing papers and speeches, and holding meetings which weren't taken care of during the week.

The demands of the job were such that it required a herculean effort from Jamie and the staff to accomplish what was only absolutely necessary in the course of a seven-day week. He had to develop and direct Michigan's economic salvation and recovery, an annual state budget, policy for the state's nineteen departments, and the state's response to crises, like floods, prison riots and red-ink on the state's books. He worked with members of the legislature to get legislation passed to implement his programs. He involved business people, labor unions, and people across the broad spectrum of the private sector in a whole host of programs. We entertained thousands at both residences to solidify support and express appreciation. He spent hours with his staff coordinating all this, including responses to several hundred invitations and several thousand pieces of correspondence received each week.

He also spent an enormous amount of time on the road, traveling to all corners of Michigan's eighty-three counties to make speeches, attend ceremonies, give and receive awards and meet with the press to advance his programs. Again, he was meeting twenty years of pent-up demand for the sight and sound of a Democratic governor.

What I've recounted here cannot begin to express the enormity of the task Jamie faced and the monumental amount of time it demanded from him. Volumes and volumes could easily be written to describe the breadth and depth of the demands and how they were met. I hope Jamie will write his own book someday to describe the reponsibilities and rewards of being governor. To anyone without Jamie's energy, drive, ambition, intelligence and expertise, it would have been overwhelming and paralyzing. He was consumed by it, and he loved it.

In the beginning, I had a measure of patience in facing these pressures. During the first year of his administration, I was busily engaged with the transition to the Residence and initiating projects in the Commerce Department. I hoped that once Jamie put Michigan's financial house in order, had his administration and staff in place and humming, and achieved a grip on the work of the nineteen departments, he would be able to bring some balance to his life. I was optimistic that after the first year or so, our lives would settle down and we would have some time to call our own. I was looking forward to the time when we could be together uninterrupted by telephone calls to take or make, when we could have family dinners together more than once or twice a week followed by a leisurely evening of relaxation, when we could make family or vacation plans which wouldn't be delayed or cancelled. That time never came. In retrospect, I realize that this was one more futile hope that things would improve. Through all the peaks and valleys of our marriage, I was sustained by the hope that at some time in the future we would "turn the corner" and come around to a life where politics was balanced with other aspects of life which were important to me. I had never lost hope before, but I now found my reserves of hope had been exhausted.

In August of 1985, I began to face the fact that the balance I desired in our marriage would never be achievable. I spent a week on a Lake Michigan beach coming to terms with what that meant. The three of us took a vacation to the Homestead Resort on Lake Michigan with Jamie's sister Suzanne, her husband Bob, and their son Rob. We usually took a beach vacation about once a year, and typically Jamie and I would sit on the beach and catch up on our reading. As I considered how I could best focus my thoughts about Jamie and our marriage, I decided writing might be helpful. I arrived at the beach with a legal pad in hand, ready to record my thoughts about our marriage, hopeful that writing might well lead me to answers I had been reluctant to put into words. I knew I could ruminate endlessly about my marriage, and my thoughts could easily go around and around in circles. I was hopeful that by putting my thoughts down on paper, I could bring logic, clarity and direction to what was on my mind. It was a measure of the emotional and psychological distance between us that even though Jamie and I were sitting on the beach side-by-side, he never asked me what I was writing. He was engrossed in a book and seemed not to notice I was doing something unusual.

It was during that week that I began to come to grips with the fact that I had many serious concerns and reservations about the life I was leading and the life Jamie and I were leading together. I began to uncover them and bring them to the light of day as I put them down on yellow pieces of paper on that white sandy beach.

I faced the fact honestly that being Governor and First Lady exacerbated the problems that had dogged our marriage for almost twenty years. I faced the fact that I was harboring a great deal of resentment because the problems were worsening instead of improving. I faced the fact that I'd lost patience with a political lifestyle. I faced the fact it was time to make a choice: I had to either choose to stay married and find a way to accept happily, cheerfully, sincerely and patiently the demands of politics and Jamie's willingness to be consumed by them, or strike out on my own to achieve the balance in my life I desperately wanted.

I attempted to look objectively at our marriage and our lifestyle. First I listed all the things which were positive. I loved my husband and admired him. I was extremely proud of his abilities, his dedication to public service and his accomplishments. I was proud to be his wife and proud of my role in his success. We had a son and lived together as a family. We were two loving parents who had provided a stable environment for Jay, in spite of the unusual life we led. We had an affluent lifestyle and opportunities to experience remarkable things, meet national and world leaders, and travel the world. I recalled meeting presidents, and visits to the White House where Jay played with Amy Carter in her tree-house on the South Lawn and where we had romped with President Ford's dogs. I reminisced about the Christmas parties we attended at the White House, the beautiful holiday decorations in the public rooms and dancing to Peter Duchin in the East Room. I smiled at the memory of State dinners there, too, where one evening my dinner companion was Admiral Poindexter, President Reagan's National Security Advisor who spent the entire evening exchanging messages with the president through an aide during the height of the Iran contra affair. I remembered that Jim Wright, majority leader of the U.S. House of Representatives and later Speaker of the House, serenaded me on my birthday in a restaurant in Madrid. I thought about our historic trip to the Mideast and our recent, memorable trip to China and Japan.

We had nineteen years of shared history, achievements and experiences. We were husband and wife, friends and lovers and partners. There was security and familiarity in our life together. I realized that every marriage has its own set of frustrations and rewards and I knew what our set was. My position as First Lady provided a forum for work I considered important and worthwhile. I enjoyed the opportunity to be a spokesperson, an advocate, and an activist.

But I also assessed the negatives of our marriage. Our marriage came after Jamie's work, and the way Jamie chose to spend his time had repeatedly demonstrated that fact. His work consumed him and he liked it that way. His choices, again, were the proof, at least in my eyes. We had no real life of our own— no home of our own, little privacy and little time to keep our marriage healthy and stable. We had little in common anymore except politics and Jay. We had difficulty communicating on a personal level, and the same problems we had had for nineteen years had never been satisfactorily resolved. I had to fit myself into the fleeting and scarce moments of his time and even that time was continually infringed upon by the demands of the job. I had only the time that was left over, which for me was not enough. I had to stand in line for his attention behind crises, budgets, programs, legislators and staff. I felt short-changed and I resented it.

Individually, each of Jamie's decisions to place our marriage second might seem insignificant, but the collective and overall effect of the pattern had emerged. He was a man whose ambition and career had consistently been of overriding importance to everything else in our lives. What reason did I have to think anything would change for the rest of our lives together? And how could I resign myself to such a life?

I kept the diary for a week because I knew intellectually and emotionally I would have to bring order and strength to this decision. The force of a nineteen-year habit was very strong. For nineteen years, I'd made my marriage my career. I'd committed my energy, my talent and my love to it. It had been my top priority and Jamie's achievements and success were my greatest source of pride. For nineteen years, Jamie's needs and aspirations, his goals, desires and expectations had come first with me. The needs of our family of three was a very close second. My own trailed far behind both. Our public life and public marriage reinforced this order.

To the public, on the surface, I had everything a woman could want. I had a handsome, successful, powerful husband, a wonderful son, an envied position and material comfort. Those factors pulled very strongly on me to maintain the status quo. I began to wonder if I could ever explain why I would walk away from that. The diary I kept that week was my way of sorting it out for myself and for others.

Jamie and I had a model political marriage and were the consummate political couple. We were effective partners in public, and we enhanced one another. We could work a room beautifully and deliver effective speeches. I could stand equally well at Jamie's side or in his stead. Our family picture on the 30,000 Christmas cards we sent each year was a study in what happy families should look like.

But privately it was a different story. In our successful pursuit of Jamie's political goals, we had lost track of each other as husband and wife somewhere along the way. We were two people who loved each other but weren't living together happily. The values I believed were important—those values instilled in me as a young person—were directing my thinking that week on the beach. The words kept ringing in my head—home and family, self-reliance, independence, loyalty, predictability, control. It became increasingly apparent to me that I was finding it impossible to reconcile those values within my marriage.

I acknowledged the fact that Jamie set the framework and the pattern of our marriage and both of us allowed his career to control it. I was basically in a take-it-or-leave-it situation. I had to live my life on his terms if I wanted to be married to him. I felt powerless to effect change in our relationship because the forces of his dedication to his work and the demands of his job were too strong for me to fight alone. I felt I had put my own life on hold for the benefit of his and this ran contrary to my need for independence and control in my life.

I acknowledged the fact that while I enjoyed the affluent lifestyle, I needed an independent professional identity and financial independence. The prospects of my being able to work at gainful employment and earn my own salary were slim. I had talked to a number of other first ladies around the country and knew the difficulties many of them had or were facing in their attempts to pursue an independent career in addition to their official roles. Many had openly expressed the frustration they felt about the constraints surrounding them and their difficulty in finding acceptable outlets for their professional talents and goals. My counterparts in other states were intelligent, talented, hardworking women who, as I, derived a great deal of satisfaction from their volunteer activities as first ladies. But many, as I, felt their volunteer work was taken for granted and underappreciated. We stood in long shadows, often feeling like appendages when, in fact, we craved the identity and individuality a professional, independent career would bring. This situation ran counter to my need for independence and self-reliance.

The word loyalty kept creeping into my consciousness, too. I yearned for the kind of devotion to our relationship that Jamie gave to his work, for the kind of fidelity he demonstrated to his career and for the intense sentiment he expressed for his dreams for Michigan.

I had an intense need for "home." In spite of its magnificence and beauty, the public fishbowl called the Governor's Residence hardly qualified as home, at least in my value system.

I fully expected Jamie to run for governor at least one more time and maybe twice. I was looking ahead to at least six or maybe ten more years of this frustration. I decided if I was going to be married, I wanted it to be to someone who would value marriage as much, or more, than a career. I wanted a husband who would express that commitment through time spent nurturing the marriage in equal measure to time spent nurturing a career.

I still loved my husband, but love alone wasn't enough anymore. I believed that one could be more lonely living in a marriage of unfulfilled expectations than living alone.

I decided that I loved Jamie enough to leave him. While I had my expectations of a husband, so he had expectations of a wife. Out of love and fairness, I acknowledged that Jamie didn't deserve a resentful partner. He deserved a wife who had patience for a political lifestyle, who would accommodate the demands willingly, who would be enthusiastic about the endless round of public duties, who would give him the happiness in a marriage that was missing in ours.

I decided the time had come for me to start owning my life,

to start owning each day. I had learned if you don't take ownership, someone else will. When it's your day, you choose how to live it. I needed decision-making freedom and had an overriding need for independence of spirit and action. I balanced these thoughts and the scales tipped to divorce.

Chapter Twenty

I was astonished how easily that decision rested on my shoulders and how comfortable I felt with my conclusion. I immediately began to look forward to life on my own, free from the frustrations and constraints which irrevocably doomed our marriage. I went so far that week as to decide on the best way to proceed with the divorce. In my diary on August 12, 1985, I established a timetable. I wanted to minimize the pain and hurt I knew our divorce would cause Jay and our family and friends. I also wanted to minimize the political damage to Jamie's career. To that end, I decided to wait until Jamie's November 1986 re-election campaign was over before filing divorce papers. I even went a few steps further. I decided not to tell Jamie about my decision until after the election in order to minimize his worries and permit him to focus his energy on his responsibilities and the campaign. I reasoned we both had worked too hard for his success to endanger unnecessarily his chances for re-election, and I wanted to be at his side to assist him in what I expected might be a difficult campaign. Equally concerned for Jay's well being, I realized he would be almost a year and a half older, and at sixteen would have a greater understanding and maturity to help him deal with our divorce.

Until the fall of 1986, I never discussed my decision with Jamie; nevertheless, it had an insidious effect. Subconsciously I began to withdraw from him and place emotional distance between us in preparation for the day when I would leave. There was a serious erosion of intimacy between us when Jamie sensed I'd given up on our marriage. By unspoken consent, he agreed and gave up, too. We began spending even less time together and shared events, happenings and conversation only when necessary. We grew farther and farther apart.

We continued to have our differences, but we were resigned to their irreconcilable nature, and neither of us made an effort to do anything about them. We danced timidly around the edges of a disintegrating marriage. I had intended to wait until after the election in November before confronting Jamie with my decision, but by October we both knew the situation was becoming intolerable, and the time had come to discuss the sad state of our marriage.

We began to talk about it in October when it became clear that Jamie's re-election was virtually guaranteed, and we began to plan the next term. Jamie took the campaign against his Republican opponent Bill Lucas seriously, and he campaigned long and hard. I made several obligatory campaign appearances and many others voluntarily, but my heart wasn't in it. I couldn't wait for the campaign to end so I could tell Jamie my decision and proceed with my plans for a new life as an independent woman.

Being First Lady both imprisoned me and empowered me. During the past four years I had acquired a significant amount of self-confidence and self-esteem. This personal growth gave me the assurance I needed to believe I could live independently. I had felt functionally single for a long time, and this bolstered my belief I could make it successfully on my own. I had spent a great deal of time in the past year since that week on the beach comtemplating, planning and looking forward to an independent life. All that was desirable in the abstract, but when Jamie

181

and I began discussing what to do about our marriage, I found I couldn't look my husband in the eye and tell him I wanted a divorce. Looking at the man I loved, the father of my son, my partner, friend, lover, and mentor, I lost the courage of my convictions.

We had many long heart-to-heart discussions about our marriage over the next few months and I found this tragically ironic. Never before, in our twenty years together, did we devote so much time to our relationship. We shared our memories of joyous times, our joint and separate accomplishments and the path through the peaks and valleys of our marriage which we had traveled together. We took some comfort in the fact that our marriage had survived difficult times before, but we both agreed that there was only a small shred of hope it could survive this time.

We were open and honest with each other about our expectations of marriage and what we each saw as our frustrations and disappointments. We talked and talked, but could find no solution to the basic problem—the fact that there existed a wide gap between what each of us wanted in a marriage. Simply stated, I wanted a husband who would place our marriage first and Jamie wanted a wife who would put his career first. Our sadness and despair stemmed from our inability to bridge that gap. We truly had irreconcilable differences. We broached the subject of divorce, but for several months, neither of us could face the fact that divorce was the ultimate solution to our differences. In the abstract, I'd made the decision to divorce Jamie a year before, but my love for him and my belief in the institution of marriage made carrying out my decision extremely difficult and painful. Jamie shared similar thoughts.

Meanwhile, we lived day-to-day, going about the business of carrying on our increasingly separate lives. As expected, Jamie won re-election to a second term, but unexpectedly, by a landslide margin. It was a sweet victory, one to be especially savored. His first term had been one of many hard-fought battles and some unpopular, but necessary, decisions. Some political observers had predicted he would be vulnerable at re-election time, and some even went so far as to predict he would be a one-term governor. They underestimated his determination, tenacity, skill and political genius. I was thrilled for him. He deserved to win, because he had effectively accomplished a great deal in his first term, and had a long agenda of issues and problems he wanted to address in his second. I was greatly relieved when the campaign ended so successfully because I felt I could leave our marriage in good conscience, if I ever summoned the courage to do so.

After every previous election, we had taken a family vacation, usually to a sunny southern spot, but this time we decided to postpone our trip. Neither of us had much enthusiasm for it, primarily because we were less and less comfortable with each other as the rift in our marriage grew wider and wider. Jamie also had found it hard to relax on some of our previous vacations in the late fall because of the enormous amount of work which had to be accomplished by the end of the year, including preparation of the budget for the upcoming fiscal year and his annual State of the State address to the legislature in January. This year there was also another inaugural to plan, in addition to the holiday festivities. We had neither the time nor inclination for leisure time together.

Jamie and I did have something in common during this time and those were our feelings of worry, anxiety and hopelessness about our marriage. These emotions were upsetting and caused us both much distress. They preoccupied us and made any enjoyment of holiday and inaugural festivities nearly impossible. We went through the motions of these celebrations with heavy hearts.

I became conscious of doing things for the last time. I had always taken great pleasure in decorating the Governor's Residence for Christmas because the scale of the house lent itself to a spectacular display of greens, lights, candles, and a fifteen-foot Christmas tree in the living room. We also decorated a smaller tree in the library with the family decorations we had lovingly made and collected over the years. I knew this year, Christmas 1986, would be my last in the Residence and I outdid myself. The house and the grounds never looked more beautiful, at least in my eyes. We hosted the many annual Christmas parties at the Residence which had become a tradition in our years there and also had our families for Christmas dinner. We had

183

enjoyed many family gatherings at the Residence, including Christmas, Easter, Mother's Day and birthday celebrations. We could easily entertain our twenty relatives from both our families with room to spare. Television viewers gathered in the library and the garden room, conversationalists chatted in the living room, dining room and kitchen, and the boys hung around in Jay's room, the basement or outdoors. This Christmas, as we formed the circle around the table and joined hands for a blessing before dinner, Jamie and I exchanged a long look which said this is our last Christmas together here. At dinner, he teased me good-naturedly about one of our Christmas dinners past when I asked Forrest, our chef, to buy a turkey which turned out to be too large for the oven and never roasted because the oven door didn't completely close. Our staff always had holidays off and I cooked the dinners, with preparation help from Forrest and the offerings of family members who brought dishes to accompany the main dish. We called that particular dinner our vegetarian Christmas because it consisted of dressing, potatoes, vegetables, salad and dessert—but no turkey! As I listened to Jamie, I realized something much more important was missing from this Christmas dinner.

I did things I knew I'd never have an opportunity to do again. My parents celebrated their forty-fifth wedding anniversary on December 27, and I decided to give them a party they would never forget. Ordinarily I would have waited until their fiftieth anniversary, but I knew, as they did not, that I wouldn't be at the Residence in 1991. I also knew they would especially relish a party there in their honor. They always enjoyed visits with us during holidays or when they came to stay with Jay while we were away. We had given similar parties for Jamie's mother when she celebrated her seventy-fifth birthday and when Suzanne, Jamie's sister, and her husband Bob celebrated their twenty-fifth wedding anniversary. Similarly, I wanted my parents to experience such a special occasion in their honor when they could invite family and close friends to a celebration at the Governor's Residence. Invitations to the Residence were coveted and cherished, and their party was no exception. My brother Larry and his wife Debbie hosted the party with us, and my parents basked in the glow of roaring fires, sparkling Christmas lights, flaming candles and the love of over one hundred family and friends who came from all over Michigan and from as far away as Florida on a cold, snowy, winter afternoon to offer congratulations.

The inaugural which followed shortly after Christmas and my parents' party was my last as First Lady, and I participated in the planning in only minor ways. Unlike our first inaugural in which I took an active role, I was relieved to let the inaugural committee organize the events. I did request that Jay hold the Bible for his father during the swearing in ceremony, where I had filled that traditional role in 1983. I also suggested that Jamie's mother lead the Pledge of Allegiance, which Jay had done in 1983. I had no official role during the swearing in ceremonies this time, and I was content to be a proud observer. Again, by unspoken agreement, Jamie concurred in my decision not to participate, and Jamie had to be reminded by Chief Justice G. Mennen Williams, the master of ceremonies, to introduce me to the audience. When Jamie introduced me as "The First Woman of Michigan," I stood at the podium beside him to acknowledge the applause, but I didn't wave as I usually did when introduced. I felt like an imposter, knowing what I knew.

In January, I took steps to disengage myself from official duties as First Lady. I closed my office in the Commerce Department with the expressed intention of devoting more of my time to my work on a master's degree at Michigan State University. My real motive remained unannounced, but my work at the university provided a legitimate reason. Two years before, in January 1985, I had begun graduate work in telecommunication with a specialty in video production, at the College of Communications Arts and Sciences. It was an effort to keep in touch with the real world beyond politics and to prepare for a career beyond public service. It offered me much relief from the demands of public life, and at the university I enjoyed being judged on my own merits because no amount of derivative power helped me pass an exam or produce a well-composed video. Education is a great equalizer, and it was a wise investment in my future. In January 1987, I had a number of courses to complete and a video production thesis to write.

I also had developed a concept for a video production company for the telecommunication department which the dean of

185

the college and my department chair enthusiastically supported. Withdrawing from my duties as First Lady, I began to make the transition from political spouse to professional woman. In February 1987, I founded TELSTATE, an audio and video production company dedicated to three objectives: to provide graduate and undergraduate students hands-on experience in audio and video production work for paying clients; to provide the department visibility for its outstanding students, faculty and production capabilities; and to provide the department with a modest source of revenue which could be used to service and purchase new production equipment. My position as director of TELSTATE was to secure clients and oversee and administer the production work of the company, which was done by students in consultation with faculty. When I began the operations of TELSTATE in February 1987, I directed the company on a part-time basis, an arrangement which worked well for me during the winter and spring of 1987, my transition period.

It was also a limbo period because I felt neither here nor there. Although closing my Commerce Department office was a major step in my process of disengagement, there were other responsibilities and opportunities which I did not wish to decline. One was the offer to write a chapter about Michigan's First Ladies in a book about the history of Michigan's governors. The author of the book was George Weeks, former chief of staff for Governor Milliken and current political columnist for *The Detroit News*. George called me in January to inquire about my willingness to author such a chapter. I immediately agreed and worked with Kelly Rossman on the necessary research and the first draft. I saw the chapter as a means to encapsulate my view of the opportunities and frustrations of the position of First Lady, and to trace the interesting ways in which the position had evolved over the years of Michigan's statehood. As I wrote the chapter, I subtly foreshadowed my divorce. When he saw my manuscript, George tactfully suggested I write the chapter in the past tense. His reason at the time was the historical nature of the book. I had grappled with that same question myself and readily agreed to his suggestion. *Stewards of the State* was published with credits to me as a contributing author just about the time our divorce was announced. It has

186

gone into a second printing, and my chapter now contains an epilogue in which I describe the dramatic change that I have made in my life since the publication of the original chapter.

Another project which required my participation was the upcoming National Governors' Conference slated for July 1987, in Traverse City. Jamie, members of his staff, and the Michigan Travel Bureau had launched an aggressive and successful effort to host the conference during the year of Michigan's Sesquicentennial celebration. Each summer, sitting governors and their families travel and meet in a designated host state. Governors compete vigorously for the honor of hosting this prestigious group, and Michigan prevailed for 1987. Traditionally, the spouse of the host governor designs and directs the three-day program of activities for spouses and children. Planning begins about a year in advance because it is a mammoth undertaking to entertain not only the fifty governors and their families but the hundreds of staff who accompany them and the hundreds of media people who follow in their wake. I worked with my staff, Jamie's staff, and my personal friend, Kathy Lewand, to plan the spouse and family activities. I asked Kathy if she would assist me in this effort because I knew, as she did not, that it was possible I would not be in Traverse City when the conference took place. Through the spring and early summer we held meetings which I directed to organize events and activities and choose gifts for our guests to take home as souvenirs of Michigan. I also sent letters with promotional materials encouraging my fellow spouses and their families to attend. All the while I doubted I would attend the events I was planning. I sensed people were puzzled about my singular lack of enthusiasm for the conference, but I knew in time they would understand.

I had been participating in the activities of the Sesquicentennial Commission as the governor's representative since its inception, and in the winter and spring of 1987, celebrations commemorating Michigan's statehood 150 years earlier were in full swing all over the state. The National Governors' Conference would be the highlight, and I fulfilled my duty with regard to that. There was one activity for which I had genuine enthusiasm and that was the 150 First Lady Award Program. It had been my idea from the outset and the Michigan Women's Commission was proceeding on schedule to nominate and choose outstanding women for the honor. Award ceremonies were planned for November 1987, and even though I knew I wouldn't be First Lady, I was determined not to disappoint one hundred and fifty women who deserved that honor. I remained committed and dedicated to this project and had Jamie's support right through the award ceremony.

We took the vacation we postponed after the election, and went to our favorite getaway spot, the Cayman Islands. We had vacationed there yearly since April of 1982, when our friends, Jim and Cathy Halverson, invited us to accompany them to Grand Cayman Island. They had discovered it several years before and raved about the beauty, the quiet and the predictably warm weather. We fell in love with it, too, and usually made it a family trip with Jay and sometimes one of his friends. This time, January 1987, Jamie and I went by ourselves after he delivered his State of the State address to the legislature. We knew it would be a bittersweet trip, and probably our last vacation together. We had mixed feelings about the trip because we weren't very comfortable with each other and our marital difficulties made things awkward and tense. In the end, we decided to go because the trip would give us some uninterrupted and undistracted time together to sort things out further. Jamie had about a week he could steal away, and we agreed that I would go down with him and stay about four days. The remainder of the time he wanted by himself so he could think and try to figure out what he wanted to do about our marriage. I found out later he had some friends join him, including Kathy's husband, Tom Lewand, who became Jamie's divorce attorney.

Our four days together were long and painful. I spent my days on the beach—reading, thinking and staring out across the ocean. Jamie played golf with the security person who accompanied us. Sometimes he joined me on the beach, but only for a short time. This was the vacation when we rented our own car and we went out to eat every evening. After dinner we went back to the condo and watched movies on video or played Scrabble. Jamie didn't really enjoy playing Scrabble, which was my favor-

188

ite game, but it gave us something to do. We tried to talk about our marriage, but found we had nothing to say which hadn't already been said many times before. We had gone round and round, agreeing that our marriage was in desperate shape, but also agreeing we couldn't face divorce because we didn't believe it was the best solution. Jamie's parents had divorced after eighteen years of marriage when he was seven, and he always had been determined that his marriage wouldn't end up that way. My parents had raised me to view divorce as a tragedy, to be avoided at all costs. In retrospect, I think we both knew divorce was inevitable, but we needed more time to come to terms with it and become convinced that there was no other alternative.

Jamie and I have talked since about the turn of events which brought things to a head and gave me the courage to begin divorce proceedings. He has told me he might have done what he did subconsciously to bring about a resolution. I don't know. I only know that the events I'm about to describe galvanized me into action.

In March, two months after our trip to Grand Cayman, Jamie announced he planned to return there for a few days for a vacation alone. Again, he indicated a need to get away by himself. He also wanted to take Jay and spend a couple of days with him in Lakeland at Tiger spring training. The plan he described had Jay returning to Michigan after Lakeland and Jamie flying south alone, with security, to the Caymans. He and Jay had made a spring ritual of visiting the Tigers in Lakeland, and the two of them loved it. I went along the first year because I'm an enthusiastic baseball fan, but discovered it's a playground best reserved for boys and men. I felt times like this which Jamie and Jay could share were very special, so I always encouraged them to go. When Jamie announced his plans for a week away, I again encouraged the visit to Lakeland, and I was relieved, if somewhat surprised, he didn't ask to me accompany him to the Caymans.

Jamie and Jay left together on a Friday evening and I made plans to visit my neighbors next door, Grace and Vern Andrews. The Andrews were frequent guests at the Governor's Residence in his official capacity as the Director of the Department of

Military Affairs and a member of Jamie's cabinet. They were also members of the Friends of the Governor's Residence, and Grace and I had become friends. I enjoyed having a friend right next door, and we often called on each other for spur-of-the-moment walks, an occasional game of golf or croquet, or lunch. We were both delighted when we discovered our shared interest in a good game of Scrabble. I walked over to their house after dinner alone, and as usual, Grace had the Scrabble board ready. They were entertaining other guests that evening, but it was very casual, and Grace and I sat down to play with several other guests kibbitzing around us. We were barely into our game when Grace asked me where Jamie was. I described his plans for Lakeland and his intention to spend a few days in the Cayman Islands by himself. Grace remarked about the coincidence of Jill Pennington and Janet Fox vacationing in the Caymans, too. I was flabbergasted and stunned at this news, but tried to cover my surprise. With other guests there, Grace didn't notice my reaction. I casually asked her about Jill and Janet. She responded that they were vacationing at Grace and Vern's home at Cayman Brac for a couple of weeks. She and Vern had become acquainted with many members of Jamie's staff who frequently attended receptions and events, and they had come to know Jill who handled Jamie's schedule, and Janet who had been Jamie's secretary for a couple of years. The Andrews were always generous in offering the use of their Cayman home to people in search of a sunny vacation spot, and Janet and Jill had taken them up on their offer.

I was staggered by Grace's innocent revelation because I had been hearing rumors for several months about an affair between Jamie and Janet. I knew he and Janet, and Jill for that matter, had a close working relationship and had lunch together in Lansing frequently. I hadn't given any credence to the rumors because Lansing is a rumor mill and abounds with new rumors everyday, each more outrageous than the one the day before. Janet had also resigned as Jamie's secretary two months earlier, in favor of a position which would be less demanding and would allow her time to finish her undergraduate degree. Jamie had also shared with me some of the health problems Janet was having and never hid the fact that he enjoyed working with her and was fond of her. Grace's innocent remark cast an entirely different light on these rumors. For the first time, I thought there might be a shred of truth in them because Jamie had never mentioned to me that Janet and Jill were planning to be in the Caymans, too. I stayed through the evening at the Andrews' as a diversion from the heartbreaking thoughts and images racing through my mind.

I agonized the entire next day about what to do. After I recovered from the shock of the news, I began to feel angry and betrayed. I can't remember what I did that day, until the evening, when I recall sitting in my office at the Residence, staring out through the windows into the night, beside myself wondering if the rumors were true. I picked up the telephone and proceeded to call several people I considered loyal friends who would be in a position to know the truth and might tell me. Luckily, or perhaps unluckily, they were all at home. Because all of them were members of Jamie's staff, with the exception of Kathy Lewand, I prefaced my questions with the statement that what I was about to ask them might make them uncomfortable and might put them in a difficult position relative to their boss—Jamie—and I would understand if they chose not to answer. Then I asked each person point-blank if Jamie and Janet were having an affair. In each case, the reaction and the answer was unfortunately a variation on the same theme. There was a pregnant pause and then a very careful answer. No one laughed and screamed, "Are you serious?" "Are you kidding?" "Whatever gave you that idea?" No one said, "No." Instead, each one responded cautiously, slowly and in essence saying, "I can't say for sure that they are having an affair. I haven't seen any direct or concrete evidence of it, but I do know they are very, very close and extremely fond of each other. I know they spend a great deal of time together." This might not have been evidence, but it was enough to convince me our marriage was over, finally and for the last time.

I picked up the phone once more that night, about 11:00 P.M., and called another friend, a man I held in the highest regard and esteem, a prominent Lansing attorney, Camille Abood. Maryalice, his wife and my friend as well, answered the phone and I apologized for calling so late. She must have noted from my voice that something was wrong because Camille came to the phone immediately and said, "Hello, Paula, how can I help you?" I hadn't yet shed a tear, but when I heard his soft, warm, reassuring voice, I broke down in tears and said, "Camille, I want to file for divorce."

Chapter Twenty-one

People have often asked me why I didn't ask, or even insist, that Jamie give up his political career to save our marriage. I could never have done that. I couldn't imagine living with the weight of a request which I considered totally inappropriate and unreasonable. I knew I could never ask Jamie, the man I loved, to sacrifice the happiness, fulfillment and success he found in his work for my personal happiness. I knew my happiness was my responsibility, not his, and it was up to me to find it.

This was one of the first questions Camille asked me when we met the next day. He had a hard time believing I was serious about my intention to file for divorce, which was understandable because he had seen only the model political partnership Jamie and I offered to the public. Like most everyone, he had no notion of our private difficulties. Camille and I spent many hours over the next week together while I described, from my point of view, the situation, the irreconcilable differences which were long-standing, my initial decision to seek a divorce in 1985, and the thought I had given it. He was astonished I was so prepared for, and so committed to, my decision. I attempted to explain to him that if, in fact, Jamie and Janet were having an affair, it was a symptom of our difficulties, not a cause of the divorce. From my viewpoint, the revelation of any affair only served to propel me to take action on a decision I had already made. In my mind, it was a moot point whether or not Jim and Janet were having an affair. Politics had been Jamie's mistress for twenty years, and I wasn't willing to pay her exorbitant price any longer.

I didn't talk to Jamie at all that week while he was away. I was relieved when he didn't call me because I wasn't ready to talk to him. I had too much thinking to do and too many decisions to reach. In meetings with Camille nearly every day that week, he tried to convince me to find a way to reconcile our differences while I tried to explain to him how irreparable things were. He resigned himself to my decision, and we began to draw up the initial divorce papers. Throughout my entire divorce, he was a constant source of strength and courage. Once he realized my decision was final and irreversible, he was my best ally. Without fail, he reinforced my intention to handle the divorce in a friendly, dignified and fair manner.

I shared my secret with only a small group of friends as I put our divorce in motion. I had ruminated about divorce for over a year, and I now had an intense need to talk this through with people I knew would listen and understand. I spent hours with my friend Kelly Rossman who listened quietly and patiently as I described my feelings and intentions. She was only slightly surprised when I announced what I intended to do. She and I had worked closely for over two years, and she wasn't completely blind to the strained relationship between Jamie and me. I sought her companionship and perspective because she was divorced and could offer insights about the course on which I was embarking. She also has a refreshing sense of humor which helped me because she brought some much needed levity to a serious situation. Another person who immediately came to my side was Kathy Lewand. She and her husband, Tom, had been centrally involved in both gubernatorial campaigns and had become our personal friends. The four of us shared many memorable times together, including an annual trip to New York City at Christmas, and Jay had accompanied their family on skiing trips and other outings. I loved Kathy as a friend and admired her uncommon good sense. I knew I could trust her to prevent me from doing anything rash. When I called her to tell her the situation, I was astonished when she said she thought I ought to move Jamie's belongings to the sidewalk and lock the door! That was only a momentary lapse on her part, and from then on her practicality prevailed. She made three round-trips that week from Birmingham to Lansing to be with me. The last person I told was Carolyn Simmons who suspected something unusual because, as Residence Manager, she was aware of the frequent visits by Camille, Kelly and Kathy.

The value of these conversations was immeasurable because they helped me clarify to others, and most of all to myself, my feelings and my intentions. I had few doubts that divorce was the right course, but I had to begin to put my feelings into words. I knew I had to be able to articulate this momentous decision sincerely and sensitively because of the public stage on which this divorce would be played. I'm blessed with an ability to fall asleep at will and sleep soundly, so nights were a needed respite from days which were filled with inner tension.

Jay had returned from Lakeland as planned and was in school during the day. He was engrossed in his own activities, including the beginning of the high school baseball season and was preparing to try out for the varsity baseball team. He was accustomed to seeing Kelly and Kathy at the Residence, and he had met Camille previously, so I don't believe Jay suspected anything out of the ordinary. Keeping things as normal as possible for Jay and on an even keel was extremely important to me.

The most difficult matter to resolve that week was how to approach Jamie when he returned from the Cayman Islands. I spent hours thinking about this and discussing it with Kelly and Kathy. I was angry and hurt, but I wanted to express those feelings to him in a broader context free of confrontation which would allow us to proceed through our divorce in a friendly and amicable fashion. I knew that together Jamie and I could bring

195

our divorce to conclusion in a way that befit our many joint successes. I didn't want to set out on the wrong foot in the final resolution of our difficulties and the final dissolution of our marriage.

After much reflection and discussion, I formulated a plan. I decided to greet Jamie at the door in a friendly way and let him unpack and catch his breath. He was arriving home about 11:00 P.M., and I knew he would immediately unpack and then go to the library to look over papers and messages awaiting him. I planned to wait for him in the library and ask him to sit down for a serious conversation. I rehearsed what I would say to him over and over. I wanted it to be friendly, reasonable, and non-accusatory, but leave no room for doubt about my convictions and determination.

He finally called me the night before he returned to let me know when he would be arriving at the Residence. I inquired politely about how his week had gone and told him I would be waiting for him when he arrived. We said good-bye after a conversation of less than a minute. Little did he know what was ahead. Kelly came over to the Residence that night to keep me company because I knew the time would drag unbearably until 11:00. We tried to pass the evening by watching television with Jay who was oblivious to our anxiety. As the hours dragged by for Kelly and me, Jay took advantage of his captive audience by giving us a full account of a two-hour movie he had just seen, while we impatiently tapped our feet and looked at our watches.

I had described to Kelly what I planned to do, and knowing Jamie was about to arrive, she became uneasy about 10:30. I told her it was all right to leave, and I spent the next half-hour in the dark of my office at the Residence, staring out the window over the front drive, waiting for the lights of Jamie's car to appear. Although I had been a bundle of nerves all week, I became calm and composed in that half-hour alone. I was at peace with my decision and convinced I was doing the right thing for both of us.

He arrived shortly after 11:00 P.M. as planned, and I went to the front door to greet him. We smiled and kissed hello and, as I predicted, he went to the bedroom to unpack. I took a seat in a chair in the library, and again, as predicted, he joined me about fifteen minutes later. He stood at his desk looking over the work stacked in front of him while I watched him silently. He looked up at me and smiled and I said, "I'd like you to sit down for a while because I have something important to tell you." He lit a cigar and sat in another chair beside mine.

I took a deep breath and told him that I had had a very difficult week while he was away. I recounted to him my visit with the Andrews and my discovery that Janet was also in the Cayman Islands. While I was talking, he had been puffing on his cigar and hadn't been looking at me, but when I mentioned Janet his startled eyes met mine. He said he thought I knew that Janet and Jill were there. I responded that I had not been aware of that until Grace had mentioned it casually on Friday. He became a bit defensive and said he had seen Janet only once, and that was when the three of them went out for dinner.

I asked him point-blank, "Are you having an affair with Janet Fox?"

He responded instantly and vehemently, "No. I'm not. I'm very fond of her and we are close, but we are not having an affair."

I answered quietly and calmly that even though I believed him, I felt deeply hurt and betrayed. I went on to tell him that during his week away, I had called Camille Abood and begun divorce proceedings. That revelation brought tears to his eyes. As I slowly described the week I had just spent, Jamie put his cigar down, slumped in his chair and cried. I talked quietly as he wept, and said I understood his tears. I said the only reason I wasn't crying too was because I had spent all my tears in the company of my friends. After a short while, he composed himself, and we talked quietly for about two hours. I knew that Jamie shared my desire to handle the subject and the decision with care and sensitivity, so we both expressed ourselves with gentleness and caution.

I shared with him my decision to seek a divorce in the summer of 1985, how I had lost the resolve to carry out that decision, and how I had found the will this past week. He reluctantly agreed that I was probably right, that divorce was the best thing for us. He expressed the same reservations about divorce which

197

we had discussed many times over the past few months, and he confessed difficulty in facing the fact that our marriage had come to this end. We agreed that we always had expected we would live out our lives together, right through retirement and old age. Divorce was an extremely disappointing and painful conclusion for both of us.

About 2:00 A.M, we had said all we could say when physical and emotional fatigue overtook us. We said goodnight and I went to our room while Jamie stayed behind in the library to begin to prepare the eulogy he was delivering the next morning at a memorial service for Sarah Power. We had many things yet to resolve, but I went to bed that night immensely relieved in the knowledge a decision had been reached in an amicable, even loving, way.

The next day dawned and was just like all the others in terms of a schedule to meet and things to be done, but of course it was different. We had made a monumental decision which was going to take some time to adjust. I was ahead of Jamie in this process because I had had a week to become accustomed to the idea and to work out some of the details in my own mind and with Camille. For Jamie, this was day one. We both felt strange in each other's presence, and it seemed artificial to carry on as usual, but that's what we did. We couldn't just put our lives on hold and talk endlessly about our divorce. Life has its own momentum, and our schedule of commitments had been planned months in advance.

That we would have to fit even our divorce around the demands upon Jamie's time became obvious. He was dressed and at his desk in the library when I left our bedroom on my way to the kitchen for breakfast. He was preparing the eulogy he was to deliver in Ann Arbor later in the morning. I planned to accompany him because Sarah Power had been a friend to both of us. In fact, I had recruited Sarah to join the Executive Committee of the Michigan Thanksgiving Parade Foundation. Her suicide was a shock which deeply saddened both of us. One of my last comments to Jamie the previous night was that Camille would appreciate talking to Jamie as soon as possible. As I said goodnight, I asked him to call Camille the next day. After breakfast, on my way back to the bedroom, I stopped in the library to see

198

how he was doing and remind him to call Camille if he had a chance before we left. Jamie looked up at me and said, "Can't you see I'm busy finishing my remarks? This is a good example of how impatient you are with the demands on me. How can you expect me to call Camille when I've got this to do?" I suppose one could say the eulogy was a more pressing demand, but our divorce, at least in my mind, was of overriding importance. That instance demonstrated how different Jamie and I were. If our roles had been reversed, I know I would have called Camille before all else that day.

We didn't come to a final decision about our divorce until May, but as time passed, we faced its inevitability and became more confident of our decision each day. I had only one lapse which came after Camille attempted to prevail upon me to reverse my course. He was determined that Jamie and I could reconcile our differences if we both put aside our pride and tried hard enough. He felt it was his duty as an attorney and his obligation as a Christian to preserve the institution of marriage. Jamie did call him, and the two of them met. Camille and I continued to talk regularly, and after one of our conversations, he convinced me to talk to Jamie about trying to save our marriage one last time. I greeted Jamie with that prospect one evening on his return home, but my heart wasn't in it, nor was his, and that half-hearted attempt was my last.

Time to deal with our divorce hinged on Jamie's schedule, and when we had time together, our conversation dealt with how we could make it as easy and painless as possible for all concerned. We agreed early that for the time being we wouldn't tell anyone else, even Jay and our immediate family, about our decision. We wanted to contain rumors and speculation and the desire of the press for sensational news. We hoped we could keep it quiet until we were ready to make a joint public announcement, and the only way to accomplish that was for as few people to know our decision as possible.

We agreed to keep up appearances and maintain our normal schedules until the time came to make our plans public. The unresolved question from March until May was "when?" There seemed to be no "good" time. Our tentative plan was to announce our divorce in August, after the National Governors'

199

Conference in July and before Jay went back to school in September. We thought it would be easier on him if the announcement took place during the summer when he wouldn't have to face questions from his classmates.

In April, we wanted to take our last family vacation together over Easter vacation. Jay had been trying to convince us to join a large group of his friends and their parents on a vacation to Florida. He had a terrific group of friends who couldn't have been nicer if we'd chosen them for him ourselves. Their parents were equally nice, and we had come to know several families casually through baseball and other high school activities. Jamie and I agreed we weren't up to maintaining appearances on a vacation to Florida with couples we didn't know very well, but we knew Jay wanted to take a vacation together and, in our own way, we both did, too.

Jamie had received an invitation to an economic conference in West Berlin, so we built our Easter vacation around a trip to Germany. We stopped in Paris on our way since none of us had ever been there. After three days of enjoyable and relaxing sightseeing, we continued on to West Berlin where our stay included a trip to East Berlin. I think both Jamie and I had some trepidation about this trip and how much we could enjoy it, but we wanted to do it for Jay. We outdid ourselves to be compatible and in good spirits, and Jay responded. As it turned out, it was a very memorable and special trip. My favorite recollection is our visit to the Louvre. I had encouraged Jay to do some exploring on his own near our hotel and pointed out the Louvre, which was located within sight through the window of his hotel room. He did, indeed, visit the museum on his own and returned very excited at his discoveries. He wanted the three of us to return the next morning so he could show us the Mona Lisa. With him proudly in the lead, showing us the way, we found her, encased in glass and surrounded by a large group of admirers. We waited on a bench until the way cleared and we had our turn to marvel. While we were waiting, a couple approached us and asked Jamie if he was Governor Blanchard. He responded yes, and they laughed and shook his hand. They were from Michigan and had been constituents when he was in Congress. Even in Paris, even at the Louvre admiring the Mona Lisa, we were not just a vacationing family of three. We were "the First Family." Introductions were made and we chatted for a few minutes. They were gracious and said goodbye after a short conversation. The three of us returned our gaze to the Mona Lisa after remarking that you never really leave the job behind. We spent another hour at the museum with no more encounters with folks back home, and Jay was fascinated by the original paintings he had seen previously only in textbooks. He snapped photo after photo, and I was pleased he found such delight in the discovery of history and beauty. The intensity of his interest and enthusiasm has been confirmed by his decision to major in fine arts at Michigan State where one of his favorite courses has been art history.

In May, it became obvious to both of us that it would be extremely difficult to hold on to our marriage until August. Our schedules were prepared several months in advance, and decisions were required regarding responses to invitations, joint appearances, the fall entertainment schedule at the Residence and the like. We tried to stall members of our staff as vaguely and diplomatically as we could, but we became increasingly uncomfortable with our happy couple charade. It was also increasingly difficult to shield our rocky private life from public view. I felt like I was leading a double life with little integrity or honesty. I was also eagerly anticipating my new life and looking forward to the freedom, independence and balance I was optimistic it would bring.

It was late on a Saturday afternoon of a warm May day when Jamie and I truly made our final decision to divorce. He had just returned to the Residence after eighteen holes of golf at the Lansing Country Club, and I was enjoying the warm sun on a lounge chair in the backyard patio. He joined me there and we were both relaxed and in a good mood. Once more, we talked about our marriage and our divorce. There was a finality to it this time, however, which I immediately sensed. "This is really it," I told myself. He rose from his chair and asked me if I would like anything to drink from the kitchen. He said he wanted to have a cold drink before dressing for a dinner he planned to attend to celebrate the opening of the new Lansing Civic Center. We sat together enjoying the the coolness of our drinks, the warmth of the sun and the beauty of the sunset over the Residence grounds.

He initiated the conversation by telling me how difficult it was becoming for him to continue as though everything were normal. He was finding that our upcoming divorce was weighing very heavily on him and making it difficult for him to concentrate on his work or govern effectively. He said he didn't think he wanted to wait until August to make our announcement, but preferred to do it in advance of the National Governors' Conference in July. Without hesitation, I agreed. I was finding the strain difficult myself and dreaded the prospect of playing hostess to several hundred people, pretending everything was normal. He said he would feel like a fraud if all his fellow governors and their families came to Michigan for the conference and enjoyed the hospitality of the Governor and First Lady, and then heard the announcement less than a month later about our divorce. Again, I agreed.

I pointed out I thought it would also be better for Jay if we made our plans known early in the summer, rather than later, because he would have the summer to adjust before starting his senior year at Okemos High School. I realized as well that if we announced our intentions in June, I would have most of the summer to get settled in my new home before resuming my work at Michigan State University in September.

The sun went down as we talked quietly on the patio, and time ran out for Jamie to dress for the dinner at the Civic Center and review his remarks. He did something then that he had never done before in my recollection. He told me he planned to call a staff person and request she call the event organizers to regretfully cancel his attendance at the dinner. He said he wanted to be able to finish our discussion and finalize this, once and for all. The irony of the situation was not lost on me. To my knowledge, this was the only time he had cancelled an appearance because he considered personal matters more important than politics. It was too bad we were discussing divorce.

We decided that evening to announce our divorce in June. The precise date was not chosen until about two weeks later after Jamie returned from a trip to Monte Carlo at the end of

202

May. We had been invited by a French company which we hosted during the Detroit Grand Prix to be their guests for the Monte Carlo Grand Prix. Jamie accepted their invitation but did not invite me to accompany him. Earlier in the year, I had indicated my desire to go, but under the circumstances it seemed best that he go alone. He was in France over Memorial Day, so I took the opportunity to go to Mackinac Island for a three-day weekend.

In the past, we had always made our first visit of the season to the island over Memorial Day and hosted a reception for the island's cottagers who owned summer homes on the island. Planning this annual get-together was something we had stalled our staff about, so no plans had been made this year for the traditional reception. Instead, I hosted a small party for my father to celebrate his birthday on May 30. I called him in advance and asked him to invite eight or ten friends for dinner Saturday evening at the island Residence. Mother and Dad were both excited at the prospect and knew their friends would be delighted to receive the invitation. Once again, I knew I was doing something for the last time when I hosted the dinner and took everyone on a tour of the Residence. It was not only the last visit for my parents, but the last visit for me. That fact saddened me, because I had become attached to the island Residence in a way I never was to the one in Lansing. It was a warm, comfortable, homey place and I had become very fond of Mary Nelson and Rollie Hill. There was no doubt I would miss Mackinac and its special magic.

The morning after Jamie returned from Monte Carlo, June was upon us and we still hadn't determined a date for our divorce. He spent the morning working at his desk at the Residence, and I took advantage of the opportunity to examine my calendar to propose a specific date. I sat down across the desk from him, calendar in hand, and pointed out that if we were going to make an announcement in June, we had better plan it now. I thought how typical it was that we were making a decision with such consequences in this manner. We had sat so many times across a table with our schedules in front of us planning our lives. One would have thought looking at us that we were deciding on the entertainment schedule for the Residence. We unemotionally and dispassionately discussed the advantages and disadvantages of one date over another and finally decided on June 16—two days before our twenty-first wedding anniversary.

There were several advantages to June 16. For Jay, it was after high school recessed for summer vacation. For Jamie, it was unscheduled, except for an evening retirement party for Bob Naftaly, his Director of the Department of Management and Budget. Jamie reasoned there would be an advantage to that because he could attend and demonstrate that he intended to conduct business as usual, even if we had announced our divorce that morning. For me, the date gave me enough time to put my affairs in order and prepare to move. We mapped out the whole scenario: we would tell our parents individually on Saturday, June 13. I planned to drive to Gaylord, where my parents were retired, in the morning and spend the day with them. Jamie planned to drive to South Lyon where his mother lived to do the same. Jay would be busy most of the day taking the ACT test. We would both return Saturday evening, in case Jay wanted to do something together. We planned to tell Jay on Sunday, June 14, and spend the entire day at the Residence. We couldn't predict his reaction, but we were naturally very concerned about him, so we wanted to be together as a family that day. We would announce our divorce publicly on Tuesday, June 16, with a joint statement prepared by us and issued by our attorneys in the morning. I planned to move out of the Governor's Residence on Monday, June 29.

We agreed on joint custody of Jay and to let him have a major say in how he would like to work that out. He had only one year left of high school, and we wanted to make his last year one that was agreeable to him and comfortable. We planned to talk about that with him on June 14. Jamie offered to assume complete financial responsibility for Jay through college.

We also decided on the division of our personal property and assets. That took us about about thirty seconds. Jamie proposed we divide everything in half, and I agreed. We decided to leave it to our attorneys to determine what half meant. We didn't want to spoil our amicable relationship by haggling over money.

It took us about an hour and a half with our calendars to work all this through, but once it was complete, we smiled with satisfaction. It was a good plan. We had made the decision and were implementing it. It felt good to move out of limbo and into action. I picked up my calendar, gave Jamie a kiss and left the Residence for my office at the university, my head spinning with everything that needed to be done in the next two weeks.

Once we determined the date, things moved quickly. There was an enormous amount to do and do quietly. We had succeeded amazingly well in keeping our intentions secret, and the few people who knew were vigilant in their promise to tell no one. A call to Camille was of immediate importance. He and I had been in regular contact, and he had been working to ready the divorce papers for filing. I needed to tell him the date had been set and discuss how to proceed to work out the property settlement. I informed him of our plans regarding the announcement to the press and indicated we hoped to have our financial settlement in place by June 16.

Jamie and I had some modest assets in mutual funds, money market funds and an individual retirement account. Dividing that in half was easy. It was harder to determine what half his salary was and how long he would pay me alimony. We let the attorneys work that out, and in the end, we agreed he would pay me alimony until December 31, 1990, the end of his second term as governor. The attorneys and their accountants worked up elaborate charts and tables to determine half of his bi-weekly salary and agreement was reached on one of those. We stayed fairly true to our intention to let our attorneys work out money matters, but occasionally they would reach an impasse. When that happened, Jamie and I would talk about it, reach an agreement fairly quickly, and announce it to our attorneys.

The most difficult part was dividing our personal property and belongings. We had two houses of furniture and household items stored in the cavernous basement of the Residence. It was like a parking garage down there and housed all our things with plenty of room to spare. The only difficulty was an extremely low ceiling which made moving things in and out a backbreaking chore. We had sold our Pleasant Ridge home in December 1986, to Carlene Bonner who had rented it from us for over two years. At that time, we consolidated all our belongings from that house and from storage where our Virginia items waited patiently and moved them into the Residence. There was no way Jamie and I could spend hours stooped over in the basement sorting through boxes, so Carolyn hired her nephew to haul all the boxes upstairs into the living room foyer. He was sworn to secrecy, as was the entire household staff.

We virtually shut down use of the Residence while Jamie and I went through the boxes which contained the story of our lives together. We divided all the wedding gifts we had moved so many times in U-Haul trailers, mementoes from our trips, china, glassware, silverware, kitchen items, linens—we went through everything. Jamie didn't want to leave the Residence after his tenure as Governor without a thing to his name with which to set up housekeeping, so we painstakingly went through everything. Our housekeeper, Jeanette, helped us unpack things so they could be sorted and then repacked. Boxes labeled with my name went to the garage and boxes labeled with Jamie's name went back down the basement. With two houses, we had almost two of everything, so sharing was accomplished quite easily. More difficult were the souvenirs, pictures, mementoes and keepsakes. Jamie and I were honest with each other about what we each wanted to keep, and when we sensed that something was especially meaningful to the other person, we parted with it without complaint. As far as the furniture, dividing that was not difficult. Again, we had two houses worth, much of it given to us by my parents when they retired. Since that furniture had special significance to me because it was furniture I had grown up with, I took that and Jamie took the furniture we had purchased while we were married.

Jamie offered to have copies made of as many of the individual photographs as was feasible and many are in this book. The only thing we couldn't divide were the family photograph albums I had lovingly assembled over the years, beginning with our marriage in 1966. Some of the later albums Jay had helped me assemble. We agreed to leave the collection intact, and decide later what to do about it. Occasionally when Jamie and I talk, I mention the albums and we agree we both want them. They remain at the Governor's Residence today.

206

As far back as January, I had been investigating homes for sale in the Okemos area. I had contacted Nancy Hodge, a long-time friend who sold real estate, and periodically she and I would spend a few hours a day looking at homes on the market. Originally, my search for a house was a last-ditch attempt to save our marriage. I desperately wanted a home to call our own, and after the sale of our Pleasant Ridge house in December, we had capital to invest. I hoped, rather unrealistically, that if Jamie, Jay and I could live in our own home, we might be able to have a more normal life and greater privacy. We wouldn't have to live in the home where we also worked constantly. I fantasized about having a home in Okemos where we could live a private life and where Jay would be close to school and his friends. I thought we could use the Residence exclusively for meetings and entertaining. I even went so far as to convince Jamie to look at one of the homes I had in mind, but his enthusiasm was less than encouraging. It was clear he would never agree to that arrangement.

In April, I had contacted Nancy, and told her I was ready to begin looking again. She assumed, and rightly so, that I was still thinking of a house for the three of us, and she showed me several houses which would have been fine for a governor and family, but hardly suitable for a single, self-supporting, independent woman. We drove around one subdivision in Okemos and I pointed out several modest homes in which I might be interested. She was clearly puzzled because they all appeared too small for our needs. After a couple of hours with Nancy, I realized I was going to have to tell her my housing requirements had drastically changed; otherwise we would waste a lot of time and I wouldn't have a place to live. I asked her to pull over to the side of the road and I tearfully proceeded to tell her of the approaching divorce. She was shocked, but stoic and supportive. My own tears surprised me because I thought I had cried them all out with Kelly, Kathy and Camille. I realized my feelings were still very raw. I had to swear her to secrecy, too, especially since her husband, Mike, was a very close friend of many people in the Blanchard administration. She said it would be very hard for her not to tell Mike, but she agreed. She was saddened by the news, but was a tremendous help to me in finding my new home as anonymously as possible. We didn't want people around the area speculating why Paula Blanchard was house-hunting.

My intention was to buy a home in Okemos because I wanted Jay to live his last year of high school in a neighborhood near his friends and near school. He had commuted from the Residence in Lansing to Okemos every day since his freshman year when we had enrolled him in the Okemos schools. For three years, the twenty-mile round trip had made it difficult for him to get together with his friends after school and on weekends. I knew he would enjoy a short trip to and from school and the ability to drop in on his friends. From a practical point of view, my purchase of a home in the community would also save Jamie several thousand dollars in school tuition we paid yearly for Jay as a student living outside the school district.

Camille was determined to dissuade me from purchasing a home, and from a financial standpoint, he was right. It really made much more sense for me to rent an apartment or condominium for the year or so I planned to remain in the Lansing area, since I intended to relocate to suburban Detroit as soon as Jay entered college. I'm sure a number of people agreed with him, but few of them raised the point with me. I was eventually able to make Camille and others understand my emotional need for my own home. It had been over five years since I had a home to call my own. It had been over five years since I had lived with my own things. It had been over five years since I had a home which wrapped its arms around me and provided me a haven. My emotional need to "nest"—to scrub, paint, wallpaper, sweep, rake, settle my belongings, hang my pictures, find a niche for all my treasured possessions—was intense. I knew that need wouldn't be satisfied if I rented a place because I wouldn't be free to make it my own.

Nancy and I were successful in finding a ranch home in the Briarwood Subdivision within earshot of Okemos High School. It wasn't ideal, but it was a home I could afford and it would serve Jay's and my needs nicely. I believed it had many features, including its location near the middle school and high school which would make quick resale feasible. Nancy and I had to do some fast footwork because the owner was in the real estate

208

business himself and wasn't as amenable to the house being shown in his absence as most owners. He was in the house the first time I visited it but didn't appear to recognize me or to be interested in introductions. As I became serious about purchase and wanted to visit the house a number of times before my final decision, Nancy had a difficult time convincing him to permit a private showing. I also wanted Jamie's opinion before I made my final offer.

Nancy arranged a viewing for us one rainy Saturday and insisted the owners be away at the time. Jamie and I were driven there by a security person who said not a word but must have wondered what was going on, if he didn't know or hadn't figured it out. We met Nancy there and Jamie did a quick ten-minute inspection. He seemed uneasy being there and didn't want to stay long, but he liked the house and thought it was just right for me. He remarked it was a house we might well have chosen together in the early days of our marriage. I signed a purchase agreement and at the closing, five days after the announcement of our divorce, the owner confessed that he and his wife had left the house that rainy Saturday as agreed, but had parked down the street within view of the front door. They had seen Jamie and me enter and leave and had recognized us. They had less than two weeks to wonder before it was clear why the Blanchards were looking at real estate.

I was eager to proceed with plans and preparations, but we postponed doing as much as we possibly could to minimize the chance our divorce would become public before we made our formal announcement. Jamie and I wanted to manage the news and the announcement carefully to contain rumors, speculation, sensationalism and exaggeration. We knew if the announcement came from us jointly the truth of our amicable divorce might have a chance to prevail. Consequently, I spent the first two weeks in June meeting and talking with Camille, dashing in and out of houses for sale, sorting out my office at the Residence and clothes closets in the master bedroom, arranging personal finances, including developing a monthly budget, reviewing my insurance policies and applying for credit cards in my own name, and maintaining my work schedule at Michigan State. I also kept a number of First Lady commitments during early June, such as speeches and appearances, including serving as Mistress of Ceremonies for the official opening of the Michigan Women's Hall of Fame in the shadow of the Capitol. Both Jamie and I did our best to maintain the essence of a normal profile during this time and the appearance that life was going on as usual. The necessity to keep up appearances when behind-the-scenes life was changing dramatically and drastically kept me continuously on edge.

We had three commitments during that time which were especially difficult. On June 6, Jamie's long-time right-hand man, Bill Liebold, was marrying Cam Dean, the woman who arranged Jamie's schedule, at the Alumni Chapel on the campus of Michigan State. We had to attend. The wedding was at 3:00 P.M. and both of us had spent most of the day talking to our respective attorneys on the telephone discussing the financial settlement. Jamie was on the phone in the library, and I was on the phone in my Residence office across the hall. At about 2:15 P.M., we both concluded these conversations and went to the master bedroom to dress for the wedding. It seemed incredible to be dressing in the same room with my husband to attend a wedding on the campus where we had met and courted after having spent most of the day discussing divorce arrangements with my attorney. Sitting through the wedding, listening to the vows, witnessing the joy of the bride and groom, and trying to appear happy for their sake was almost too much to bear. I thought of our own wedding day and our dreams of spending the rest of our lives together. I didn't doubt my decision to marry Jamie or divorce him, but the disappointment that our marriage was ending wrenched my heart.

The following day, Sunday, June 7, we attended our nephew Rob's graduation from Okemos High School and a family celebration at Suzanne and Bob's home afterward. None of our family knew of our decision, and it was a sad day for both Jamie and me, but especially for me. I loved Jamie's family—his mother, his sister Suzanne, who was like a sister to me, his brother-in-law Bob, and their boys who were like brothers to Jay. They had become my family, too, and I knew things would never be the same between them and me again. I realized the next time I talked to them or saw them, they would know about our divorce and our relationship would be irrevocably changed. I hoped I would be able to stay in touch with them because they had been an important part of my life, but we wouldn't be "family" anymore. The bittersweet and harsh realities of divorce were becoming painfully clear.

On Monday, Jamie and I appeared together at his annual fundraiser in Greektown. Every year Ron Thayer planned a June event which was more spectacular and successful than the one the previous year. On June 8, 1987, several hundred people attended Jim Blanchard's "Shish-K-Bash" in Greektown, and most of them stood in a long receiving line to shake hands with us. One entire block of Monroe Street—Greektown's main street—was closed to traffic as people browsed in and out of restaurants feasting on fine Greek food and drink. We only heard reports of the wonderful party below us because we were on the second floor of Trapper's Alley in a receiving line for nearly three hours. My patience wore thin quickly, but I was happy in the knowledge that this was the last receiving line I would have to stand in. Only once did I try to move the line along more rapidly and that occurred when an overly made-up and very drunk young woman draped herself over Jamie and insisted on planting wet kisses on him. I hurried her along to Martha Griffiths standing beside me who skillfully passed her to the security person standing at the end of the line. When the line dwindled to a few stragglers, I stepped out on an outdoor balcony to observe what we had missed. It was a warm summer evening and the people below us were having a wonderful time. I promised myself I'd come to the party next year and join the crowd on the street—which is exactly what I did.

On Saturday, June 13, Jamie and I began to defuse the suspense we were experiencing by sharing our secret with our parents. We made our separate journeys. I went north to Gaylord and Jamie went south to South Lyon. I had called my parents earlier in the week to tell them that I'd like to drive up and visit them on Saturday. I didn't reveal anything of what I wanted to talk to them about, and I tried to keep my voice normal and casual so they wouldn't sense anything wrong. I didn't want to discuss divorce over the telephone, and I was relieved when they didn't inquire about the purpose of my visit.

211

I felt guilty, however, because they expressed delight at the prospect of having me all to themselves for a day.

I had plenty of time to think about what I would tell them on the three-hour drive to Gaylord. One of the members of the security detail drove me up there because I wasn't sure what kind of shape I'd be in for the return trip back to Lansing later that day. When I arrived about 2:00 P.M., only my father was home. Mother was at choir practice as she had told me she would be. It was a blessing because I expected my mother to be extremely upset, and I could count on my father to help me console her if he already knew the situation. He and I kissed and embraced fondly as always, and sat down together on the front deck of their cozy home in the woods under the poplars. I felt the weight of a momentous decision as my father looked at me expectantly. He knew me well enough to know I had something important on my mind. He also knows I am a direct and straightforward person, so he wasn't surprised when I came right to the point. He was, nevertheless, astonished and sad-dened by the news. I had heard him describe divorce as a trag-edy, so I was prepared to have him advocate reconcilation, counseling, even a trial separation. I, in turn, was pleasantly surprised and relieved when he said quietly, "Paula, I'm very sad to hear this. But I trust you to know what's best and to do what's best. We've always been proud of you, and you've never disappointed us. We love you and we'll do everything we can to help you." I never loved my father more than when he said those words.

We had about an hour together to talk further as I told him how I had decided on a divorce in 1985, why I had taken so long to act on it, of our plans to announce it and my plans for the future. We were talking quietly when my mother pulled in the driveway. She climbed the steps to the deck and looked at us curiously. I knew she suspected something was out of the or-dinary because she has a mother's sixth sense. We gave each other a hug and a kiss, and she held me at arm's length to give me a long look.

"All right, what's wrong?" she said.

"Paula has something important to tell us," replied Dad. "Why don't you sit down with us?"

He started to tell her but I interrupted him. Again, I didn't waste any words because my mother appreciates directness even more than I do. When I had told her, she put her head in her hands and cried. She was saddened, but more than that, worried. She was worried how I would manage alone. When I explained to her that I looked forward to my new life eagerly and with confidence and optimism, she was taken by surprise. When I told her, "Enough was enough, mother. I'm ready to take control of my own life again," she slammed her fist on the table and exclaimed, "I don't know how you've stood it as long as you have." That energized her into action and she went into the kitchen to prepare lunch for all of us.

I spent the rest of the afternoon sharing my feelings, thoughts and plans with my parents. They couldn't have been more sensitive, loving, understanding or supportive. This was immeasurably comforting and reassuring to me and while I have always been grateful to them for more things than I can count, their support, encouragement and assistance through my divorce has been their most treasured gift to me. When I left late that afternoon, they had already made plans to arrive at my new home on moving day to help me make beds, unpack boxes and convert a house into a home.

When I returned to the Residence, Jamie had returned from the visit to his mother. He reported she had been loyal and supportive of him, but not our decision. She and Jamie's father ended their eighteen year marriage in a divorce which she strongly opposed. She opposed ours as well, principally because of her concern for Jay's happiness and well-being.

We had two more hurdles to jump—telling Jay and making our public announcement. As we planned, we told Jay our decision the next day, Sunday, June 14. Jay is a night owl like his father, so we knew we'd have the morning to plan what to say to him before he was out of bed. We had talked about it many times before, but when the day dawned, Jamie and I were pale with dread. Above all, we wanted Jay to know he was loved, treasured, and not in any way responsible for our divorce. We also wanted him to know that Jamie and I still loved each other, but were no longer compatible. It was also important for him to understand that he wouldn't have to choose between us or lose either one of us. We planned to be friends and continue to do things as a family whenever it was possible and comfortable. These were important things for Jay to understand, but they were also complex adult concepts. We knew he undoubtedly could comprehend them on an intellectual level, but we also knew it would take a long time before he would be convinced in his heart of their truth. We realized we would have to prove our sincerity by our actions.

Jamie and I were up early that Sunday and spent most of the morning discussing what we would tell Jay and how. As we predicted, he slept in until noon, and we kept checking all morning to see if he was up and about. When he did rise, we gave him time to go through his morning routine of breakfast and a shower, and then we called up to his room from the bottom of the stairs. We told him we'd like him to come down because we wanted to talk to him about something important. He bolted downstairs and we went to the garden room where Jay sat on one couch and Jamie and I sat next to each on another.

Jay said, "What's up?"

Jamie started the conversation, but I can't remember what he said. My eyes and thoughts were focused completely on Jay. I watched his face change from curiosity to shock to sadness. I watched him cry and then immediately compose himself. He was not quite seventeen, but he felt the responsibility to be a man.

He took the news calmly as he knew he was expected to do. He is his father's son, and he had rarely, if ever, seen his father overreact to anything. Jamie was his role model and Jay loved and admired him. Jamie talked for quite a while explaining why we had come to our decision. Both of us repeated over and over how much we loved Jay and how nothing that he had done caused us to come to our decision. We both kept talking to give Jay time to compose himself and gather his thoughts.

When he was ready to speak, he didn't comment on the divorce. Instead, he had some practical and natural questions. He wanted to know where he would live. I explained my plans to purchase a home in Okemos, and I could tell he was pleased and relieved at that news. We told him we hoped he would want

214

to share his time with both of us, but we would leave it up to him to work out an arrangement which would be most comfortable for him. Since he had his own car, he would be able to go back and forth easily and at his convenience. Privately, Jamie and I thought he would probably spend the school week with me and see his dad on the weekends, and that is basically how it worked out.

After about an hour, I could tell Jay wanted some time alone to think about this unexpected and jarring news, so we told him we planned to be home all day if he wanted to talk more about it. He answered that he wanted to go upstairs to his room so we all stood up and gave each other big hugs. He came down a short time later and asked if he could keep some plans he had made for the day with his friends. He did not seem to know quite what was expected of him. I also think he felt a little uncomfortable with the dramatic change in his life, and it was a natural inclination to want to be with his friends. We told him it was perfectly all right to keep his plans and in fact, we were all going to have to go on with our lives and adjust slowly, day by day. When Jay left the Residence, Jamie and I hugged each other with relief. The person we loved most in the whole world had taken the news calmly and seemed able to accept it. We also knew this was just the beginning for all of us in dealing with it emotionally.

Jamie and I spent the rest of the day at the Residence and worked on the statement we would release to the press in two days. I wrote the first draft on my computer in my Residence office, and together we revised it several times. We spent nearly a day on a one and one-half page release because we wanted the tone and the message to convey our sincere feelings and desires. We hoped the statement would communicate our decision and contain enough information for the press. We wished to avoid a media feeding frenzy. Our conversation with Jay and drafting the release are the only two things I remember about that day. Both were quite enough for one Sunday.

On Monday, each of us followed our customary routine. Jay spent the day with friends, I went to work at the university, and Jamie went to his office in the Capitol. Months before, I had scheduled an evaluation of my master's thesis for June 15, and

I decided to proceed with it. Four professionals had agreed to evaluate the half-hour television show I had produced for the Arts and Entertainment cable station a year earlier, and I felt obligated not to inconvenience them by cancelling our session at the last minute. Two Michigan State professors, a television producer and director, and an Oscar-winning filmmaker joined me on Monday afternoon to view my production and make an oral and written critique. If I seemed preoccupied and distracted that afternoon, they understood why the next day. I told only one person at the university of our plans—Tom Baldwin, acting chair of the Telecommunication Department. I alerted him to the events of the next day, but asked him to keep the news confidential until we released our statement. I gave him a copy of the statement and asked him to respond to any calls from the press. I also asked for the day off on Tuesday. He was dumbfounded but agreed and honored all three requests.

Late Monday afternoon, a summit meeting was held between all parties—an agreeable and friendly one. Jamie and I and our two attorneys met in the living room of the Residence to dot the "i's" on our financial agreement. This meeting was the result of hard work and negotiation on the part of our attorneys and our determination to stay as much above the fray as possible. We were fortunate that our attorneys agreed with that strategy and were willing to hammer it out between themselves. The avoidance of a dispute over money contributed significantly to the amicable settlement and divorce which Jamie and I achieved. I will be eternally grateful to Camille Abood for the skill and grace with which he handled my part in our divorce. He was in the unenviable position of being a Lansing attorney on the opposite side of a powerful and popular governor. The tact and skill with which he handled the situation is evidenced by the fact that he and Jamie still play golf together on occasion.

Tuesday, June 16, was quiet and rather anti-climatic as it turned out. It went according to plan and without a hitch. At dinner the previous night, the three of us talked about what would occur the following day. We explained to Jay the legal proceedings, and we gave him the release to read. We told him to be prepared for questions from people since it would be on the noon and evening news and in the paper Wednesday morn-

216

ing. He said he wasn't going to say much about it to anyone because it was our decision and it was a private matter. As always, Jay was a real trouper. He never complained, he never protested, and he never questioned our decision. He just trusted us and was philosophical beyond his years.

On Tuesday morning about 10:00 A.M., our attorneys arrived at the Residence. Jamie and I greeted them together in the living room. They wanted to confirm that we were, in fact, intending to proceed. It was our last chance to change our minds before the divorce papers were filed. Jamie and I turned to each other, smiled, nodded our heads in agreement, and signed the final documents. Our attorneys departed with the legal papers and our press statement in hand. They intended to go to Circuit Court immediately to file the papers and have our statement distributed almost simultaneously to the Capitol Press Corps.

We had kept Carolyn Simmons apprised of events, and she was prepared to answer the telephone and take messages. Jamie and I had each made our own lists of people we wanted to telephone immediately, and as soon as Camille and Tom left, we went to separate telephones to make our calls. We had planned to spend the entire day at the Residence on the telephone. We agreed that Tom and Camille would respond to all inquiries by the press and their response would be to refer all media to the statement we released. Jamie and I wanted to spend our time talking to friends, relatives and associates. We also knew if we stepped out of the Residence, we would be beseiged by the press.

I called my parents to tell them events were proceeding as planned. They offered to call close members of our family, including my brother, and I thankfully accepted. I knew the calls I was about to make would be emotionally draining and I planned to make as few as possible. Jamie called his sister Suzanne first who asked if she could come over to see us. She came immediately and talked to each of us separately. When she and I talked, we hugged and cried and promised to try to stay close. She had seen our difficulties for years, but had kept her concerns about our marriage to herself. She was saddened, but not surprised.

Her reaction was the exception. First, I called my loyal as-

217

sistant, Steve Thomas, who was stunned to silence. He came to the Residence immediately for a copy of the statement and we spoke only a few words. Following my call to Steve, I called a number of close personal friends and associates who I wanted to hear the news from me first. Almost without exception, they were flabbergasted, but extremely supportive and encouraging.

I made my calls within a period of about two hours. Jamie was constantly on the telephone all day. I don't know who he called, other than Suzanne, and I didn't ask him. His list, naturally was much longer than mine. After my calls were complete, I was at loose ends. I had talked enough about the divorce for the time being. I roamed around the Residence, but didn't dare leave, because the press were camped out in front. I wandered into the garden room where Jamie was making his calls, but he was uncomfortable talking while I was present, so I left. Carolyn was fielding call after call in her office so she couldn't keep me company. Jay had disappeared with friends. I was too distracted to read, or pack or concentrate on anything, so I sat in my office in the Residence and stared out the window at the press staked out at the end of the driveway. It occurred to me that this day was proof of my captivity. I sat gazing at the neighborhood which had been my home for five years, and as I looked at the Andrews' house next door, I remembered a secluded short-cut between their yard and the Residence. I knew I could dash over to Grace's and remain undetected by the press. I immediately called Grace, with whom I already had spoken, and told her I wanted to come over. She told me to come right away. That visit was one of three I made to her home that day. I scurried back and forth across the short cut between our backyards to check on messages with Carolyn, to return some telephone calls, to wave to Jamie through the door to the garden room as he made call after call, and to chat with Forrest in the kitchen where he made me a sandwich for lunch.

Grace had set up the Scrabble board as a distraction for me, and she and I were playing a game as the 5:00 P.M. television news from Grand Rapids flashed across the screen. The lead story, with a photo of Jamie and me at the Inaugural Ball six months earlier at the Gerald R. Ford Museum, heralded the news: "Paula Blanchard says 'So Long' to the Governor."

218

The living room of the Governor's Residence in Lansing.

Dancing with Jay at Larry and Debbie's wedding reception in October 1983.

We cheered the Detroit Tigers to victory in the World Series at Tiger Stadium in October 1984.

Jamie and I visited an
irrigation project in the
Sichuan Province during
our trip to China in June
1984.

Arriving for a White House
State Dinner in February
1985.

Celebrating my forty-first
birthday at the Governor's
Residence in Lansing,
November 1985.

Jamie and I on vacation in the Cayman Islands in February 1986.

Friends and I on the porch of the Governor's Residence on Mackinac Island in 1986. Left to right are: Liz Thomas, Grace Andrews, Carolyn Simmons, Karen Hoffecker, Kelly Rossman and Nancy Hodge. In front are Mary Nelson (center) and Pat Glazer.

Cutting the cake at the party we hosted in December 1986 at the Governor's Residence to celebrate my parents' 45th wedding anniversary. Pictured are my father, mother and I. Behind us are Jamie, my brother Larry and his wife Debbie, and Jay.

Attending a retirement party honoring G. Mennen "Soapy" Williams at the home of our neighbors Vern and Grace Andrews. Pictured with us are Soapy and his wife Nancy.

Jay takes his role seriously at the 1987 inaugural ceremonies.

My official photograph as First Lady.

Giving regards to Nancy
Reagan following a White
House luncheon she hosted for
governors' wives in February
1987.

We posed for a family picnic photograph in the backyard of the Residence
in Lansing, which was later reproduced on the state map.

Promoting Michigan products.

Speaking from a train on a
Whistlestop Tour
promoting train travel
during Michigan Week in
May 1987, less than a
month before we
announced our divorce.

Jay, Jamie and I had lunch at this bistro during our
visit to Paris, April 1987.

Jamie and I presented Santa with a license plate for his sleigh at the Michigan Thanksgiving Parade in November 1987, less than a month before our divorce was final. Pictured left to right are Detroit Mayor Coleman A. Young, flanked by one of Santa's elves and Tom Adams, Chairman of the Michigan Thanksgiving Parade Foundation.

Lt. Governor Martha Griffiths, Jamie and I leave the memorial service for Sarah Power, the day after I told him I had filed for divorce.

Fall 1987 in front of my home in Okemos.

Jamie and I were proud parents at Jay's graduation party which we hosted at the Governor's Residence in Lansing in June 1988, nearly a year after I left.

In September 1988, I took Jay to London for a week-long visit as a high school graduation gift. Here we are greeted by one of the wax figures at Madame Tussaud's.

Getting settled in my new career as associate vice president at Casey Communications Management in September 1988.

Chapter Twenty-two

M ichigan law requires people who are seeking a divorce which involves children to wait six months before the divorce can be ruled final by a judge. We waited six months and five days, and each one of those 188 days was a gift. People, including my mother, tried to persuade me to attempt a reconcilation with Jamie during that six month period, but every day increased my confidence I was doing the right thing by staying my intended course.

On Wednesday, June 17, I couldn't wait to get on with preparations for my move and my new life. I was up early to read the morning papers which carried front-page headline stories of our divorce. I was relieved to read that, with the exception of only one person who claimed to be our friend, the press had been unable to convince anyone who knew us to make a comment. The stories were fairly accurate and well-contained. Only one reference bothered me. An unnamed person had witnessed my impatience with the inebriated woman who had made such a spectacle over Jamie at the Greektown fundraiser and felt justified in claiming that I had been rude to people in the receiving line that evening. Apparently, that unnamed person saw only that one incident and didn't observe the several hundred supporters I greeted warmly during the three hours I shook hands.

I had been a prisoner in the Residence the day before, but on June 17 I was free! The word of our divorce was out and I could get on with my life. I left the Residence the first thing in the morning for my Michigan State office where I intended to keep several previously scheduled appointments. People stopped in my office all morning to commiserate with me, but I would have none of it. I quickly dissuaded them from any notions that this was a tragedy. I understood their surprise and shock, but I hoped they would understand that this was a course I had chosen and one I desired. Many couldn't understand it then, and many people can't understand it to this day. They have a hard time believing I would choose to walk away from a life and marriage most people envied. The press did follow me, and I held interviews outside my office door with curious students and bystanders as witnesses.

The next ten days were consumed with dividing our belongings and packing for the move. Carolyn's nephew began the systematic process of hauling boxes upstairs for sorting which were then either delegated to the garage or returned to the basement. That process took the better part of ten days.

I continued to go to my office at the university to conclude my part-time work for the year as TELSTATE Director. I also had a productive conversation with the chairperson of my department, Dr. Bradley Greenberg. I proposed to return in September to direct TELSTATE for an academic year on a full-time basis and complete my master's thesis, the only unfinished element of my degree program. He was enthusiastic and we reached an agreement on the terms of my employment and salary. I was ecstatic because it meant I could continue to develop, implement and streamline my special project, TELSTATE; I had secured full-time employment for the next year at a salary which would support my needs; and I had the summer off to relax, travel, and redecorate my house. I was delighted things were falling so handily into place.

On Thursday, June 18, Jamie and I celebrated our twenty-first wedding anniversary. We had a quiet dinner—just the two of us—at the Lansing Country Club. We shocked each and every other guest there when we walked in the club and continued to surprise them as we held hands across the table during dinner. We reminisced and talked about the future. It was a bittersweet evening as I felt sad and excited at the same time.

On Monday, June 22, Camille and I attended the closing of the home I purchased—the house about which Camille had severe misgivings, but the house I was thrilled to own. I felt proud, independent and capable to be purchasing my own home. It might not have been good for my checkbook, but it was great for my emotional and mental health.

I took possession of the house that week, and Jay and I went there together for the first time over the weekend. He had asked me the address and had driven by it with his friends. He also told me word was all over the high school and Okemos that I had purchased the house so when we moved in, my neighbors were well aware who the new occupants were.

When Jay and I arrived to look the place over, his first interest were the bedrooms. There was a master bedroom and three smaller bedrooms. I told him he could have his choice of one of the three for his room, and he chose the one I expected he would—the one across the hall and down from mine, the one I considered the nicest. He helped me move things in, vacuumed and dusted his room, and put shelf paper in the kitchen cupboards. He was the most kind and considerate son, and it reassured me that he seemed to be feeling some claim on this house as his own. He grew restless after several hours and left to visit friends. I think he was excited that he could drive around the corner to drop in at a friend's house, and he wanted to try it to see what it felt like. It would no longer take him ten miles and a twenty-minute commute to see friends. It wasn't long before he brought a carload of them to the the door to give them a tour of the house. I realized then how much I had missed having Jay's friends drop in during the past five years. They came by the Residence with Jay, but they never dropped in to inquire if Jay was home or to just say hello because it was ten miles out of their way.

Movers were due on Monday, June 29, at 8:30 A.M. to transport my furniture and belongings from the Residence to 2115 Belding Court. I spent all day Sunday at the Residence doing last-minute packing and putting things in order. I worked most of the evening until about 11:00 P.M. when I joined Jamie in the library to watch the late evening news. He was sitting in his favorite chair in front of the TV smoking a cigar and reading the paper. I sat down on a couch across the room. He looked up and asked how it was going, and I said I was packed and ready. We sat silently and watched the news together. When it was over, I rose and said I would be going to bed. I walked over to him and with my hand on his shoulder, I bent to give him a kiss. He returned my affection and said he would be in to say goodnight in a few minutes. After I was in bed, the same bed we had shared for the five years of our life together in the Governor's Residence, he came to sit at my side. We put our arms around each other, and he told me what a wonderful wife I had been to him for twenty-one years. I said I wasn't sorry I had married him, and I'd do it all over again, even if it did end in divorce. I fell asleep quickly, as usual, and didn't wake until early the next morning with Jamie asleep beside me.

By 8:00 A.M. I was dressed and ready for the movers who arrived at 8:30. I was busy all morning supervising their activities from the garage where all my belongings had been housed and organized in preparation for the move. I knew Jamie was leaving the Residence about 10:00, and I wanted to be sure and catch him before he left to say our last good-bye. Just before ten o'clock I went into our bedroom and found him putting on his suitcoat and making last minute adjustments to his tie. We looked at each other and I said, "Well, this is it. This is the end of our marriage." And with that, I started to bawl. It was a totally unexpected reaction to a scene I had visualized in my mind many times over the past few months. I thought I was completely ready and psychologically prepared for this moment and to a degree I was. But my heart, which I had enclosed so tightly in layers of protective reason, cried one last time.

He put his arms around me to comfort me and said, "We'll talk often, we'll see each other, and we'll be friends."

I said, "I know, but it won't be the same."

He told me once more what a wonderful wife I had been and turned away to leave the room. He paused at the bedroom door and waved. I sat down on our bed and had a good, deep, heart-wrenching cry. I must have cleansed my heart because I haven't cried over our divorce since.

By mid-afternoon of that day, I had moved out of the Residence and into my new house which immediately became a beehive of activity. My parents arrived as promised shortly after the movers departed. Jay came and went with several groups of friends. Forrest, the Residence chef, brought a cooler of food as a housewarming present. Several of my new neighbors dropped in to welcome me with homemade bread, plants and good wishes. And a delivery man from the florist shop arrived with a bouquet of a dozen yellow roses, my favorite flower, with a card inscribed, "I hope you enjoy your new home. Love, Jamie." My parents dug right in and we made beds, unpacked boxes, washed dishes, and started making my new house a home. I loved every minute of it.

Neither my parents nor I tolerate disorganization well, so we worked like beavers. We had only two days because I had made plans to leave on Thursday, July 2, on a week-long trip to Italy with Carlene Bonner. We were going to Viareggio, Italy, to commission papier-mache heads for the Michigan Thanksgiving Parade from world-renowned papier-mache artists who work and reside in Viareggio. My parents and I were successful in unpacking the necessities and getting my kitchen organized. Jay moved into his room, hung up some posters, and took care of his own necessities—hooking up the TV and the stereo.

I was thrilled by the prospect of the trip to Italy. I hadn't been there before and I had never vacationed with anyone other than family. Carlene and I get along famously and I expected we would have a great deal of fun and a wonderful time. I wasn't disappointed. We discovered we both like to vacation the same way—rise early, sightsee until we drop, have a leisurely dinner and go to bed before midnight. We rented a car when we arrived in Rome, and with Carlene at the wheel and me navigating, we roared around Italy having a marvelous time. We visited Rome, Florence, Viareggio and Pisa in six days and we saw everything which was humanly possible to see in that time. We had so

223

many memorable moments. I recall our pre-dawn visit to St. Peter's in Rome where we shared the square with only a few pigeons and a couple of priests and nuns scurrying to prayers. Opera was never more beautiful than the outdoor, under-the-stars performance of Aida at the Roman Baths. Highlighting our trip was our visit to Viagreggio and our tour of the artists' studios to view their magnificent and larger-than-life papier-mache art. I'll never forget the intense and vociferous negotiations which were conducted over the commission of the papier-mache heads. Everyone was yelling and gesturing at the same time—the artists in Italian, the interpreters in Italian and English, and Carlene in her own version of Italian. I quietly photographed these lively proceedings. On our last afternoon, we had pizza in the shadow of the Leaning Tower in Pisa and almost missed our plane back home because the service was so slow.

All my memories of that trip are sweet, but the sweetest was a trip unencumbered by an entourage and uninterrupted by business and politics. I felt light and unburdened, invigorated and free.

I returned home full of energy to put into my new life. The summer months flew by as I scrubbed and swept the house clean, painted and wallpapered, and situated my beloved belongings. I spent hours arranging and rearranging furniture, pictures, knick-knacks and mementoes. I found a place for everything and loved browsing through my own home, fondly picking up things and setting them back down. I felt as if I had rediscovered part of myself in having my own posessions around me.

I hired Dan Crow, our hardworking and faithful employee at the Residence who was studying at Michigan State for a degree in landscape architecture, to landscape the yard and repair the fence around the back. Dan worked evenings and weekends, after putting in a full-day and week at the Residence during the hottest summer in recent history and performed a miracle. He trimmed trees and bushes, repaired the fence, planted shrubs and groundcover, and transformed the exterior of the house. He did many little extra things for me without being asked, and I deeply appreciated his friendship and loyalty.

224

My parents were frequent visitors that summer, and they worked hard during every visit to help me hang drapes, paint, wallpaper, haul furniture and do a hundred other chores and jobs. As always, it was a labor of love, because the heat of that summer was nearly unbearable and my house wasn't air-conditioned. I minded the heat, but I loved my new home so much I couldn't bear to complain—at least not very often.

I loved living independently and exercising the wonderful freedom which gave me self-determination and control of my own destiny. I was living my own life, not someone else's. I owned my own home—and my own time. I couldn't remember being happier. I liked answering my own phone when it rang, but I was afraid to miss calls when I was away so I installed an answering machine. I also liked answering the phone when the calls were for Jay because it gave me some insight into his activities. I didn't have that advantage at the Residence when he had his own phone line directly into his room or the general number was answered by the staff.

I thought I was eager to begin dating until a man I knew called and asked me to accompany him to dinner. I told him I was flattered, but felt it best to wait until the divorce was final in December. It was clear to me during that conversation, when I felt like an awkward teenager, that being in the company of a man on a date was going to require some adjustment.

I relished the freedom to come and go at will in my own car, without requesting transportation from security or alerting the guard at the Residence where I was going and when I'd be back. I enjoyed the challenge of keeping my own financial records, managing my money and paying my bills. I was elated to earn my own money, carry my own money, and make decisions about what to do with it. For the first time in my life, I was living independently, and for the first time in my life, I felt like an adult.

Upon seeing me on the street, in stores or at events, people I knew remarked how wonderful I looked, how relaxed and glowing. Women I didn't know who recognized me stopped to commend me on my courage and told me I looked terrific. One woman whom I know casually told me I was a walking advertisement for divorce. I appreciated their compliments and thanked them, but I was continually surprised. I knew I felt marvelous inside, but I couldn't see much difference when I looked in the mirror. I began to wonder if I had looked awful before the divorce and didn't see it. I observed that it apparently suprises people to see a divorced woman looking well and happy.

I spent a great deal of my time becoming reacquainted with my family and friends. It was wonderfully refreshing to expand my social life beyond the small circle of political friends Jamie preferred and to engage in activities other than politics. And I found out who my real friends were. They were the ones who called frequently, arranged outings with me, sent me "hello" cards and didn't worry about whether "the Governor" would be angry at them for being my friend. Some people I thought were my friends just couldn't bear risking the disfavor of the governor by showing me friendship. They didn't call, but I understood and forgave them. They felt they had to choose between Jamie and me, and many chose Jamie. Politics has a powerful grip on people, and very few people wanted to risk the friendship of a popular governor who would probably be in office for several more years. That situation was compounded by the fact that most of our friends were also employed by Jamie or appointed by him to positions they coveted.

I also entertained in my new home. Kelly Rossman and Grace Andrews were frequent guests. I renewed a friendship with Cathy McCoy who was my college roommate in the sorority house and a bridesmaid in our wedding. She was living in the Detroit area and called shortly after I moved to Okemos. She visited twice in the fall to attend Michigan State home football games with me, and she and I hosted a party for area sorority sisters before the homecoming game. I take particular delight at Halloween, so I staged a mystery game and costume party on Halloween night for eight friends, all of whom entered into the spirit and came in full regalia. And at Christmas, Jay and I decorated the house, inside and out, with all our family Christmas decorations and had a few friends over for a casual get-together. I truly rejoiced in my own home and proudly shared my abode with friends and family.

I regretted missing the National Governors' Conference at

the end of July for only one reason—I wouldn't have a chance to say good-bye to some of the other first ladies with whom I had become close. I talked to Jamie about my desire to see them privately during their visit to Traverse City, and he agreed we could work something out. It had been reported in the press that I would not be in attendance, and articles and columns had been written about my absence speculating about who, if anyone, would be at the governor's side. I didn't want to do anything to fuel the flames of the speculation or spoil a conference which others had planned for over a year. The conference was a rare opportunity to showcase the beautiful area of Traverse City and the state of Michigan with opinion leaders and media from all over the country, and I didn't want to turn it into a soap opera.

Jamie and I agreed that I would drive up to my parents' home in Gaylord, located about an hour from Traverse City, where I would be picked up by a security person and driven to the Grand Traverse Resort, the conference site. We decided that I would visit in the mid-afternoon when people would be engaged in various conference activities, and I could slip in and out of the hotel unnoticed. He asked me whom I would like to see, and I gave him the names of Kitty Dukakis, Hillary Clinton, Dagmar Celeste, Jane Sinner and a few others. Jamie planned to speak with Hillary and ask her to arrange my visit.

Everything went according to plan until we pulled up in front of the Grand Traverse Resort. The place was deserted, except for one man standing at the curb with his back to us. As we pulled up and stopped the car, he turned around to face us. I recognized him too late as Roger Martin, a reporter for The Detroit News. There was no escape; he recognized me. I acknowledged him with a curt hello, and he smiled like a cat who had caught a canary. He returned my greeting and we said no more. It was an emotional reunion with my friends, and I assured them I was just fine. They could tell that was true by looking at me and talking with me, and we promised to stay in touch. They were loyal to their promise, and I remain in touch with two or three of them.

I paid a modest price for that visit but it was worth it. The next day a small article appeared in *The Detroit News* with the scoop that I had attended the Governors' Conference. I had been seen entering the building the previous afternoon. Tom Scott, the governor's spokesperson, denied any knowledge of my visit, saying neither he nor the governor knew anything about it. That statement made me very angry because it made me look like an unwanted party crasher when, in fact, both Jamie and I had taken great care to prevent just such a perception. The following day, in a smaller article, in an obscure place in the newspaper, Tom Scott issued a retraction. Yes, he announced, the governor had been aware in advance of Paula Blanchard's visit, and she had his blessing to visit privately with some of her friends among the first ladies. That correction was some consolation, but not much. The greatest comfort was the knowledge that soon I wouldn't need a husband's permission to visit my friends.

Although I didn't miss the all-consuming nature of politics during our separation, I thought about Jamie frequently during those six months, but those thoughts diminished as time passed. At first, I found myself continually wondering what he was doing, where he was, what events he was attending, and what was going on at the Residence. My life had been so completely driven by his career and his daily schedule that it took several months before I released myself from the habit of working my life around his.

As I expected, I sorely missed my summer on Mackinac Island. My good friends there, Mary and Robert Milton, sensed that might be the case, and they extended an invitation to me to visit them for a week in August at their Mackinac Island home. I gladly accepted their invitation and enjoyed a delightful week at their lovely summer cottage up the road from the Grand Hotel where they put me up in their daughter's bedroom with a beautifully framed view of the Mackinac Bridge. Mary and I spent a least part of every day on her horses, riding through the peaceful, quiet woods on Mackinac. I also had a chance to visit my former boss, Fred Holt, and his wife, Fran, who have a summer place at British Landing on the far side of the island. Fred and Fran vacation there every year during the last two weeks of August, and I rode one of Mary's bicycles out there for an afternoon visit. I took several bicycle rides that week, one of which took me past the Grand Hotel golf course. As I approached what used to be the sixth green, I noticed a familiar figure waiting to putt. Sure enough, it was Jamie, playing a round of golf with Tom Lewand. I waved gaily as I sailed by and shouted hello. They both waved back, looking a little startled to see me. I was on my way to the East Bluff to visit Tom's wife, Kathy. The ride took me right past the Governor's Residence, and since the kitchen faces the road I was on, I called hello to Mary Nelson on my way by. I called her later on the telephone to make sure she had heard me, but she hadn't. As we chatted, we spoke about how much we missed each other. When I was certain Jamie had left the island, I called Mary again to arrange a visit to the Residence to pick up some things I had left behind on my last stay there in May. Rollie Hill helped us pack two boxes, and his face and Mary's were as sad and long as mine as we said good-bye. I've since talked to Mary nearly every time I visit the island, but I've never been back to the Residence. It's just as well, I think. The few times I've been invited to events at the Lansing Residence, it has felt awkward and strange to be there under such different circumstances.

Jamie and I talked frequently during those six months. During the summer, Jay kept an irregular schedule between my house and the Residence. Since it was so hot and Jay loved air-conditioning like his father, he spent many summer nights sleeping at the Residence. We left it up to him to decide when he wanted to stay with me and when he wanted to be with his dad, but we insisted that he inform both of us where he would be and when so we could maintain some measure of supervision over his comings and goings. Jay cooperated, and Jamie and I were in regular communication about Jay's activities and his whereabouts. We also had some final decisions and arrangements to discuss regarding our divorce and the financial settlement.

When school started in September, Jay began spending the school week with me and weekends with his dad. This worked out well for all three of us because it saved Jay a daily commute to school, and gave Jay and me a chance to develop a fairly regular schedule during the week. Jamie also had more time to spend with Jay on weekends than he had during the week, and he made a special effort to save time to do things together with Jay. The two of them developed a very close and warm relationship. Once again, I was struck by the irony. I think Jamie and Jay probably spent more time together after our separation and divorce than they might have if Jamie and I had stayed married.

Jamie and I wanted to assure Jay that even though we were divorcing each other, we weren't divorcing our family of three. We felt the timing of our divorce was better for Jay before his high school graduation than after because we would have a year to prove we could still be a family and do things together before he left home for college. We had always had a large family birthday celebration in October because so many birthdays fell in that month. Jay's was on October 1, my brother Larry's was the third, Rob's was the fifth, and his brother Jeff's was on the fifteenth. We decided to continue that tradition this year as well and gather the whole family together at my new home for the celebration. Fifteen of us in all—including Jamie, his mother and her husband Baxter, Suzanne and Bob and their three boys, including Jeff's wife Mary Ellen, my parents, and my brother Larry and his wife Debbie—crowded into my small family room for a Sunday evening dinner of chicken and birthday cake. It was a far cry from our gatherings at the spacious Governor's Residence, but it felt good to me to have all of us together.

Jamie remembered my birthday in November, too, and came to my home bearing a large, personally-wrapped present. He had asked Jay what I needed, and Jay reminded him I didn't have a VCR. I had the television and the stereo, but no teenager's home is complete these days without a videotape player. Jamie can take a hint, so it was a VCR which I unwrapped on my forty-third birthday. My parents had come down from Gaylord to celebrate with me and Jay was home, too, when Jamie stopped by to wish me happy birthday. All hands were on deck to watch while Jamie gallantly and successfully installed and hooked up the newest electronic gadget at Paula Blanchard's new home.

As December approached, Jamie and I began to discuss the date our divorce would become final. We were both ready to bring it to a conclusion, but unfortunately the end of the six-month waiting period fell just before Christmas. We debated the pros and cons of finalizing it before Christmas or waiting until after the holidays. Either way, it would fall during the Christmas season. We couldn't wait until January because I planned to leave on January 3 for three weeks in India on a production trip for a television program I was co-producing about an ancient Indian dance form. We finally decided on a date prior to Christmas which again demonstrated to Jay that, in spite of our divorce, we would be celebrating Christmas as a family. Plans had already been made to have a joint celebration for our two families at Suzanne and Bob's house on Christmas Eve.

We chose December 21 as the date, for what reason I can't remember now. Camille, always sensitive, requested a private hearing from the judge assigned to my case. That request was granted for 4:00 P.M. Camille had requested late afternoon because he knew members of the press would be less likely to be looking for stories in the filing room at that time of day.

I met Camille in his office about 3:00 P.M., and he briefed me about what to expect during the hearing. There were several pro forma questions he would ask me for the record. He expected the judge to ask some questions of me as well, and he indicated what he thought those might be. He listened to the answers I planned to give and was completely satisfied with my responses. Then we sat chatting comfortably and quietly for a few minutes in his office while we waited for the time to pass until it was time to go to court. I always enjoyed my conversations with Camille. He was calm, steady and completely reassuring. He always confirmed the faith I had in my own judgment, supported my optimism about the future and boosted my confidence. His constant support and encouragement were a source of immeasurable strength to me.

About 3:45 P.M., he and I walked across the street to the Lansing Circuit Court to the chambers of Judge James Giddings to bring my twenty-one years of marriage to a quiet end. As we sat waiting in the reception area outside Judge Giddings office, I thought about how differently most marriages end compared to how they begin. Weddings are joyous, colorful and festive occasions with music, dancing and feasting with family and friends. Divorces are solemn, quiet, lonely and grim. I also silently observed that while I had been nervous during my wedding ceremony, I was calm and composed during my divorce proceedings. The law did not require Jamie or his attorney to be present, and neither was there. When we entered the courtroom from the back through the same door as the judge in order to avoid the public areas outside the courtroom, it was dark and empty. Only the judge, Camille, a court reporter and I were present. We rose when the judge entered the courtroom, and I was asked to take the witness stand. I sat alone in the witness chair as Camille asked me questions about the cause of our divorce and its irreconcilable nature. Most questions required only a yes or no answer from me. Then the judge asked me some questions about the divorce settlement and the financial arrangements upon which all parties had agreed. My voice echoed in the empty courtroom as I responded. The judge did not look at me, and I felt sorry for him. Who would want to be the judge who had to rule on the divorce of Governor and Mrs. James J. Blanchard? There were a few minutes of silence, interrupted only by the click of the machine the court reporter used to record my final answers as Judge Giddings reviewed the divorce papers. After a minute or two of deafening silence, he announced his consent to our divorce. The deed was done. I stepped down from the witness chair and both Camille and I thanked Judge Giddings for the special consideration he had given us with a private hearing. He was gracious and wished me the best.

Camille and I proceeded to another room where the papers were officially filed. The woman behind the counter accepted the papers from Camille and went through a series of procedures without a second glance, as though they were everyday divorce papers and nothing extraordinary—which, of course, to her they probably weren't. By 5:00 P.M., Camille and I were on our way out the door, having successfully evaded the press and curious bystanders. At that point, I felt hollow and numb. December 21 is the shortest day of the year, but it had been bright and sunny when we entered the building. Now darkness was approaching and a cold wind was blowing across Michigan Avenue as we crossed the street. Camille took my arm and asked me if I wanted to go to Jim's Tiffany Restaurant for a cup of coffee. I gladly accepted and for the next hour I felt the comfort of his companionship. He asked me if I could join him and Maryalice for dinner, but I indicated I had made previous plans. I knew he was curious so I told him my secret. Jamie and I were having dinner together at the Radisson Hotel. He was surprised and delighted that we had persevered and remained amicable.

It was too early to meet Jamie, so I went home to Okemos to call some friends and share the events of the day. Jay had plans for the evening, and the house was quiet when I arrived. I still felt a funny empty feeling so I decided to take a bath which has always been one of my prescriptions for relaxation. As I slipped into the warm water and laid my head back to relax, I felt a sense of peace and contentment begin to replace the hollowness inside me. I also felt a sense of accomplishment that we had been successful in our marriage and successful in bringing it to a loving and congenial conclusion. After the luxury of a half-hour bubble bath and consideration of the positive aspects of what I had done and what lay ahead, my frame of mind had completely reversed itself, and I was bubbling. The melancholy of my hour in the the courtroom began to recede and I jumped into my robe and called as many friends as I had time to call before I had to dress to drive to Lansing to meet Jamie. My friends asked how I felt, and when I tried to describe my feelings I realized they were too complex for a concise description. I fell back on the use of a cliche, which is handy in just this sort of situation, and said, "I feel free as a bird which just escaped its cage."

Jamie and I planned to meet in the lot behind the Capitol at his parking space and ride over to the Radisson together. The prospect of riding in the back seat with him with two members of his security detail in the front seat didn't appeal to me at all. I wanted some privacy to tell him about how it had gone in court and to share my feelings with him. It was a beautiful, crystal-clear night, and I suggested we walk over to the hotel. It was cold, but the walk was not far and it would take us past the Christmas tree in front of the Capitol. I hadn't seen the tree lit at night yet, and I was anxious to do so. From our yearly trips to New York City at Christmas which always included a visit to see the tree at Rockefeller Center, Jamie had conceived the idea that Michigan should have a tree taller than the one in New

233

York. It was a great idea and certainly appropriate, considering the fact that Michigan grew more Christmas trees than any other state in the nation. He had, indeed, been able to secure a Christmas tree taller than the one in Rockefeller Center, and it stood towering above us in all its lighted glory as we walked by.

We were seated in a private booth in the hotel restaurant where we had dined many times before. Our waiter approached the table and said, "Good evening, Governor. Good evening, Mrs. Blanchard." Jamie and I looked at each other and laughed out loud. That broke the ice, and we had a warm and comfortable evening together. It seemed a fitting close to our marriage that we could enjoy each other's company after all our years together.

We walked arm-in-arm back to the parking lot after dinner, past the sparkling Christmas tree standing tall under a full moon in a clear, dark sky. It was cold, but we stood for a minute between our cars for another good-bye. As a finale, we kissed and congratulated ourselves that we had handled our divorce so graciously.

On my drive back home, I was filled with a sense of well-being and satisfaction. I knew I had done the right thing and had done things right. I had no doubts about the future because I believed in my Grandmother Beardslee's credo, "Things always turn out for the best." It had been my experience they always had and there was no reason to believe they wouldn't in the future. My independent life was taking shape more quickly than I expected it would. I felt enormous gratitude to Jamie, Jay, my parents, my friends, my attorney Camille, and my associates who had supported me in the most dramatic and difficult decision of my life.

When I arrived home, things were still quiet. Jay wasn't home yet because Christmas vacation had begun and he was still out for the evening with his friends. I wasn't tired or ready to go to bed, so while I still had my coat on, I took out the garbage and the newspapers for morning pickup. I came in the house and changed into a warm robe, plugged in the lights on the Christmas tree in the family room, and lit a fire in the family room fireplace. I went to my bookcase to look for a special book I knew I had put there and turned on some Christmas music on the stereo.

I sat down by the light of the tree and the fire and opened my book. It had been given to me several years before by Jamie's mother who inscribed it with a note that said, "You should write a book, Paula." I opened it to the first page, which was blank, like all the others. I picked up a pen and wrote the words, "December 21, 1987. Today, I began a whole new life by ending one that lasted twenty-one years. Today, I divorced my husband. . . ."

Epilogue

I 'm celebrating three years of independent living—of being separated and divorced.

In that time, I've travelled to Italy for a week with a friend. I've journeyed to India to make a movie. I took Jay to London on a graduation trip, and I toured France and Germany for ten days with a man I thought I might marry.

I've purchased, decorated and improved two homes and sold one.

I bought a new red four-door sedan and sold a two-door white convertible.

I finished coursework on a master's degree, directed a video production company, and am pursuing a career in public relations as an associate vice president with Michigan's largest public relations firm, Casey Communications Management, Inc.

I read the accounts of Jamie's wedding to his former secretary Janet Fox, and I rejoiced that my decision to divorce him was reconfirmed by what I saw and read in the newspapers. I felt pleased for Jamie that he had a partner who didn't seem to mind that their honeymoon had to be postponed because of pressing political matters, like walking the Mackinac Bridge the day following their wedding. I was even more pleased for myself that it was she and not me.

I think about Jamie nearly every day, and he has told me he does the same. Sometimes, but only rarely, I miss my old life, but usually the memories are enough.

I've changed my life dramatically. As First Lady, I walked a public tightrope balancing my husband's, my family's and my own needs with the demands of public life. In the spring of 1987, I decided to come down off that highwire and put my feet back on the ground. I walked away from the circus of politics in an effort to simplify and redirect my life and bring balance to it.

I now live independently, exercising a wonderful freedom which accords me self-determination and places me in control of my destiny. I am living my own life, not someone else's. I own my own home and my own time. In fact, I own each day.

As I expected, there is a price to pay for this independence, just as there was a price to pay for marriage. I've found loneliness a good buy compared to the exorbitant price politics demanded. And I can drive a hard bargain with loneliness, unlike politics, singlehandedly. In many cases I've outwitted loneliness completely.

I feel a tremendous sense of satisfaction with my life—the past, present and future. I cherish my memories of Michigan's people, places, products and pride. I have a sense of well-being that I enjoyed, in many ways, an extraordinary marriage, and that I used my position as First Lady wisely and well. I have no regrets that I was there and no regrets that I left.

My years as a political spouse have been chronicled and now I can close the book on a life which began on June 18, 1966, when I was a nervous bride glimpsing my future. The next chapters of my new life now remain to be written, and every day I confidently turn a new page.

* * *